Social Phenomenology

Social Phenomenology

Husserl, Intersubjectivity, and Collective Intentionality

Eric Chelstrom

LEXINGTON BOOKS

Lanham • Boulder • New York • Toronto • Plymouth, UK

Published by Lexington Books
A wholly owned subsidiary of The Rowman & Littlefield Publishing Group, Inc.
4501 Forbes Boulevard, Suite 200, Lanham, Maryland 20706
www.rowman.com

10 Thornbury Road, Plymouth PL6 7PP, United Kingdom

British Library Cataloguing in Publication Information Available

Library of Congress Cataloging-in-Publication Data

Library of Congress Cataloging-in-Publication Data Available

ISBN 978-0-7391-7308-4 (cloth : alk. paper)—978-0-7391-7309-1 (electronic)

⊖™ The paper used in this publication meets the minimum requirements of American
National Standard for Information Sciences—Permanence of Paper for Printed Library
Materials, ANSI/NISO Z39.48-1992.

Printed in the United States of America

To my family, for their enduring patience.

Contents

Acknowledgments

This project began in a seminar on Husserl, developed into conference presentations, then a dissertation, and now the present work. Along the way there are numerous conversations I've been grateful for with colleagues and peers. To all who've I've spoken with about Husserl, intersubjectivity, collective intentionality, the mind and more, from professor to peer to student, thank you all.

Special gratitude is necessary for Kah Kyung Cho, Jorge Gracia and Kenneth Shockley, without whose prodding and guidance this would never have taken shape. I must thank Andrew Spear and Amanda Hicks for their tireless devotions to all things philosophical and for making "Philosopher's Alley" what it was while these ideas first began to germinate and take shape. Also, to the philosophy faculty at Hamline University, who first ignited my interests in philosophy and what it means to truly engage a topic.

My gratitude to Lexington Press's editorial team and to Connie Van Dyke for their assistance in getting the manuscript and its index into something presentable.

Usage of materials from Dorion Cairns' translation of Edmund Husserl's *Cartesian Meditations* (1999) by kind permission of Springer.

Portions of Chapter 4 appeared in print previously as "Pluralities Without Reified Wholes: A Phenomenological Response to Hans Bernhard Schmid's Collectivism" in *Investigaciones Fenomenológicas*, Issue 3, 2011; published here with the kind permission of the Sociedad Española de Fenomenología.

Finally, to my family, which has grown since this work first began, I am ever grateful.

Introduction

If the social world is dependent on achievements of beings with sufficiently sophisticated systems of consciousness, then the intentionality of consciousness is foundational to the social world. Intentionality is essential to any and all *socially constituted* beings. As such, the theory of intentionality one assumes in one's theorizing can have enormous implications for one's social ontology, one's theory of the nature of the social world. Both phenomenological philosophy and participants in contemporary discussions of collective intentionality accept a foundational role for intentionality in relation to the social world. Phenomenology offers a rigorously worked out methodology for the analysis of intentionality. The view of intentionality found in the phenomenological tradition is distinct from those common to analytic philosophers, and arguably much richer. The approach of the present work is to bring phenomenological philosophy into dialogue with collective intentionality literature. Specifically, a background in Husserlian phenomenology will be brought to bear in weighing in critically on the collective intentionality literature. The result is the beginnings of a distinctive non-atomistic, non-collectivistic account of collective intentionality, one expressly concerned with being consistent with a broader theory of consciousness. Specific attention is given to the notion of a plural subject, the subject of collective experience or collective action, the "we." This work argues that a number of contemporary discussions in the literature on collective intentionality are confused in ways that can be corrected, or at least illuminated, when informed by Husserlian phenomenology.

This is a work in social ontology. Social ontology is the study of the nature of social reality, or more carefully the social domains of reality. Key to understanding the social world is understanding the role consciousness plays in the constitution of social objects. The social world is distinguished from the natural world as that domain which is dependent on consciousness. There could be no social world if there were no beings with consciousness to constitute it and experience it. Collective intentionality is the directedness of consciousness in a first person plural form. Collective intentions are intentions that can be stated in the we-form. A collective intention claims extension over a plurality of subjects, not the singular subject alone.

This work addresses issues associated with a phenomenologically informed non-atomistic individualist position. Phenomenology is the study of consciousness qua consciousness. Phenomenology is also a tradition and a methodology, central to which is the analysis of the intentional achievements of subjectivity. The word achievements is used to denote that consciousness is not purely passive in nature. The phenomenologist may understand the following as an extended reflection on intentionality's plural form manifestations. This work is heavily informed by the phenomenological tradition, especially in relation to the works of Edmund Husserl. The author understands Husserl's extant writings on intersubjectivity to point to a phenomenologically motivated position of non-atomistic individualism, the same position many of his early critics took while believing they were lamenting characteristics of Husserl's thought. Two of those early critics who have had an enormous influence on the later reception of Husserl were Martin Heidegger and Jean-Paul Sartre. Emmanuel Levinas follows with equal force, but a distinctive emphasis.

A non-atomistic position is one that treats subjectivity as immersed in relations to others, denying the atomistic conception, which claims that the subject is an island unto herself and all relations to others are secondary to her being. The denial of atomism asserts that one's relations to others is in some important regard constitutive of one's being. One cannot be the sort of subject one is without others.

An individualist position argues that consciousness is only found in individual subjects and not in collectivities. Collectivism claims that groups or collectivities can themselves be conscious over and above their individual memberships. Some are motivated to collectivism on the belief that group agency can only thus be properly understood. However, such an understanding is not necessary. The collectivist preys on an ambiguity. One argues that the basic sense of agency is unique to conscious beings, and nonetheless argues that there is a different and derived sense of agency that can be ascribed to groups or collectivities. Group agency would, on such a view, be dependent on individual agency, and not entail a commitment to collective consciousness. Rather, group agency would be a result of the collective intentional achievements of individual subjects, even if not reducible to the agency of any one individual nor a summative expression of individual agent intentions. The view argued here is that group agency must be dependent on individual agency as agency depends on consciousness and consciousness is only found in individual subjects.

The phenomenological tradition is one that has consistently aimed towards taking a middle position between atomism and collectivism or holism. J.N. Mohanty argues well for phenomenology's rejection of both extremes. Mohanty:

> [I]t would be best to begin by recognizing [the truth of]…the rejection of atomism, be it psychological, semantic or epistemological. Neither a mental act nor its sense nor its referent stands, each by itself, as an autonomous unity. A men-

tal act belongs to the mental life of its owner, just as a sense points to other senses and a referent to other entities in its world. But rejection of atomism need not entail holism. Truth must lie in between these one-sided abstractions. Phenomena themselves do not speak for either.[1]

By extension, the individual subject does not stand free of relations and dependency on others, the individual is always part of a social context. Mohanty argues that a satisfactory theory must account for *both* the individuality of the particular phenomenon *and* the context that makes that individual what it is.[2] Further, he argues that phenomenology has supplied two key concepts towards achieving an adequate account: the distinction between dependent and independent meanings and the concept of horizon intentionality.[3]

The former distinction allows one to assert that words, for example, have individual meanings, but that those meanings are not independent. Similarly, one may defend the individuality of particular subjects while maintaining their dependence on social structures. As such, Mohanty argues that, contra-holism, one must maintain a distinction between the *evidence* one has for ascribing thoughts or characteristics to individuals, and the thought or characteristic ascribed to the individual herself. Paraphrasing Mohanty, the recognition of the primacy of the individual as the basic locus of agency and consciousness, in relation to whom social institutions and practices are built up, "is not only historically a basis of western logic and epistemology but also, phenomenologically, an incontrovertible thesis that any holism can deny only at the risk of its own credibility."[4] Contra-atomism, the individual is not the whole, nor is the whole capable of being understood only in terms of individuals.

Further, the concept of horizon in phenomenology places the individual and whole together into a nuanced dynamic relation.

> We grasp a sense…within a horizon containing pointing references to what lies beyond and around intentional expectancies that demand the movement of thought beyond what is thematically grasped. But a horizon is a horizon *insofar as it lets the thematic figure stand apart*. Holism cannot account for this thematic grasping of atomic or molecular sense. The totality to which holism appeals is a metaphysical construction, while the horizonal character of all thematic apprehension is a phenomenological feature of all experience.[5]

Atomism is inadequate insofar as it discounts the importance of the thematic whole, or the social context. Holism is inadequate because it discounts the importance of the individual and treats the individual as mere instance of a kind.

None of this is to discount the importance of social context or how social practices inform experience. Rather, phenomenology is clear that social practices are founded on the achievements of subjectivity. "The idea of social *praxis* as constituting the whole is incurably intentional. …[H]olism presupposes the concept of intentionality, rather than being able to either eliminate it or to explain it."[6] As such, an analysis of a social practice, a social or collective action, a social institution, etc., presupposes intentional achievements of individuals. Social practices and institutions arise only on the basis of individual subjects accepting or affirming their being, perhaps begrudgingly or while disapproving of their content. Nonetheless, the individual alone is not sufficient to make them social. To become part of the fabric of the social world requires collective acceptance or adherence. That's not to say the individual is not herself dependent on the social. Rather,

> The intentional acts performed by individual egos have a primacy that needs to be preserved...as against both causal and holistic explanations. This is not to say that any and every individual ego is the primal source of constitution of all those meanings it intends. On the contrary, most of the meanings that an individual ego intends are taken over from a tradition within which it finds itself. It may also be that in intending a sense (or, what is its correlate and reverse achievement, in interpreting a speaker), one makes use of a fairly large, already available, network of senses and shared background beliefs; but those other senses *had* their 'primal institution' in intentions of other egos, and those beliefs are beliefs shared by a community of egos. Though there is more to the intended sense than a particular act intending it may be aware of, what we are referred back to are themselves other actual or possible acts of individual egos: beliefs, expectations, thoughts, and the like.[7]

Atomism errs in treating the individual as being autonomous or independent in a totalizing fashion, failing to respect that autonomy is not a given, rather an achievement.[8] And the achievement of and meaning given to autonomy depends on the social context one finds oneself in. Holism errs in mistaking that individual achievements constitute and maintain the whole at a primitive level. Each position is an extreme insofar as each seeks to understand one pole of the relation in terms of the other. Atomistic thought aims to understand social wholes in terms of individuals. Holistic thought aims to understand individuals in terms of social wholes. A moderate position, on the other hand, treats neither individual nor whole as inherently given in isolation from the other, and aims to explicate the dialectical and dynamic nature of their relation.

This work aims to engage both analytic and phenomenological philosophers, hoping to offer some productive bridge between those traditions. In relation to the analytic literature on collective intentionality, it offers critique and another theory of intentionality to be considered in relation to the foundational elements in our discussions of social phenomena. In relation to phenomenological philosophy, it explores a new avenue for discussions of intersubjectivity and social phenomena. Specific to Husserlian phenomenology, it offers a way to move forward in discussing the higher-order intersubjective or social wholes that Husserl refers to in the later sections of his *Fifth Cartesian Meditation*, and provides a way to continue exploring the full range of intersubjective phenomena without having to settle with any finality the disputes over Husserl's treatment of one's experience of an other as other.

Phenomenology is a rich tradition. Not presupposing one's audience extensive familiarity with phenomenology or the same understanding of Husserlian phenomenology or its history, some review is prudent. Dan Zahavi has noted, "Husserl came up against intersubjectivity in the course of analyzing the constitution of objectivity, reality and transcendence, since these categories simply could not be constituted on a solitary egological basis."[9] Husserl's problem, according to his critics, was that he needed to provide an account of intersubjectivity that is consistent with his project, or accept that phenomenology as he developed it was somehow fundamentally flawed. On closer inspection the problem is not one of knowledge, but adequate description of the forms of intentionality manifest in the experience of others. "The other is given in its bodily presence as a *lived body*, a body that is actively engaged in the world."[10] The experience of lived bodies is not constituted in the same manner as the experience of other physical bodies.[11] This motivates a number of phenomenological descriptions to rely on reference to *empathy*. "Empathy is defined as a form of intentionality in which one is directed towards the other's lived experience."[12] It is important to note that by reference to the intentionality of the experience of an other, whether couched in terms of empathy or not, phenomenologists are speaking of the *experiences* themselves, of something that is expressly non-inferential in nature. "In empathy, we experience the other directly as a person, as an intentional being whose bodily gestures and actions are expressive of his or her experiences or states of mind."[13] More to the point, "We are not dealing with any kind of inference, but with an actual *experience*, the structure of which Husserl attempts to uncover."[14] As such, "Phenomenological views, then, involve non-mentalizing, embodied, perceptual approaches to questions of understanding others and the problem of intersubjectivity."[15]

The task for the phenomenologist becomes how to explicate and describe one's intentions of others. The phrase "intentions of others" is potentially ambiguous as it contains a potential double genitive. To clarify, I do not mean others' intentions, but one's consciousness of another as part of one's own experience, the experience of another as other. The experience of an other as other, more generally the experience of otherness, is captured in phenomenological literature by the term alterity. Included in the task of phenomenology is clarifying what counts as fulfillment conditions for what one experiences where one has intentional contents that refer to others, i.e. what sort of evidence is manifest to experience in relation to the experience of others.[16]

> The second- (and third-)person access to another person differs from the first-person access to my own experience, but this difference is not an imperfection or a shortcoming. Rather, the difference is constitutional. It is what makes my experience *of the other*, rather than a self-experience.[17]

Husserl's problem is primarily a problem with how one accounts for others in a manner consistent with the intentional nature of consciousness and which respects the phenomenon of the other.[18] To complicate matters, there is an irreducible asymmetry in the experience of the other. Zahavi captures it clearly:

It is essential to the phenomenological description of the subject-subject relation that it involves an *asymmetry*. There is a difference between the experiencing subject and the experienced subject. But this asymmetry is a part of any
correct description of intersubjectivity. Without asymmetry there would be no
intersubjectivity, but merely an undifferentiated collectivity.[19]

Additionally, "…it is only because the foreign subject eludes my direct experience…that he or she is experienced as an Other at all."[20] As such, it is not without reason that discussions of intersubjectivity in phenomenology cut to the core
of the discipline, and represent a nexus at which the whole set of resources developed in phenomenological theory come to be marshaled. The issue of being
able to adequately describe the experience of others takes on further urgency
when it is shown that the very sense of objectivity depends on the content of
experience's having the sense of being available to other subjects, i.e. as a content that is not idiosyncratic to oneself. As John Drummond has it:

> As instantiated, [quality and matter of the intentional act] are the real contents
> *by* which *this* act is directed to an object. As essential, they are intentional con-
> tents that transcend any particular subjective or psychological realities and are
> thereby capable of grounding an *intersubjective* awareness of an *objectivity*.[21]

Phenomenology's understanding of intentionality is not the same as that
found in contemporary analytic philosophy. Phenomenology utilizes an understanding of intentionality similar to that offered by Franz Brentano.[22] A key difference between the phenomenological view and alternatives found outside of
phenomenology is that, in phenomenology, "intentionality is entirely internal to
episodes in consciousness–to *experiences*, broadly conceived–and does not consist in, or merely essentially involve, a relation of reference to anything in the
world outside of consciousness."[23]

Intentionality is a term with an unfortunate history in English-language philosophy. "In the phenomenological tradition, this idea, that consciousness is
always consciousness-of-something, is referred to as the intentionality of consciousness."[24] In English, 'intention' can refer either to a cognitive act, the act of
one's consciousness being oriented toward or directed at an object, event or state
of affairs; or that which represents or embodies an expression of one's will to
action. One should thus be careful to distinguish between intent [*Absicht, volun-
tas*] and intention [*Intentionalität, intentio*].[25] My use of terms like 'intention,'
"intentionality," "intentional content" relate to intention in the *Intentionalität*
sense unless otherwise noted. Intention is also sometimes confused with intension, a logical characteristic of linguistic utterances whereby one refers to the
meaning of a term.[26] Contrary to these unfortunately common and pervasive
equivocations, "Intentionality is a ubiquitous character of consciousness, and as
the phenomenologists put it, it means that all consciousness (all perceptions,
memories, imaginings, judgments, etc.) is *about* or *of something*."[27] As such, the
phenomenologist tends to argue that experience "always involves reference to
the *world*, taking that term in a very wide sense to include not just the physical

environment, but the social and cultural world, which may include things that do not exist in a physical way."[28]

Amongst analytic philosophers, John Searle has perhaps come closest to articulating the nature of intentionality in a manner consistent with phenomenological philosophy. Searle defines intentionality thus: "Intentionality is that property of many mental states and events by which they are directed at or about or of objects and states of affairs in the world."[29] As such, it is a mistake to think that intentionality is something that must necessarily be linguistic in nature or that it is something necessarily volitional in character. Even if volitional intent is intentional in the wider sense, in that it is directed at some object, event or state of affairs, it would not follow that intentionality in the wider sense–applicable to states of consciousness or mental states–would in all cases be volitional. One doesn't choose the objects in one's perceptual field, even if one can choose to attend to this or that object in particular.

Nor is intentionality only what is immediately given to consciousness in the sense of one's immediate object of thought or interest. There are myriad intentional achievements operative in and constitutive of even the simplest everyday experience. These include the temporal-, spatial- and bodily-dimensions of experience, the social horizons, linguistic horizons, and generative and genetic dimensions of experience, as well as the variant perceptual modalities, and perhaps other possibilities. Zahavi points this out in detail:

> In his analysis of the structure of experience, Husserl pays particular attention to a group of experiences that are all characterized by being conscious *of* something, that is, which all possess an object-*directedness*. This attribute is also called *intentionality*. One does not merely love, fear, see, or judge, one loves a beloved, fears something fearful, sees an object, and judges a state of affairs. Regardless of whether we are talking of a perception, thought, judgment, fantasy, doubt, expectation, or recollection, all of these diverse forms of consciousness are characterized by intending objects and cannot be analyzed properly without a look at their objective correlate, that is, the perceived, doubted, expected object.[30]

One can see then, that intentionality is manifest in experience, and manifests in distinctive manners, not all of which can be treated with a reductive understanding of intentionality as either a property of linguistic utterances or an overly simplified sense of comportment. Any instance of intentionality in consciousness is constituted by some act of consciousness–e.g. seeing, believing, imagining, etc.–standing in correlation to some content or object–e.g. a ball, a unicorn, the shade of blue on the inseam of one's shirt, etc. Each of the various act-types and content-types, and their many combinatorial possibilities, produce distinctive evidentiary requirements and require their own analyses. Believing that it is raining is different from believing that it is snowing or hoping that it is raining. Phenomenology seeks to excavate and bring to clarity the multitude of intentional act-content correlations in experience, as they are both explicit and implicit in everyday experience, and to then assess their evidentiary statuses.[31]

Searle offers a useful distinction between three senses of the primary sense of intentionality: intrinsic, derived and as-if. Intrinsic intentionality is the intentionality proper to consciousness. Throughout this work, it is taken as given that it is a mistake to think intentionality can be understood independent of reference to consciousness.[32] Further, even if there could be reasons for distinguishing between mind and consciousness, throughout I use those terms interchangeably, unless otherwise noted.[33]

As-if intentionality is where intentional characteristics are attributed to something metaphorically, where one ascribes intentional features to something that could not bear those characteristics. For instance, one might describe their car as happy or their computer as uncooperative. Strictly speaking, cars are not either happy or not happy, and computers are incapable of cooperating or of being uncooperative as they respond to the user's commands relative to their coded programming. The object to which the intentional state is attributed in the case of as-if intentionality does not actually possess intentionality in the relevant capacity.

Finally, derived intentionality is where something possesses intentionality, but the reason for its having intentionality is a dependence relation on beings that possess intentionality intrinsically. This form of intentionality is very important for understanding collective intentional achievements. To clarify derived intentionality, Searle uses the examples of a sentence in a language and a stop sign. Sentences possess intentionality; sentences are about something. However, a sentence's intentionality is not intrinsic to the sentence itself, as a set of written marks or uttered phonemes. Sentences only have intentionality because their speakers, and their linguistic communities, make them so. The same is true of stop signs, the physical object is given the status of something intentional, but only because certain beings with consciousness make it so. Even if conscious in some manner, squirrels don't accept one's shout to get out of the way or the stop sign as being about much of anything. What's more, the intentionality of derived intentionality is only accessible to beings with consciousness. As such, Searle argues, "Linguistic meaning is a real form of intentionality, but it is not intrinsic intentionality. It is derived from the intrinsic intentionality of the users of the language."[34] The position Searle takes, of the intentionality of language being dependent on the intentionality of consciousness, is not unique to him alone. That view is also found in Husserl's *Logical Investigations*, as well as in William of Ockham's *Summa Logicae*.[35]

In addition to the intentionality of individual consciousness in regard to its own individual perceptions or beliefs, there is intentionality that extends beyond oneself so as to include others. There are not just experiences *I* have alone, but experiences that are *ours*, that *we* have together. This capacity to experience or act together with others is not unique to our species either. "Many species of animals, our own especially, have a capacity for collective intentionality. By this I mean not only that they engage in cooperative behavior, but that they share intentional states such as beliefs, desires, and intentions."[36] Collective intentionality is intentionality that expresses itself in the form of "we intend *x*," as distin-

guished from individual intentionality which expresses itself in the form "I intend *x*."[37] For instance, "*we* believe that the game is tomorrow" is distinct from
my believing it to be so and *your* believing it as well, just as "*we* will root
against the Yankees" is distinct from *my* rooting against the Yankees and *your*
rooting against the Yankees as well. Each of us could individually hold the same
belief or take the same action, but just because you do so and I do so, it does not
follow that *we* do so *together*. I can root against the Yankees in my home, and
you in yours, or you at the game. There's nothing shared in such coincidental
agreement. Collective intentions include others in one's intention, necessarily
involving the component of our doing such and such together.

There are two additional characteristics of intentionality that need be identified for present purposes. First, intentional states establish their conditions for
satisfaction or fulfillment or what would constitute their being evidenced.[38] That
one's consciousness is directed at or has a given content about something in the
world does not in itself mean that the world actually is as such. One's believing
that *x* is the case does not make it so. "[Phenomenology] seeks to be critical and
non-dogmatic, shunning metaphysical and theoretical prejudices, as much as
possible. It seeks to be guided by that which is actually experienced, rather than
by what we expect to find given our theoretical commitments."[39] For instance, if
I experience the sky as blue, the intentional content of that experience is fulfilled,
verified, or evidenced by the sky's being blue. If I believe that "there is a unicorn in the corner," my belief has intentionality, has meaning. That said, however, the belief "there is a unicorn in the corner" is an empty intention, an intention
that cannot be evidenced or fulfilled–as there are no such things as unicorns.
Similarly, if I believe that "Tim likes peanut butter," that is evidenced or satisfied by Tim's liking peanut butter.

Second, intentional achievements can be founded on other intentional
achievement and thereby iterated. One intention can be founded on another, and
systems of intentional states might thereby be ordered in dependence relations
relative to other intentional achievements.

> To say that an act is founded upon another means that it (a) presupposes that
> other act as necessary and (b) builds itself upon that act's matter or noematic
> sense so as to form a unity with it. Founded acts can also be objectifying; judg-
> ing a state of affairs would be an example of a higher-order objectifying act.[40]

There are two initial reasons this is important to the present discussion of collective intentionality. First, a recognition of the capacity for one intention's being
founded on another allows one to offer a preliminary remark on the issue of
whether or not collective intentions are formally individualistic or not. Formal
individualism holds that all collective intentions are in the form of individual or
"I" intentions, as opposed to plural or "we" intentions. The capacity for intentions to be founded on one another allows one to understand we-intentions as
basic, that is not reducible to I-intentions, but to respect that we-intentions may
be grounded on I-intentions. The formal individualist is correct that one's collec-

tive intention, we-intention, cannot be founded on another's intentional states–as the consciousness of the other is inaccessible to one in any immediate sense. However, the formal individualist is incorrect if they assert that one can't have an intention that aims its extension across a plurality of individuals.

A second point is that normative contents can be understood in their dependence relation to more basic intentional contents. For any normative content n, n represents some object, event or state of affairs x in relation to a possible state of affairs that represents how x ought to be, in context C. Collective intentionality often entails certain practical or axiological content. As Drummond puts it,

> Practical or axiological intentions, for example, when their specifically practical and axiological moments are abstracted and isolated, are "non-objectifying," since they present only an aspect of an object but do not present that object in its own right. However, practical and axiological intentions are necessarily founded on objectifying acts.[41]

One can thus understand that much of what is discussed in the collective intentionality literature, whether in terms of objectifying or non-objectifying acts, may be understood as a discussion of founded intentional acts. For instance, the rules of chess are a systematic set of declarative prescriptions *about* the pieces' individual capabilities and powers and also *about* how the game ought to be conducted. That is, collective intentional achievements about the rule-properties of a given chess piece are dependent on there being some item that is the piece in question or something to which the status of having that power is applied. Other examples of dependent and iterated or founded intentional achievements include higher order mathematical proofs and social institutions. The former are dependent on more primitive intentional achievements having to do with the properties and functions associated with numbers and the basic characteristics of numerical relations. The latter are founded on a number of other achievements, individual recognition that there is some interest that ought to be satisfied, individual acceptance that this institution is empowered to serve that interest, an articulation of that interest in relation to lived experiential contexts in which it arises, the normative representation of the object of that interest definitive of the interest's satisfied and unsatisfied forms, and so on.

Returning to the main issue of discussion it should be apparent that any instance of derived intentionality must always have a founded nature. This does not prevent the products of such acts from being foundational to further founded acts. However, more primitive intentional achievements ground such acts. As such, any description of founded acts that are presented in such a manner whereby they stand in contradiction to or with incoherence in respect to that which they are founded upon are inherently problematic descriptions of said acts.[42] That is, any derived intentional achievement is ultimately grounded on some intrinsic intentional achievement(s). If derived intentional achievements are treated as basic or explicated in a manner inconsistent with their grounding phenomena–the intentional achievements that initially provide the lived experiential ground for their being–then, such analyses are in error. For those familiar with Husserl, this is, in effect, the line of argument he offers in *The Crisis of the European Sciences and Transcendental Phenomenology*.[43]

Husserl's most well-known analysis of intersubjectivity is found in *Cartesian Meditations*. There, Husserl addresses intentions directed at other subjects and asks as to the possibilities associated with evidence. Again, remember that 'intention' does not necessarily involve a sense of volition or action in the phenomenological tradition. Husserl's principal focus is on the recognition that the other is other, a conscious subject unto their self, as manifesting in one's experience. That basic intentional achievement of recognizing another subject as other, in turn, would be foundational to any collective intention that would extend to the other as a possible party to the specified act-content correlation. In order that the other is accepted as other, that their alterity is preserved, it is essential to the experience of the other that their consciousness and intrinsic intentional states be inaccessible to one in an original sense. There is an essential asymmetry in the experience of the other. As such, the only kind of evidence one's intention of the other is capable of is an indirect form of adequate evidence. Adequate evidence is always open to modification and the possibility of error. Evidence of the other as other is indirect as one cannot have direct experience of the other's consciousness itself. To have such experience would mean sharing the same stream of consciousness, in which case the other is not other at all. As such, the best evidence one has of the other in their otherness is that available through indications of their consciousness, not their consciousness itself.

Most of the literature on intersubjectivity in the context of Husserl has focused on the above line of argument, and tends to worry whether Husserl is a solipsist. Much of that literature, at least in the English-speaking world, also tends to misconstrue the point of Husserl's analyses. Most discussions of Husserl's writings on intersubjectivity treat Husserl's analysis as though it were another instance of the problem of other minds, as an epistemological quandary about one's knowledge of other minds. Husserl's concern, however, is only to show how the evidentiary possibilities associated with the experiences of the other as other *must* be structured. That evidence *must* be incomplete and nontotalizing in virtue of the nature of alterity inherent in the experience of the other. Husserl is not arguing as to *whether* one experiences others, rather he is working out *how* such experiences function. Yes, he expressed the added motive of showing that critics who claim that phenomenology is essentially solipsistic are in error. It seems reasonable to accept his claim that others are already meaningfully present in experience, and to accept that one can never have complete or perfect evidence of others. Further, an additional reduction to the "sphere of ownness" or bracketing of others would not be necessary unless they were already present in one's lived experience in a deep and irreducible way.[44]

If Husserl's problem were insoluble, it would be hard to understand why he then argues that the social world itself is predicated on intentional achievements.[45] Intentional achievements, accepted by pluralities of subjects, are constitutive of social objects and institutions, as they are distinct from natural kinds.[46] For instance, that a green-black inked, rectangular-shaped piece of cotton fabric paper has a certain value for exchange is entirely dependent on a peoples' collective acceptance.[47] That a gesture is insulting or friendly, that this is a game of chess, that the World Cup crowns the international soccer champion, that a word connotes a given meaning(s), etc.; all of these are instances of socially constituted objects, events, or states of affairs. The very possibility for socially extended meanings is dependent on intentionality and consciousness. That dependence is not understood in reference to individuals in isolation from one another, but to individuals collectively recognizing, acknowledging, agreeing to or accepting some meaning, significance, status or plan of action. To be clear, individuals' acceptance of something collectively does not imply their endorsement. Otherwise all members of a society or group with oppressive norm structures would have to be understood as accepting and endorsing the norms of their society or group.

As stated earlier, this work argues that a number of contemporary discussions in the literature on collective intentionality are confused in ways that can be corrected, or at least illuminated, by considerations informed by Husserlian phenomenology. Specifically, it is argued that such discussions sometimes fail to maintain a distinction between intrinsic and derived intentionality. In doing so they mistakenly attribute intrinsic intentionality when it is not present, namely to groups or collectivities of subjects as distinct from the individuals who compose them. The sources of the confusion are, at least, fourfold: 1) Confusion arises as a result of the ambiguity in the English-language word "intentionality," which bears two distinct senses that are not carefully distinguished by some parties to discussions of intersubjectivity in phenomenology and collective intentionality. Volition to act is not the same as directedness of consciousness. 2) Confusion arises through a tendency to equivocate between or collapse the distinction between an intentional state and the success in evidencing, satisfying or fulfilling its conditions for satisfaction–as prevalent in the externalist trends that are dominant in contemporary analytic philosophy. 3) An appreciable confusion arises on the basis of an intuition to the effect that focus on individual subjects alone cannot adequately account for social phenomena. There is a difference between the social phenomena and the individual's role relative to those social phenomena. While something social is not reducible to the individual, it is nonetheless dependent on consciousness. And consciousness only manifests itself in individuals; this claim will be supported rather extensively in chapters one and two. One can end in confusion if they significantly reduce or eliminate the place of individuals in relation to the social world; thereby glossing the founding role achievements of consciousness have for the social world. The social world is a world that is social only in virtue of there being conscious agents to experience it as social. 4) Finally, there is too much trust placed on linguistically expressed intuitions about social phenomena without sufficient critical analysis of the phenomena intended and whether such utterances represent adequate or defensible ways of speaking about the phenomena they aim to describe. At times, there appears to be insufficient systematic concern beyond the narrowly confined problem that is the focus of one's immediate attention.[48] Some philosophers, like some scientists, are sometimes too hasty to draw global conclusions from arguments that only warrant qualified conclusions, conclusions dependent on the host of background assumptions.

A concern for consistency across a wider set of considerations than the immediate problem taken in isolation, in addition to a concern for doing justice to the phenomena, is not something unique to phenomenological philosophy or foreign to analytic philosophy.[49] Arguments here offered on collective intentionality are informed by phenomenology, with its traditional concerns for context and careful attention to detail of description,[50] as well as the types of issues philosophers working more directly in the analytic tradition are concerned with. It is important that my readers understand that where I contrast phenomenology with analytic philosophy, the purpose is to draw attention to a difference between authors and their background assumptions. The aim of such comparative claims is not to raise the specter of an unbridgeable divide between irreconcilable traditions or assert the superiority of one tradition over another.[51]

In what follows, the confusions enumerated above are addressed in relation to the ideas of collective consciousness and plural subjects, both of which represent possible conclusions that can be drawn from research into intersubjectivity or collective intentionality. Intersubjective experiences are not indicative of collective subjectivities or collective consciousness. Collectives or plural subjects are not themselves conscious beings. This is so even if a collective forms a plural subject, a unified subject or group agent with attributes or powers distinct from those the individuals who compose and participate in it have.

My concern is that even if collectives or plural subjects can have attributes or powers distinct from those of their individual members, it does not follow that their attributes or powers are the same in kind as those of their individual members. That is, even if a collectivity or plural subject might "have" intentionality in some way, it isn't necessarily the case that its intentionality is intrinsic, as that would imply consciousness, which is implausible. Rather, I argue that these are not instances of intrinsic intentionality, but derived intentionality. That one speaks in everyday parlance sometimes of collectivities or groups as though they have intentionality in an intrinsic sense, e.g. as possessing a mind of their own, can be misleading. That is plural subjects are like stop signs in that they can embody intentionality in a derived sense, but not intrinsic sense. They are more interesting than stop signs, however, as individual agents–conscious subjects–participate in them and give plural subjects a dynamic character that inert artifacts like stop signs lack. That's a reflection of plural subjects being embodiments of networks of collective intentional achievements. For instance, Michael Bratman rightly argues that in cases of complex coordination, it is implausible that all individual subjects have cognizance of the specific acts all other participants have in achieving the group goal. As such, Bratman endorses the view that it is sufficient that they share some general goal and the participants' sub-plans mesh.[52] Accepting the convention of a stop sign requires only awareness of its conventional function and acknowledgment that the convention holds. Plural subjects, on the other hand, are at least an order of magnitude more complex.

Here, then, is a brief synopsis of each of the chapters of the work. It is worth noting that chapters one, two, and seven share a common focus around the issue of collective consciousness; chapters four through six are focused more directly on the phenomenology of plural subjects:

Chapter one argues that the phenomenology of plural subjects does not imply any robust notion of collective consciousness. There I critique the view that a plural subject itself, the subject of collective intentionality, is thought to have consciousness over and above the individuals who constitute that subject. I do not deny that there are plural subjects. Rather, I deny that plural subjects are entities endowed with consciousness in their own right; I deny that there is collective consciousness. These arguments are buttressed by an understanding of the nature of consciousness and intentionality from the Husserlian tradition. This helps establish an understanding of those two central concepts for the rest of the work. Both this and the subsequent chapter are motivated by the view that an adequate account of agency must be consistent with the philosophies of mind and consciousness.

Where chapter one's emphasis is specifically phenomenological in character—oriented at the intentional achievements relating to the experiences of plural subjects—chapter two examines the metaphysical or ontological requirements for there to be collective consciousness. Chapter two argues that there is no successful metaphysical justification for collective consciousness, and a commitment to collective consciousness is in many cases inconsistent with commonly held positions on the nature of mind. This also affords an opportunity to place the understanding of consciousness and intentionality into discussion with the analytic discussions of mind. A theory of agency ought to be consistent with theory of mind. That means that a theory of collective agency must establish how it is related to minds. Do collectives themselves have minds or is collective agency a by-product of individual minds standing in the right sorts of relations? The former claim is problematic and does not sit well with established understandings of the nature of mind or consciousness. The latter is the sort of view that a theory of collective agency should aim to offer.

Chapter three develops a phenomenological view of plural subjects. The account builds on the discussions of the nature of intentionality and consciousness developed in the first two chapters. The account developed owes a great deal to an essay by David Carr on the phenomenology of plural subjects. Plural subjects are the "we" of a collective intention. Following Carr, I argue that plural subjects do not imply collective consciousness, and are not reducible to individual intentions represented in the first-person singular. My position is developed in a manner congenial to the contemporary literature on collective intentionality and defends a modified version of Carr's view from challenges such a view is liable to. In particular, I contrast the developed position with that of Hans Bernhard Schmid's phenomenologically informed collectivism.

Schmid's collectivism is given more direct treatment and criticism in the fourth chapter. Schmid is one of the few phenomenologists working actively on collective intentions. He develops a collectivist account of collective intentionality. Schmid argues that individualist accounts are inadequate, that they are unable to account for normativity and collective action. Contra-Schmid, it is argued that a non-atomistic subjective individualist position is able to account for the largely passive constitutional maintenance and attendance of the social world in a manner consistent with experience. Specifically, I respond to what Schmid sees as any individualist's two primary obstacles: normativity and relationality. Schmid argues that individualist accounts of collective intentionality fail to be able to account for the normative force of collective intentions as well as to the intersubjectively relational dimension of collective intentions. I show that an individualist account can respond to his challenges. I show how an appreciation of the nature of phenomenological evidence and horizon intentionality actually favors the individualist approach to collective intentionality.

Since the account developed in this work aims to strike a third way between atomistic individualism and collectivism, it is good to examine an alternative attempt at forging a middle way. Margaret Gilbert's theory of collective intentionality is both important to contemporary discussions of collective intentionality and attempts to avoid the excesses of both individualism and collectivism. It is argued that there are problems with Gilbert's account, problems that a more complete understanding of intentionality, like that found in phenomenology, can remedy. Gilbert appears to assume that all intentions are volitional in nature, a presupposition found in analytic philosophers. However, if a view of agency is to be sound, it must be consistent with the nature of the mind and consciousness. As such, if a view of agency presupposes a problematic conception of intentionality, and intentionality is fundamental to consciousness, then the resultant account will not be sound. The chapter includes discussion of Aron Gurwitsch's social philosophy to show that, despite differences, Gilbert's and phenomenology's approaches to social ontology share much in common, and serve as fruitful ground for additional dialogue.

The sixth chapter defends the Husserlian phenomenological approach from two criticisms motivated by realist concerns, one first offered by Barry Smith and the second from Hans Georg Gadamer. Smith argues that Husserl is ill equipped to answer for there being a plurality of worlds, a charge that is echoed in his criticisms of Searle's theory of collective intentionality. A world, in the phenomenological sense, is a totality of reference or meaning. As such, it is acceptable to speak of each individual or community as having its own world. A potential problem arises in that there may be disagreement across worlds. I argue that shared experiences and a shared framework for experience represent an adequate basis for plurality and that differences can largely be accounted for as unproblematic where one holds to the Aristotelian principle that particularism does not entail relativism.[53] Gadamer's criticisms are based around how he believes one should best understand the social dimensions of the intentional horizons of consciousness. I argue that Gadamer's notion of the fusion of horizons does not impart a clear criticism against the Husserlian paradigm, and can be accounted for by a subjective individualist position, relying on Gurwitsch's discussions of fusion from a subjective individualist perspective in my defense. I argue that both challenges fail against a more nuanced understanding of Husserlian phenomenology.

The final chapter defends Husserlian phenomenology's methodology from a challenge by Robert Sokolowski. Sokolowski sharpens the perennial challenge that Husserl's phenomenology is solipsistic in nature. The consequence for this, if accurate, is that Husserlian phenomenology would be incapable of accounting for any social phenomena. I argue that it is a mistake to think that Husserl's phenomenology is solipsistic in nature or committed to solipsism. I argue that the alternative methodological approach of the sort Sokolowski offers does not succeed and that a more complete understanding of Husserl shows his philosophy and its methodology are not committed to solipsism.

As Husserl would say: *zu den Sachen selbst!*

Notes

1. Mohanty 1984: 28
2. ibid: 29
3. ibid.
4. ibid: 30
5. ibid: 30-31
6. ibid: 31
7. ibid: 32
8. This squares with the analytic debates on atomism, which tend to follow Charles Taylor's classic paper, "Atomism" (Taylor 1979). Meijers 1998 is a good overview of the state of the debate on atomism v. holism.
9. Zahavi 2001: 16
10. Gallagher & Zahavi 2008: 183
11. In the phenomenological literature this is captured through the distinction between *Lieb* and *Körper*. One experiences a mannequin as having only *Körper*–a body, as mannequins are experienced as inanimate and insentient beings. That is distinct from the experience of an animate or sentient being, which is experienced as having *Lieb*–a lived body.
12. Gallagher & Zahavi 2008: 183
13. ibid: 183
14. Zahavi 2003a: 113
15. Gallagher & Zahavi 2008: 183
16. Husserl distinguishes between various kinds of evidentiary fulfillment. While I grant there is the appearance of something in common with the traditional problem of other minds, that is simply not what the phenomenological issue consists in. Further discussion of this issue goes beyond the scope of the present work.

17. Gallagher & Zahavi 2008: 187

18. Husserl is breaking with the Modern's conception of the mind–what we might call the "theater model." Much of the difficulty with understanding Husserl can be explained in lieu of his rigorous attempts to revise philosophy around the intentional model of the consciousness (See Null 2007a & Gurwitsch 1964).

With respect to Husserl not being concerned with a problem of solipsism, see Hutcheson 1980

19. Zahavi 2003a: 114

20. ibid.

21. Drummond 2003: 68

22. "Every mental phenomenon is characterized by what the Scholastics of the Middle Ages called the intentional (or mental) inexistence of an object, and what we might call, though not wholly unambiguously, reference to content, direction toward an object (which is not to be understood here as meaning a thing), or immanent objectivity. Every mental phenomenon includes something as object within itself, although they do not all do so in the same way" (Brentano in Gallagher & Zahavi 2008: 109).

23. Meixner 2006: 26

24. Gallagher & Zahavi 2008: 107

25. Searle addresses this distinction in Searle 1998: 85-86

26. "One of the most pervasive confusions in contemporary philosophy is the mistaken belief that there is some close connection, perhaps even an identity, between intensionality-with-an-s and intentionality-with-a-t. Nothing could be further from the truth. They are not even remotely similar" (Searle 1983: 24). Intension is a logical characteristic of sentences and statements. Intentionality is the power of consciousness whereby consciousness is directed at or about something. Confusion persists, at least in part as Searle notes, owed to that statement about intentionality possessing intensionality, i.e. reports about and descriptions of experience and consciousness are conflated with the states of affairs they describe (ibid: 24 & Ch. 7). See also Lowe 2000: Ch. 9

27. Gallagher & Zahavi 2008: 7

28. ibid.

29. Searle 1983: 1

30. Zahavi 2003a: 14

31. For further detail and insight into the disputes within the phenomenological tradition about intentionality, as well as those specific to Husserlian phenomenology, as to the nature of intentionality consult, Gallagher & Zahavi 2008; Zahavi 2003a; Drummond 2003; Moran 2000, 2005; D.W. Smith 2007; Sokolowski 2000; Strawson 2005; Gurwitsch 1970; Null 2007a, 2007b, 2007c.

32. Phenomenologists are not alone in insisting on respect for consciousness as essentially first-personal in nature. Analytic philosophers sympathetic to this view include not only Searle, but also David Chalmers and E.J. Lowe. Both Searle and Chalmers, in a manner typical to some analytic philosophers, tend to frame discussions of consciousness in qualitative terms–informed by and framed in reference to Locke's distinction between primary and secondary qualities.

"Husserl would consequently reject the widespread view that only sensory and emotional states have phenomenal qualities" (Gallagher & Zahavi 2008: 115). The phenomenological view is contrasted with the reductionist and eliminativist positions of those like Daniel Dennett and Paul and Patricia Churchland respectively.

33. For instance, one might argue that minds are dependent, emergent systemic level properties of brains, similar to Searle's larger view. Similarly, one might argue that consciousness is a dependent emergent property of minds. Such a distinction is not specific to the focus of this work.

34. Searle 1992: 79

35. Those who argue that language is basic to consciousness tend to confuse the epistemology with the ontology. Something's being first in the order of knowledge is not proof of its being first in the order of being, or vice versa.

36. Searle 1995: 23

37. "Intend" in each case is a general term; variant act-types of intention can be substituted for greater specificity.

38. See also the discussion of evidence in Zahavi 2003a: 31-35

39. Gallagher & Zahavi 2008: 10

40. Drummond 2003: 83

41. ibid.

42. For instance, in phenomenology, the sense of one's agency is dependently related to one's experiential awareness of one's agency. Animals and small children are not agents in that they are unaware of the self-directed nature of their activities, i.e. they don't experience themselves as directors of those activities: "In its proper sense, we understand agency to depend on the agent's consciousness of agency. That is, if someone intentionally causes something to happen, that person is not an agent of (even if they are a cause) if they do not know that they have intentionally caused it to happen. ...The kind of conscious knowledge involved in agency does not have to be of a very high order; it could be simply a matter of a very thin, pre-reflective awareness, and in most cases it is just that. Sometimes, however, there may be an explicit consciousness of acting for reasons. ...The *sense of agency* (or self-agency) for my actions, then, may involve a thin, pre-reflective awareness of what I am doing as I am doing it, or it may involve a more explicit consciousness filled with well-developed reasons" (Gallagher & Zahavi 2008: 158).

43. Husserl 1970

44. Husserl 1999: §§44-47

45. ibid: §55ff.

46. In the phenomenological tradition we emphasize the subject's role in intentionality, not just the object or content side of things. This leads us to speak of intentional acts as achievements, especially where the acts are predicated on or founded on other acts. The basic idea is an emphasis on how consciousness is not merely passive in nature.

47. For fuller treatment, consult Searle 1995

48. This is an interesting facet of the collective intentionality discussions as they first began to develop. More to the point, much of the divergence of the variant positions depends on what draws their authors to the issue. Some are motivated by concerns for theories of action, some from more explicit normative concerns, others from the position of philosophy of mind, still others are drawn by issues in philosophy of language. If one treats a multi-faceted problem from a singular view without concern for the larger picture, or on the assumption that a given orientation is more basic without adequate argument, one is bound to end up in a position that does violence to the phenomena. This is part of the merit of phenomenological philosophy, which asks one to set aside their particular theoretical quibbles and put the phenomena first. Doing so can sometimes result in something consonant with one's prior theoretical commitments, or can issue in revisions for the better. Not doing so, however, can lead to forced explanations, peculiar entities, and conclusions contrary to how experience is actually structured, i.e. scientism. A counter-intuitive position on the basis of research done is not problematic in itself. A conclusion motivated only by narrow theoretical interests or theoretically convenient definitions, however, is likely to be problematic and not representative of the phenomena themselves. More succinctly, vigilance is necessary to avoid drawing unjustified global conclusions about the phenomena, where more specific, qualified conclusions are what are generally offered. This includes where one approaches a problem from a particular type of concern and attempts to conclude something about the object of study independent of that concern. For example, the study of human nature *qua* biology or *qua* economics is never the study of human nature *qua* human nature.

49. This harkens back to the methodological orientation of Aristotle, respecting how the degree of precision one's investigation can take is dependent on its subject-matter and that it is foolish to expect a degree of precision greater than that which the subject-matter warrants. Further, there is an imperative to respect the limits of one's investigations and methodologies (Aristotle *Nicomachean Ethics* I.3). Hence, phenomenology embraces the complexity of phenomena and conscientiously aims to avoid offering reductive or eliminative arguments so as to preserve said complexity in analysis.

50. "Analytic philosophers typically try to solve fairly delineated philosophical problems by 'reducing them to their…parts and to the relations in which these parts stand.' Continental philosophers typically address large questions in a synthetic or integrative way, and consider particular philosophical issues to be 'parts of larger unities' and as properly understood and dealt with only when fitted into those unities" (Prado 2003: 10). C.G. Prado's volume is a good start at opening the meta-dialogue about differences between traditions and to address how the nature of philosophy on the whole needs both approaches. It is a false dilemma to insist that one tradition's approach is inherently more philosophical than the others, not to mention question begging.

51. Shaun Gallagher and Dan Zahavi have both made expressed efforts to engage analytic philosophy into dialogue with phenomenology. Alva Noë and Evan Thompson have each had success in crossing the supposed divide. D.W.

Smith emphasizes the common ground of both analytic philosophy and phenomenology at their inceptions, pointing out that their divergence occurred during
the mid-twentieth century (D.W. Smith 2007: 22-25). In a similar vein, Amie
Thomasson has argued that analytic philosophy itself was largely developed in
continuity with phenomenology, not in opposition to phenomenology as has
been commonly assumed (Thomasson 2002).
     52. Bratman 1999
     53. Nussbaum 1993

Chapter 1
That Experience Does Not Motivate a Robust Claim for Collective Consciousness

Groups or collectivities are experienced in everyday life as unified objects of concern and unified subjects of action. In the contemporary collective intentionality literature one refers to such groups or collectivities as plural subjects. A plural subject is any group or collective of individuals whose unity is not accidental and in relation to which either its participants recognize said unity or said unity is presupposed by those individuals' actions. While it is clear that collectivities can have characteristics or properties that their participating subjects don't have, it's not obvious what should be said about plural subjects themselves. For instance, even if a plural subject has a particular stance on something, what might be called a belief, e.g. a corporate or national policy, a group's opinion, etc., even if few of its members agree, it's not obvious that plural subject itself possesses consciousness or "has a mind of its own." Further, it's not clear why one would have to accept that by claiming plural subjects can embody intentions or be engaged in actions, one thereby must commit oneself to the position that the plural subject itself is conscious. It is not clear why one would have to accept that the plural subject itself is conscious or has a mind even if one accepted plural subjects could be attributed beliefs or responsibility for actions.

Strangely, the view that plural subjects are conscious agents in their own right appears to be given credence by a number of individuals.[1] Given the *Citizens United* decision of the United States Supreme Court, and the trend in favoring corporate interests over individual interests, the issue is becoming more pressing in recent years. In this chapter I argue that something's being a plural subject does not entail its possessing consciousness. In this chapter, and the next, I accept Kay Mathiesen's three conditions for the experience of plural subjects (plurality, awareness, collectivity), but argue that they do not entail a commitment to collective consciousness.[2] The title of Mathiesen's paper, "Collective Consciousness," I take to be misleading, and here aim to explore why that is so.[3] My arguments take her paper as a point of departure because she purports to offer an account that is consistent with the philosophy of the phenomenological tradition. In this chapter, I respond to her paper critically with the specific con-

cerns of the phenomenological tradition, arguing that in said tradition, consciousness can only be intrinsic to embodied subjectivities, of which collectivities are not instances. As such, I rely on a distinction between intrinsic and derived intentionality. I argue, views which attribute collective consciousness to
groups on the basis of their expressing intentionality conflate derived intentionality with intrinsic intentionality, and on that basis ascribe consciousness to plural subjects over and above the individuals who compose them. I don't deny that
Mathiesen is outlining a reasonable set of criteria for plural subjects, only that
she overreaches if her conclusion is that one can meaningfully attribute consciousness to plural subjects. For instance, she asserts that collective consciousness "needs no argument. Collective consciousness...is a familiar and ubiquitous part of our world. It is as common as families, clubs, tribes, churches, states,
and ethnic groups."[4] The argument appears to be that when one participates in
action in concert with others, that they sometimes represent a collective subject,
with its own consciousness. I aim to show that there is no adequate phenomenological basis for collective *consciousness*, despite there being good evidence for
collective *intentions*. I argue that there are not sufficient grounds to believe that
plural subjects are conscious in their own right. One should treat the status of the
collective entity, the plural subject, at least as tenuously as the individual subject
in a phenomenological analysis.

Theories of collective consciousness are often motivated either by 1) that
groups or collectives can bear predicates that their individuals either do not possess or whose individual members, on their own, might affirm the contrary; or 2)
the recent acceptance of a more robust role for socially conditioned beliefs, e.g.
one might argue that all minds are socially embedded or that all experience is
linguistically conditioned, therefore, socially conditioned. These are insufficient
grounds for extending the notion of consciousness to groups or collectives. I
agree that some who are critical of the idea of collective consciousness are motivated by fears of collectivity, a fear of individuality being subjugated to a collective whim or rule by the uncritical beliefs and actions of the many, etc. However, adherents of a view of collective consciousness seem to arrive at their
position either on the basis of uncritical metaphysical conclusions or reifications
of grammatical objects in displacement of *bona fide* phenomenological evidence.

One type of argument for collective consciousness might look roughly as
thus:[5] Normally, I experience my own intentions and action. Sometimes, my
intentions and actions are part of a collective or group activity; I can be part of a
"we." When acting as an individual, I am the subject of my acts and intentions.
Being a subject implies having consciousness. When acting as a group, we are
the subject of our acts and intentions. Since being a subject implies consciousness, the group must have consciousness. Call this the argument from subject-
status.

An alternative line of argument might argue from the position that intentionality requires consciousness. Individual intentionality is part of individual
consciousness, or dependent on individual consciousness. Insofar as there are
collective intentions, collective intentionality must either: (1) be part of a collec-

tive consciousness or (2) be dependent on collective consciousness. That is, collective intentionality implies collective consciousness in the same way that individual intentionality implies individual consciousness. Call this the argument from intentionality.[6]

Both arguments are *theoretical* arguments that refer to the phenomena they aim to describe obliquely. They are concerned more with satisfying theoretically motivated definitions and holding argumentative ground in the face of a challenge rather than the Aristotelian principle of the preservation of phenomena. An example of this is how research search engines sometimes change their format, claiming to make it more intuitive and user-friendly. The changes, however, are generally only intuitive to the programmers and habits individuals express in the non-academic usages of Internet search engines. Such changes fail to respect that academic research needs are more targeted and specifically oriented, that they differ from general Internet searching, in addition to what might be more intuitive for those operating in the underlying programming language. Since the purpose of an academic database is to serve academic interests, those interests establish the criteria as to whether or not the revisions are for the better or worse. If a database's aim is to assist academic interests and its claim to having succeeded in implementing improvements is based on programmers' interests, making academic research more difficult in practice, then the database's managers would be wrong to assert that they have offered the improvement in question. This is a mistake that could be alleviated by attending more carefully to the phenomena–who uses its database, why, and how they think (e.g. within disciplinary confines, primarily being interested in articles, etc.).

Consider also persons who uncritically apply rules without attending to particulars.[7] This is not to claim that the problem lies in challenging "common sense," but in glossing over or being inattentive to the phenomena that a given theory professes to describe. Both the argument from subject-status and argument from intentionality are flawed on their own terms, they fail to disambiguate their subject matter. The more direct concern is that phenomenological investigation does not support a case for collective *consciousness*, at least not without supplemental argumentation.

One of David Carr's basic insights is that there are everyday cases wherein one experiences being a part of a "we" and that the experience of a "we" is not reducible to an "I" experience. For example, if we go to the baseball game it is not the same as saying I went to the baseball game and you went to the baseball game. "We" connotes a sense of *togetherness* that is left out by the conjunction of individual claims. Even if we both, as a matter of fact, went to the game, we may not have done it together; we might not have *shared* the experience.[8] There are phenomena that are intrinsically intersubjective or plural in form and they cannot be adequately accounted for with reference to conjunctions of individual experiences. Take for example, playing baseball: one cannot play a game of baseball without others. Individual descriptions of actions taken in reference to the conjunctions of events constitutive of such a phenomena cannot themselves constitute the activity in question as such. Baseball games require subjects act-

ing together with one another in a cooperative effort.[9] What this means is that
we regularly experience meaningful attributions and projections in plural form,
establishing some ground for the legitimacy of "we-intentions," i.e. experiences,
from a phenomenological perspective, wherein others are directly referenced as
part of the subject of the intentionality manifest to one's experience.[10]

The potential value of Carr's contribution to a phenomenological analysis
of plural subjects is hard to understate. Carr works within the limitations of a
strictly *phenomenological* analysis, resisting any urge to argue from metaphysical impulses.[11] "The reality of the intentional subject–singular or plural–may
seem a pale thing to those whose notion of reality is tailored to the hard physical
world. And it may be difficult for them to fit such ephemera into their seamless
ontology. But that is their *theoretical* problem."[12] Tackling a theoretical problem
is not itself a bad thing, but it does not guarantee that one's subject matter is
representative of the world of experience; phenomenology directs its analyses on
the experiential world explicitly. "For all of us, outside the constructed worlds of
our theories, selves, our own and others, and the communities to which we belong, are as real as anything we know."[13] "For the phenomenologist it is this
reality that counts."[14]

Returning to the main argument, advocates of collective consciousness appear to equivocate between two things: 1) an individual's consciousness of their
plural subject experience(s), i.e. an individual's consciousness of their individual
relation to or participation in a collective; and, 2) collective consciousness, the
consciousness the plural subject or collective itself might have. To be clear, I
argue against (2) the claim that collectives themselves are conscious, and do not
here offer an argument against the claim that there is a modification of individual consciousness relative to plural subject or collective experiences. I do, however, count the choice of 'collective consciousness' as a name for such phenomena to be entirely misguided and inappropriate.[15]

Mathiesen proposes three conditions for collective consciousness. Again,
she also asserts her position is supported by phenomenological evidence, a claim
with which I disagree. After clarifying the three conditions for collective experience, I argue that the claim that plural subjects have consciousness is implausible whether it aims to deploy an argument from subject-status to collective consciousness or an argument from intentionality to collective consciousness. A
diagnosis is offered in the end that the arguments may either be conflating a
grammatical subject or subject of action with subjectivity, or confusing something's expressing intentionality and something's having the capacity for intentionality intrinsic to it.[16] Something's being expressive of intentionality can
function in derived capacities–as inanimate objects can express intentionality–
where that is not indicative of, nor sufficient justification for the judgment that
the thing in question itself possesses intentionality in an intrinsic sense or that
said being itself possesses consciousness.

Before moving on, it is useful to disambiguate the distinction between subject and subjectivity. This is the distinction between a subject in the grammatical
sense (of a sentence), the logical sense (subject-predicate relation), the sense of

action (principally what the action should be attributed to), and an *experiencing* subject (subjectivity). Subjectivity thus refers to a conscious being, i.e. a subject who *experiences*. It is important also to distinguish subjectivity from the subject of experience: *who* experiences from *what* is experienced. Groups might be experienced by one as a unity, but that doesn't necessitate that the group itself is the same sort of subject that an individual is. I don't deny that plural subjects are subjects in the grammatical, logical, or action based senses, while I do deny that they are subjectivities. I deny plural subjects are conscious entities in their own right, thereby denying them intentionality in an intrinsic fashion.

Why make such a distinction? For example, there are actions that are performed by groups (i.e. plural subjects) that are not reducible to actions predicable of individuals. Unless one counts the plural subject as the subject of action and counts it a subject with some independent status of its own, as distinct from its member individuals, one cannot address these actions. The range of specific plural subject actions that cannot be readily accounted for without significant loss of meaning, some hardly able to be made sense of at all, by reducing them to individuals' acts are non-trivial. For instance, if one corporation acquires or merges with another, one nation goes to war with another, etc., it's not clear that a summation of many individuals' actions can adequately account for what happens. Indeed, the individuals' actions are often done as party to the plural subject's aim. Given such considerations it seems quite clear that plural subjects are subjects. However, there's nothing about treating groups as subjects that necessitates that the plural subject itself represent, or be itself, something with its own subjectivity.

Collective Consciousness

Mathiesen's position is "that individuals can share in a collective consciousness by forming a collective subject and that they do so by modeling within themselves the states of consciousness of the collective."[17] She identifies three conditions for collective subjects: plurality, awareness, and collectivity. Each of the alternative theses she discounts is supposed to violate at least one of these conditions, those theses will be directly examined in the next chapter. Mathiesen states her position in further detail. "When we take the collective (as opposed to merely plural) perspective, and thus form a properly *collective* subject, we take the perspective of the collective of which we are members."[18] This is possible, she claims, in virtue of simulation and empathy wherein we project and " 'simulate' the states of a collective subject of which we are members."[19] In a way, this is to claim that we can take on the perspective of the collective. Elsewhere Mathiesen claims that we adopt only the perspective of the other *members* of the collective, not the *collective* itself.[20] If she means to refer to taking the perspective of another individual or a group as an analogical act of judgment, this is not really collective consciousness. In that case, the term 'collective consciousness' is misleading.

The three criteria for collective experience are said to function together in the following way. Collective experience is plural in that it is composed of multiple persons. "The individual members of the collective are aware of the contents of their collective consciousness and the intentionality of the collective is derived from that of its members."[21] It is collective in virtue of the "shared conception of the collective" dependent upon the relation of its members.[22] In other words, her concept of collective consciousness consists of multiple persons being aware of their collectivity and what, as a collective, they have in common. This also satisfies the awareness condition.

In another paper, Mathiesen offers further clarification of the awareness condition.[23] She specifies that she's not requiring awareness per se of collectives, only the *capacity* for reflection on one's beliefs and desires.[24] In support of the discussion there, she points out that individuals are not always aware of their own beliefs and motivations. She adds: "we each have a duty to reflect on what we do and on the sorts of beliefs and desires that such actions express."[25] Awareness, then, requires only the capacity to reflect on beliefs and desires. If collectives have this, then they satisfy the awareness criterion.[26]

Beyond the ambiguity of the three conditions on Mathiesen's account, a first concern is that it is in no way obvious how sharing beliefs and ways of understanding the world requires *collective* consciousness. That is to say, it is unclear how consciousness itself could be collective in nature or how there could be a consciousness of a collective. Second, the awareness criterion is potentially too strict, possibly ruling out almost all everyday group experiences from qualifying as being collectivities. This would be especially problematic in virtue of her claim to the ubiquity of collectivities in experience. Third, the emphasis on individuals and their role in this view potentially empties this of being anything authentically collective. It becomes unclear what is *collective* about her picture of collective *consciousness*, beyond the plurality and awareness criteria.

The Awareness Condition

Regarding the first concern, that it is in no way obvious how sharing beliefs and ways of understanding the world requires *collective* consciousness, it is clear that one wants to be able to differentiate accidental cases of shared beliefs and attitudes, from those unified in a community of subjects acting together intentionally. What is not clear is why communities must manifest a notion of collective consciousness. Communities could share beliefs and perspectives in virtue of a shared history, which does not require any extra or added consciousness to the individual consciousnesses of their members. To distinguish from accidental cases of agreement, there must be some sense of identification of the individuals as being participants in a plural subject, wherein one's experience is in a we-mode. One's identification as part of a "we" seems essential to the case for collective consciousness.[27] Identification in a "we" in no way implies that "we" has consciousness, which is what the term collective consciousness suggests. In other words, consciousness of a collective, a "we," even identifying oneself as being part of one, does not imply collective consciousness. A shared sense of collective doesn't necessarily require much in the way of substantive commitment. It could mean no more than that we identify as a group or member in a group. For instance, people in line together at the DMV might identify as a group, expressing their solidarity in the face of nauseatingly soulless bureaucracy. That does not commit them to having anything else in common or generate a collective consciousness.

If the awareness condition requires awareness on the part of individual members of a collective as to the contents of their shared beliefs and attitudes, it would seem that nearly no group has collective consciousness. For instance, children often share beliefs and attitudes of their families and communities; yet do not always have awareness as to *what precisely is shared*. This is evidenced where they meet with surprise those who have differences with themselves. One might think that dissenting views internal to a group–for example, Democrats, Republicans, Americans, etc.–would undermine the awareness criterion as well.

One might argue all that the awareness condition requires is awareness of what is common to members, what makes them members of *this* group. Even here, some identify with and participate in groups sometimes without said awareness regarding what makes them the group they are, e.g. cliques or political affiliations. Some vote by party without much, if any, awareness as to that party's platform contemporarily or historically. Not all participants in a group participate for the same reasons, nor seem to be required that they be aware of another's having distinct reasons from oneself. For example, Log Cabin Republicans, social conservatives in the religious right, and libertarian minded economic conservatives all participate in the Republican voting bloc for distinctive reasons, and social conservatives are sometimes blind to other motivations for voting with that bloc. As such, there is reason to hesitate about too stringent a requirement for awareness of what constitutes group membership. Of course, this still allows that awareness of group identity could be negatively constituted, as being a member of this group is defined as being opposed to members of some other.

Additionally, one might argue that to be aware of what is shared would require knowing *who* all is part of one's "we." Such a requirement would pose an unnecessary burden on subjects. No one American knows all other Americans, and if all Americans have in common is the label and a citizenship, even if they don't all understand or agree as to precisely what is entailed in that, it would seem to trivialize and make arbitrary the collectives one could identify with. We could call, for instance, all Americans who are blonde and 5'8" a collective in virtue of that commonality, even make all of them aware of that commonality. It's not clear as to how that would represent a meaningful grouping as far as belief-sets, attitudes, or actions are concerned. It's not that it can't be treated as such, but that it generally is not, and all of those persons possessing the right trait being made aware of their commonality isn't itself sufficient for group membership–hence the additional conditions of plurality and collectivity.

A more plausible understanding of the awareness criterion, would be to argue that only a sense of the criteria for membership be necessary to satisfy the
awareness condition, such criterion could represent a basis for solidarity and
thereby the collectivity in question.[28] This view has the benefit of capturing intuitions about how larger collectives or collectives distributed over spatial or temporal boundaries can maintain some cohesion and sense. However, it appears in
practice that individuals sometimes accept rather vague or indeterminate criteria
as sufficient for identification of membership. Take for instance the recent
movements in American politics, the Tea Party and Occupy Wall Street. Both
movements were supposedly unified before having any clear or articulate sense
of what their unity meant, arguably they still struggle in that respect. As such, it
appears that the group of all 5'8" blonde Americans *could* serve as a basis for
identification with a collective and through which one might act as a group, even
if highly unlikely.

There is a further concern, however, that something is not adequate in such
an account to the types of lived personal experiences we have in smaller groups.
The direct contact with and awareness of others in a personal manner, in lived
experiential contexts, seems to add something significant to the nature or dynamic of a collective. This doesn't pose a problem for the general account, as
knowledge of membership or identification criteria could still be sufficient in
such cases. However, it does point to a potential sub-category of collectives
whose awareness conditions are more stringent, and which are reflected by the
personal awareness intuition expressed above. There appears to be something
more meaningful happening in cases of collectives that require some intimacy of
contact in addition to spatial and temporal proximity.

The Collectivity Condition

The dependence on the individual could be thought to undermine the collectivity condition. Collectivity is clearly supposed to be differentiated from plurality in that a collective has some permeating commonality or principle of unity
that is not required by plurality alone. A mere collection of people is not a collective. But if one requires that there be both a collection and an awareness of
being a collective, either collectivity seems to punctuate the conjunction of those
two conditions, or it amplifies them in some unclear manner. Larry May, among
others, has argued that there is an awareness of our sense of solidarity with others, a sense of a common cause or common purpose through which one orients
their action in the context of plural subject (group or collective) behavior.

> Solidarity is a relationship which exists among individuals, but it is not itself
> merely a function of the individual psychological states of the members of the
> group. The relationships themselves not only influence the psychological states
> of the members, but they facilitate the ability of these members to engage in
> joint action. ...each chooses to act in solidarity with the others, and each there-

by comes to do these things which facilitate the actions of fellow group members....[29]

Solidarity is a product of individual recognition of common purpose that enframes one's thoughts and actions in a manner directed through that common purpose. Marion Smiley underscores that for May, and others, "group solidarity does not *require* group self-consciousness."[30] In other words, one may have awareness of one's comportment being directed on the basis of solidarity with others and express collective intentionality, without the *collective* itself thereby expressing any consciousness of its own either independent of or additive to the individual members.

A problem seems to originate from the ambiguity inherent in the idea of collective consciousness itself. When one speaks of collective consciousness they could refer to either some thing or entity in its own right *or* something shared by individual conscious agents. If the latter is the case, then 'collective consciousness' refers only to shared states of individuals, and the collectivity criterion appears to add a binding "we" component. A "we" identification by the individual refers not to a collection of persons, but a collective of persons with some commonality(s).

That the identification is the *individual's* and that any "intentionality of the collective is derived from that of its members" must give us pause about how it is that there is any collective consciousness or even a collective subjectivity at all.[31] To speak of plural *subjects*, collective *subjectivities*, and collective *consciousness*, all as roughly equivalent sorts of notions is misleading, and strongly suggestive of some thing or entity in its own right. It reifies our interactions with others, endowing groups with a property or capacity beyond that of their members. To give a simplistic example: assuming a set of two parental figures, does a child address one, two or three *subjects* when they respond to their parents? One could argue that a child responds to one subject: their parents as a whole. One could argue that a child responds to two subjects: their parents as individual persons who both share a role in common. Or, one might argue that a child responds to three subjects: their parents as a unity in addition to the individuals composing that unity separately.

There is reason to think that there is ambiguity in how "subject" refers in these cases. "Subject" might refer to subjectivities, entities endowed with consciousness and intrinsic intentionality. "Subject" might also refer to a sense-unity in experience. Individualist views can answer the question of quantities by specifying that there are two subjectivities, even if there is another possible subject to experience–the unity of sense that represents a whole to which the subjectivities proper are parts. To what or to whom the child addresses depends on the specific act-content structure of the particular intentional state. This is evidenced by how children smoothly and intuitively redirect their responses to maximize their interests. The child addresses *one* group, their parents. But they may address each parent individually in an attempt to undermine the parental unity in a manner to their benefit. Their "parents" is a complex phenomenal whole (unity in experience), two parts of which are subjectivities in their own right; those individuals are the only subjectivities. If the whole is counted as an intentional agent or subjectivity in its own right, endowed with consciousness, then one's position is strongly collectivistic in kind. Though it's not entirely clear what is being referred to exactly.

There are good reasons to hold that groups can have properties their individual members don't. That is not itself something problematic. A problem arises if we allow that attribute of groups to be promiscuous, if *any* property can be predicated of groups. It is not clear whether consciousness is something that can be ascribed to or predicated of groups, or that subjectivity is something that can be predicated of groups. In the case of consciousness, the group does not have all characteristics shared by its members. That is, consciousness and subjectivity are characteristics or properties of group members—excusing that awkward way of speaking about such matters—that groups themselves cannot and do not possess. Just as no person can divide and replicate themselves in the same way the cells of their body can, no group is a subject endowed with consciousness. No group ingests or urinates as its members can. What is conscious about a group or collective, especially if it is entirely dependent on the consciousness, subjectivity and intentionality of the individuals who comprise it?[32] In short, to argue groups or collectives are conscious is to commit the fallacy of composition, unless one can offer independent reasons for thinking it is conscious.

In the end, all that seems to be required is that *individuals* have a mode of consciousness whose content transcends their individuality. It is not just in the sense of one's being conscious of the chair in the hall, of being conscious of an object other than oneself. Rather, it is that *individuals* can be conscious of *other subjects* as other and in virtue of that are potential candidates for being party to collective experiences and actions, partners in a "we." We can come together to found complex forms of social interactions, predicated upon our individual capabilities and beliefs. This is what Husserl's discussions of higher order pluralities and social subjectivities represent and attempt to describe, a shorthand way of referring to intersubjective achievements at various levels of founded meanings. Collective intentionality as a mode of individual consciousness does not require or imply collective consciousness. Phenomenologically, there appears to be no concrete experience of a conscious group or collective to which one could appeal as unambiguous evidence for collective consciousness. One experiences groups and collectives as real phenomena with certain regularities of form and function. Claims of collective consciousness apart from individual subjects being essential constituents of the relevant sorts for groups or collectivities appears not to be motivated by the phenomena themselves. Such a position appears to be motivated instead by theoretical considerations, pre-commitments to describing phenomena in a given way—regardless of what the phenomena themselves offer as evidence.[33]

In the context of the overall argument, then, one is pointing out that our experiences are only ever our own and that the experience of other subjects in the robust sense—as other experiencing subjects, i.e. subjectivities—does not include groups or collectives, but their members only. One does not experience their group as itself an entity with consciousness, and really not as having a mind in a literal sense either. One does not experience plural subjects as themselves conscious either in one's firsthand experience as a member, nor as an outsider, even though one experiences plural subjects or collectives as something distinct from and not reducible to individuals. Descriptions that suggest consciousness are best taken metaphorically or as elliptical descriptions of much more complex phenomena. The view that plural subjects have consciousness, then, is likely motivated by theoretical concerns that are separate from experience itself.

Further, the appresentational manifold of expectations associated with the experience of a plural subject does not match the cases of other subjects. Plural subjects don't bear the same anticipatory dimensions in experience that individuals do. One doesn't expect groups or collectivities to act as individuals act. More to the point, in the case of groups to which one is a part, there is a lack of alterity associated with the group itself. Alterity, being the essentially open-ended otherness of another subjectivity, is always present in the experience of other individuals. While there may be a sense of something alien associated with groups to which one is not a member, the group itself still doesn't impress itself upon one as another individual does. A group's alienness is more readily discernable; one can grasp a sense of a group's nature in a way that one cannot with another individual. This isn't to say that one can ever understand the totality of a group, though that is doubtful. Rather, it is to argue that the limits of our grasping group natures are either epistemic and not ontological in nature, or they are epistemic and ontologically dependent on the alterity of their participant members. Another possibility is that perhaps the alterity of the members, especially when directed as a unit under the organizing principle of the group, whereby they determine each other in a way inconsistent with the other's alterity, acts as a kind of bad-faith denial of one's subjectivity, which contributes to the alien nature experienced in association with groups. That is, perhaps it is actually that submitting to group unity denies or constricts one's subjectivity that is experienced as alien in association with group experiences. Perhaps it is not the alterity of the other that is experienced, but a collective negation of alterity.

Phenomenologically Motivated Concerns

David Carr has argued there are two senses of transcendence in Husserl and has established clearly that transcendence is one of the main motivating factors in Husserl's account of intersubjectivity. "Transcendence is conceived as non-reducibility of what is meant to the particular act or acts [of consciousness] in which it is meant. But the meant surpasses any particular act or acts by always being the reference point to other *possible* acts implied in any *actual* one."[34] Those who object that phenomenology is inherently solipsistic do so in virtue of a problem of transcendence. "[Phenomenology] can account for the weaker sense of transcendence (the transcendence of my particular act or acts) because of its concept of the relation between actuality and potentiality in the stream of consciousness."[35] The stronger sense of transcendence is what is invoked when one identifies something, especially in the natural attitude, as being objective. "The objective is not only irreducible to any particular acts of mine; it is also not reducible to *all possible* acts of mine, my whole actual and possible stream of consciousness, because it is identically the same for others and their acts as well."[36] In Husserl's words, "It must now be made understandable how, at the founded higher level, the sense-bestowal pertaining to transcendency proper, to constitutionally secondary *Objective transcendency*, comes about–and does so as experience."[37] The weak sense of transcendence is transcendence of one's actual acts. The strong sense of transcendence is transcendence of one's actual and possible acts. As Husserl states: "...that I can become aware of someone else, presupposes that *not all my own modes of consciousness are modes of my self-consciousness.*"[38]

Our interactions with others are dependent on intentional contents (others' acts of consciousness) that are strongly transcendent, i.e. that there be consciousness other than one's own that is intended as being transcendent of one's own consciousness and not as limited to one's own subjective or idiosyncratic intentional content(s) of *their own* consciousness. *Otherness* is not the experience of something as dependent on *me,* but the experience of something that *my* experience can never fully encompass.

Collective intentions are inherently transcendent in the strong sense in that they implicate others and their intentionality in one's intention.[39] In neither case is one engaged in a sort of constructivism:

> It is a matter of examining this experience [of the Objective world as continuously experienced and habitually accepted] itself and uncovering intentionally the manner in which it bestows sense, the manner in which it can occur as experience and become verified as evidence relating to an actual existent with an explicable essence of *its* own, which is not *my* own essence and has no place as a constituent part thereof, though it nevertheless can acquire sense and verification only in my essence.[40]

Rather, one is examining the intentional formations that are not reducible to one's own, and that are constitutive of the meanings one experiences in phenomena. In some cases, those intentions are individual in form, and not contingent on what the individual intends; for example, a visual experience of Niagara Falls. In other cases, those intentions are collective in form, and contingent upon the many individuals agreeing on a more or less determinate content; for example, that a certain person is the President or that a given article of green and black inked cloth paper has such a monetary value for purposes of exchange. The key point for Husserl, and why phenomena must come first not only in an epistemic sense, is that the meanings and their verification in evidence are only possible through acts of individual subjectivities; but, phenomena inform our ontology as well, against which our claims are liable to evaluation. Arguments on collective intentionality are liable to consistency considerations with the ontology of consciousness, as intentionality is primarily a characteristic of consciousness. If decisions are necessary for actions, consciousness is necessary for decisions. Allowing for a collective consciousness would mean some new form of subjectivity capable of experiencing and verifying meanings. "It is to the I as an *individual* subject or person, rather than to any sort of plurality, that intentionality properly belongs."[41] Beyond metaphorical attributions or a derivative status ascription, there appears to be no good evidence for collectivities having that capability independent of the individuals, who compose them, and their acts, founded or unfounded.

Reviewing Again the Three Conditions of Collective Experience

One may ask if in emphasizing the individual in the manner done here whether or not one violates the proposed plurality condition. For instance, by emphasizing the individual, one might be understood as de-emphasizing the group or hinting toward a reductivist account of a group. Individualist positions that couch collectivity and collective intentionality in relation to individual consciousness may *prima facie* seem to violate the plurality condition. Whether or not this is an actual case of violating the plurality condition depends entirely on how one specifies what that condition actually requires. Is it that there be a plurality of subjects as a matter of fact? That wouldn't be a purely phenomenologically motivated position as Mathiesen has claimed to offer. Instead, such a position is an object-position (with extra-experiential criteria), referring to objects in the world independent of experience as its condition. The difference is whether or not one's counting the plurality condition to range over objects in the world or the form of the content of one's consciousness. The way plurality factors into the phenomenal meanings, *intentionally*, is in the structure of the intentional content itself–or, alternately, as a different intentional act-type. That is, either in a mental content that is plural in form or in an intentional or conscious act of a we-form or we-mode. Even if modes of intentionality don't themselves represent anything, modes clearly do affect and *modify* the intentional content itself. The plurality of principal importance phenomenologically is plurality in *meaning* of experience, i.e. in consciousness, not objects in the world as such. The plurality at an object level represents the conditions of verification or evidence for a given plural-meaning state, not the condition for a plural-meaning state in consciousness itself. If that were not the case, it would be impossible to be mistaken in relation to we-structured intentions. Also, it would be impossible to *imagine* or *remember* a genuine we-oriented intention. One could never project forward about what one and their friends might do at a future time, as the object-level state of affairs did not exist.[42]

One now has at their disposal a way of better understanding the difference between plurality and collectivity as conditions for collective consciousness. Plurality is a condition affecting the intentional form of one's acts of consciousness. Phenomenologically, the plurality condition is that of an intention or experience in we-form. Collectivity is a condition adding a sense of togetherness, and thereby modifying the subject-relation to the content of an intentional act. There plurality may be satisfied by accidental cases of we-formations. For example, "we (referring to all in attendance) witnessed the game ending out at the World Series." If this is what Mathiesen understands by her conditions for collective consciousness, they really represent little new beyond Carr's precedent findings. As Carr notes:

> There are, of course, different uses of 'we.' I may say of you and me that "we saw" the Eiffel Tower, but that implies hardly more than a common object. We may have seen the tower at different times, or at the same time but unaware of each other's presence. Little is lost if we substitute for the "we saw" a simple conjunction: I saw the tower *and* you saw it. But, if we see it *together*, something essential to the experience is lost when that substitution is made, since in this case each of us saw the tower and was aware that the other was seeing it too.[43]

Perhaps it is that sense of we-together in the experience and not merely an object of experience in common that underlies the collectivity condition.

Now, however, there may be an issue teasing apart the collectivity and awareness conditions. Carr, as noted above, argues that the strong sense of "we" involves that "each of us saw the tower and was aware that the other was seeing it too." One can ask what is added by collectivity, if one has plurality (we-intention) and awareness? One could claim that meeting the plurality and awareness conditions may still fail to capture something important. Say that I'm aware of your viewing the tower at the same time as I, perhaps because we spoke on a cell phone while trying to come together at the tower. Here, one might argue collectivity is missing. But, it's not clear why collectivity would have to involve spatial proximity. Why might cell phone contact not be sufficient? It seems that plenty of strong we-intentional states could arise in the context of a teleconference, an Internet chat, a videoconference, etc. Certainly business teams where each individual is working from a separate location and collaborating remotely are still collectively intending.

It's not clear that plurality or awareness, independently or in conjunction, necessarily includes the sense of togetherness. For instance, if we change the communication between us as we are trying to meet at the tower to text messaging there does appear to be some significant change. I can be aware of your also being in the presence of the tower, and hold that we are both seeing it. But the connection between our experiences has been modified. With texting, there is less of a sense of togetherness, arguably none, than there is available through the phone conversation. What's changed appears to be the qualitative character of our experience.[44] Collectivity will then be taken as a qualitative condition affecting the we-form of one's experience, plurality a formal condition, i.e. that the experience is in plural- or we-form. Awareness can then be understood as an epistemic condition for the subject of collective intentions.

What can one say about the *phenomenology* of collectivities or groups? What phenomena may be motivating the view of a collective consciousness? Mathiesen herself appeals at one point to Margaret Gilbert's theory of plural subjects. For Gilbert, individuals form plural subjects when they come together, "as a body," when they act as one.[45] For Gilbert, a collective intention is the intending of the group, and is not derived from the intentions of the individual members. Though, all group members share a joint commitment to that intention.[46] In contrast to Gilbert's view, and speaking directly from the perspective of phenomenology, is Carr's articulation of the plural subject. Carr explicitly avoids weighing in on what one precisely commits oneself to ontologically or existentially when speaking of plural subjects.[47] However, he acknowledges that "we do exist and participate in such communities–indeed they are very important parts of our lives. We do say *we* to each other and we mean something real by it. For the phenomenologist it is this reality that counts."[48] That is, experience as *meaningful* or meant as real is what phenomenology comments on first. To Carr, plural subjects are constituted in basically the same way as individuals– "in and through a series of experiences and actions by way of a reflexive, narrative account of that series."[49] Further, "Like the *we,* the I exists as the unity of a multiplicity of intentional experiences and actions, a unity not postulated in advance but constituted in and through that multiplicity."[50] In other words, one can, and often does, refer to groups they belong to or oppose as things it makes sense to individuate. At the same time, whatever unity these groups or groupings have is based in some shared experiences, beliefs, actions, etc., of the individual members. Yet the group itself has no being apart from our engagements in, against, with, etc. it. If the relations no longer obtain, there will no longer be any collective or group.

There is one final concern about the notion of collective consciousness as it is presently being discussed. One might object that the position formed here is dependent on a position like Searle's in relation to collective intentionality; one accepts collective intentions, but requires their expression be limited to the individual. Hans Bernhard Schmid identifies this as a position that is individualist about collective intentionality's subjectivity, but collectivist about collective intentionality in a formal sense.[51] Perhaps one might motivate a case for collective consciousness if one endorsed a position that was both subjectively *and* formally collectivistic. Basically, if one accepts the form of collective intentions, we-form intentions, and accepts that these intentions are dependent on collective subjects, this might imply a theory of collective consciousness.

The argument here is principally that collectivity does not imply some new form of consciousness. Even if one claims that collective intentions extend across subjects necessarily–that an individual alone could never have a collective intention–there's no reason to accept that the intention is 'located in' or is the act of some superagent over and above the individuals who compose the group. It is far more reasonable, even on a subjectively and formally collectivist view, to claim that the intention is only partially realized in each individual of some set of individual consciousnesses. Does this mean that one participates in another consciousness? That is not clear. What still seems to be unclear is how one individual experiences another's partial contribution to the whole. At best, a subjectively collectivist position seems to be referencing *as one* a set of individuals' intention*s* per some shared aim. This, however, is not a phenomenological notion, but one referencing a state of affairs independent from the subjective standpoint. This is far less radical than claiming that the intention be a part of some new entity, a collective consciousness that itself *experiences* the intentional content. Collectivity could be preserved, most plausibly, by distributing collective intentionality across subjects acting *as if* a single subject, while retaining act-content functionality at the level of individual subjects, not at the level of the plural subject state of affairs. Such a view avoids hypothesizing an entity above and beyond those already present while preserving the operative sense of something's bearing meaning or being directed across a unified set of individual subjects. Barring the introduction of some argument to the conclusion that it is necessary to consider such entities, there is no reason to accept them.

The Arguments from Subject-Status and from Intentionality

To return to the arguments for collective consciousness presented in the introduction, the argument from subject-status and the argument from intentionality, one must ask which, if either, might be associated with Mathiesen's view and whether either argument is viable. At first blush, it appears that her argument might be seen as approaching collective consciousness by the argument from subject-status. Recall two passages quoted previously. First, "that individuals can share in a collective consciousness by forming a collective subject and that they do so by modeling within themselves the states of consciousness of the collective." Second, "when we take the collective (as opposed to merely plural) perspective, and thus form a properly *collective* subject, we take the perspective of the collective of which we are members." These seem to suggest that a version of the argument from subject-status might be operative.

It has been argued that this line of argument relies on an ambiguity in the sense of "subject."[52] When the argument claims "Being a subject implies having consciousness" it means subject in the strong sense of having subjectivity,[53] not being a subject in a grammatical sense or subjective form of intentionality. Grammatical subjects don't have consciousness; pointing to the way we speak about subjects is insufficient evidence on its own in order to warrant such a view. If one intends something in the form of "we intend *x*," it does not follow that the "we" represents an *experiencing subject* in its own right. Otherwise, a "we" that a child intends, ranging over herself and her stuffed animals would be its own plural subject, having its own consciousness. The stuffed animals are not subjects in the robust sense of having subjectivity. Nor is there subjectivity ranging across the set of child and stuffed animals in any way other than the child's subjectivity alone.

What about groups of conscious subjects engaged in collective action? What about an orchestra or football team for instance? After all, these are the types of cases Mathiesen refers to. Could the argument from subject-status apply to such cases? Still I believe no. Here the problem is that one infers from subjects having subjectivity that their acting in concert implies some additional subject. In other words, one commits the fallacy of composition. Instead of attributing properties or powers to groups as such, one can appreciate that groups might express certain characteristics only in virtue of their memberships. There are two separate claims I would make here. First, that a group might analogically express certain behaviors or characteristics is no evidence that groups are intrinsically a certain way, e.g. if a group is said to have a certain kind of character or thoughts of its own. Second, if one experiences groups primarily through interactions with individual subjects, it shouldn't surprise one that a group can, by extension, seem to express powers or characteristics those individuals possess. That individuals can act in groups and lend their powers to groups isn't evidence that groups themselves possess the same powers or characteristics of the individuals necessary to their composition.

What might explain why groups exhibit such qualities? It will help if one reminds herself of Searle's distinctions between intrinsic intentionality, derived intentionality, and as-if intentionality. These present us with three alternative ways of understanding collectives. First, one might claim that they only express as-if intentionality, i.e. they don't express intentionality in fact, but we speak of them as if they have intentionality. This is too weak a claim, as collectives do have intentional characteristics and can engage in actions directed at some end. The remaining alternatives, then, are between whether collectives possess intrinsic intentionality, where collectives themselves are conscious beings; or, collectives possess derived intentionality, where collectives are not themselves conscious, but nonetheless can express intentionality.

To attribute to collectives intrinsic intentionality and by implication consciousness, however, is to reify the collective and treat it as an instance of subjectivity in its own right. It is here that one asks for evidence to the effect that a collective is conscious. It appears that there is an equivocation between the subject of an action and the subject in a cognitive or experiential sense (i.e. subjectivity). While one may make attributions of actions to inanimate objects like computers and machines or weather systems one doesn't thereby attribute consciousness or intrinsic intentionality to those objects, they don't possess subjectivity. Collectives may also be meaningfully given ascriptions as subjects of action, but the leap to subjectivity or consciousness does not appear warranted in that the mere presence of intentionality is insufficient, as the intentionality may only be derived intentionality. The intentionality of collectives might be no more than an extension of their being constituted by and participated in by the subjects who function in and often represent them. Indeed, such a view postulates less while having equivalent explanatory power. The onus is then on those who seek to attribute intrinsic intentionality and thereby consciousness proper to collectives to demonstrate how descriptions of collectives that only attribute intrinsic intentionality to individuals are inadequate.

What's more, the phenomenology seems to be against such a view in cases like these.[54] What are our experiences of groups like, both in dealing with them as other or as participants in them? A telling type of case is where we try to deal with a corporation or group, in a customer service capacity for instance, over a defective product perhaps. In such cases we often deal with some individual or set of individuals as representatives of the corporation or company. In particularly frustrating instances they deny or complicate our requests by appealing to corporate or company policy. Even if we become irritated at the exchange, we often accept that the individual or individuals we are interacting with are not responsible for the policy or policies that are the source of our irritation.

What happens in such cases? First, there is a sense formed that one is dealing with a group of peoples, the corporation or company, not all of whose members are empowered to respond the way one hopes. One experiences the customer service agent as a representative of that corporation or company, albeit with determinately finite powers. One appreciates that there are those who have the power to handle our request, as is often occasioned where one asks for management to avoid dealing with floor employees, on the belief that they possess greater amounts of the relevant power to serve our request. Next, one tends to place responsibility on the corporation or company as opposed to its representative(s), sometimes the representative(s) at hand shares in our frustration, shares in shifting responsibility to some indeterminate subject. In the absence of a determinate individual subject to bear responsibility, that responsibility remains attached, not to some indeterminate subject, but is affixed to the determinate object that is the corporation or company. That is, one treats them *as* subject. The phenomenologist might even argue that experiences like this are the phenomenological basis for the legal treatment of corporations as persons. One hastens to add that the legal convention is not itself sufficient for moral status as persons equivalent with individual subjects, as the *Citizens United* decision appears to claim.

Consider how one likes some companies and dislikes others, likes some organizations and roots against their competitors, etc. It's not that one has no determinate intentional content. These are definite things to which our attitudes, affects, etc., are directed. In important respects, however, our experience of these *as* subjects in some sense is not at all like the experience of another person as subject. What differs importantly is that groups, organizations, companies, etc., all represent abstract entities on an order different from the concrete individual persons in our experience. Even where experienced *as* subject, they are not experienced as *subjectivities*–as subjects who experience or have consciousness in their own right. Rather, they are more abstract sorts of subjects–subjects in a grammatical sense, or subjects in the sense of a distinct unity of moral consideration. Thus, the argument from subject-status fails on account of there being no determinate evidence in support of the claim that collectivities are subjects in the same manner that individuals are.

Perhaps the view might be said to tacitly offer an argument from intentionality. It was said that it is individuals who take the perspective of the collective, who model such a perspective. Being able to construct a perspective does not entail the existence of any entity who actually has said perspective. Mathiesen insisted that, "...collective consciousness and the intentionality of the collective is derived from that of its members."[55] This may be taken to claim that since there is intentionality of the collective, that collective must have consciousness. As we have already seen above, it's not clear that collective intentionality is the *collective's* intentionality, as something distinct from that of individuals. Rather, collective intentionality may only be another mode of intentionality of individual subjects. In her own arguments against an emergentist view of collective consciousness Mathiesen states: "If one wants to give up the view that consciousness is a phenomenon that crucially includes such features as awareness, and call all self-organizing entities conscious, then there are multiple collective consciousnesses in a very trivial sense."[56] To identify anything responsive to its environment as actually exhibiting intentionality, not merely metaphorically, is to denude the concept of intentionality of its specific nature. If this is accurate, then one would be attributing awareness not just to individuals, but to the collective, if she claims the collective has its own intentionality. This means that a group like the Target Corporation is aware! The members who constitute the employees of Target are aware, sure. But the corporation itself? What is it aware of? In requiring a sense of awareness to intentionality, which requires no more than that *experiences are experienced*, one seems to pass to an absurd consequence, one that is not supported by the evidence. Target itself doesn't experience anything, only its employees do. Surely there's nothing it is like to be the Target Corporation.

One might claim that the Target Corporation had a rough week or that it had a good week. However, that doesn't imply that the Target Corporation is itself conscious. Such language is metaphorical language. It might require that the Target Corporation be an agent of some kind, that it can make decisions and bear responsibility for its decisions in a manner that doesn't entail individual members of its corporate entity have the same properties. But why think only conscious beings can be agents? It seems clear that conscious beings acting together can construct a derived capacity for agency, one that is parasitic on their being conscious agents participating in a deliberate decision making process but which does not itself result in consciousness for the collective agent itself. Derived agency would be distinct from the intrinsic agency that conscious beings like us have. Accepting collectives can possess a derived agency is more palatable than collective consciousness.

One doesn't experience groups, like the Target corporation as themselves being aware of anything and it's not clear why one should believe they are aware otherwise. One can experience collectives as being responsive to them in a manner analogous to individuals. That doesn't commit one to believing collectives are conscious entities in their own right. Such talk is best understood as shorthand for intentions on one's part that some indeterminate member(s), indeterminate to one's experience that is, act in a role as agent of the group and it's not that one takes the corporation writ large to be *who* responds to one's requests. This is all to say that we don't ascribe a stream of consciousness with intrinsic intentionality to groups, there is no apperceptive attribution of (intrinsic) intentionality or consciousness–no filling out–of these abstract entities in the way we do with concrete individuals.[57] If one were to ascribe a stream of consciousness to a group, surely that intention would fail to be evidenced, and we would identify that intentional content as confused or improperly formed. One can see this if they consider how plural subjects or collectives are constituted in and through the intentional acts of individuals. Without individuals' intentional maintenance, plural subjects dissolve. Were plural subjects to possess intrinsic intentionality, they would–in "having a mind of their own"–be capable of self-maintenance in respect of their constitutions independent of, or perhaps even absent of, any individuals whatsoever. Mathiesen herself denies this possibility by her appeal to the individual's necessary role in relation to plural subject constitution.[58]

That collective intentions of individuals, when shared and used as bases for further intentional formations, especially when formalized in institutional structures and policies, can give us the impression of that body of individuals as uniquely intentional should not surprise us. One also experiences non-player characters in role-playing or video games as expressing intentionality. Something's expressing intentionality is, however, not sufficient evidence for its being an intending subject or intrinsically having intentionality–it does not imply that the object expressing intentionality is itself the cause of its intentional expression. As Searle has noted, stop signs express intentionality. What differentiates stop signs from the non-player characters in games is that the latter is a far more sophisticated instance of derived intentionality. Groups, like non-player characters in games, should be thought of as sophisticated instances of derived intentionality. Though, groups are even more complex in that they consist of systems of derived intentionality that can be modified by those subjects with influence *and* groups are constituted by living subjects with intentionality and consciousness in their own right in a way in which game characters and stop signs are not. Even if there are plural subjects to which things can be predicated, that does not imply that there is collective consciousness. Of course, this will require us to further elaborate the nature of plural subjects, and just how strong a view of plural subjects is plausible. That is the subject of the following chapters. The key point for present purposes is that the argument from intentionality depends on ambiguity, conflating derived intentionality and intrinsic intentionality. Derived intentionality does not imply consciousness as intrinsic intentionality does; otherwise things like stop signs would be conscious. There is no clear evidence for collectives possessing intrinsic intentionality.[59]

With the phenomenology not nearly as clear-cut as Mathiesen appears to have assumed, and the theoretical claims her position appears to be dependent on themselves fraught with ambiguity, what might one conclude in regard to her arguments? The argument from subject-status conflates subject in a grammatical sense, or the form of our experience (as in the case of one's experiencing being a part of a "we"), or being the subject of action, with subjectivity (an *experiencing* subject). The argument from intentionality conflates derived and intrinsic intentionality. One can endorse Mathiesen's three conditions for collective experience: plurality, awareness, and collectivity, but disagree that they represent conditions for *collective consciousness* in the more literal or robust sense. Rather, they can be said to represent conditions for *plural subjects*. And by that, all one needs mean is that they represent conditions necessary to the experience of intentionality in the we-mode or experiences of objects constituted in and through systems of we-intentions, e.g. corporations. Collective consciousness, however, is something entirely different.

Notes

1. Burns & Engdahl 1998, Migdley 2006, Combs & Krippner 2008, Ziman 2006, Pandey & Gupta 2008
2. Mathiesen 2005
3. Mathiesen argues that plural subjects can be counted as moral agents in Mathiesen 2006a. My argument here is neutral on the question as to whether plural subjects can be moral agents, unless consciousness is a necessary condition for moral agency–not an implausible intuition–in which case my view implies a denial of plural subjects' being moral agents in a direct sense. For a denial that plural subjects are moral agents that accepts they can be held responsible sometimes for pragmatic reasons guided by convention, see Velasquez 2003. See also the general discussion in Smiley 2008. My concerns in this work are not morally oriented, but to provide criticism of the social ontology informed by the approach of and tradition of phenomenology.
4. Mathiesen 2005: 233
5. This argument, and the one that follows, are my analytical reconstructions of what appears to be underlying *prima facie* plausible arguments for there being collective consciousness. I believe both arguments, while logically valid, are unsound.
6. The following passage is indicative of an alternative way of thinking about this, one that does not entail acceptance of collective consciousness. "The collective intentionality theory holds that—in contrast to mere strategic individual-mode action—truly social action is essentially we-mode action based on collective intentionality. The claim is that in truly social action, agents instinctively switch to we-mode psychology and frame the situation at hand in irreducibly collectivistic terms so that the instrumental rationality of social actions is assessed in terms of what is rational for the group to do. In short, the rationalizing question behind strategic individual-mode action is what I should do in this social situation to realize my ends (be they egoistic, altruistic, or what have you), whereas the question motivating we-mode action is what we should do in order to realize our goals" (Saaristo 2006: 41).

7. Kant gives a number of excellent examples of this sort of phenomenon in both "An Answer to the Question: What is Enlightenment?" (Kant 1983: Ch. 2) and *Anthropology from a Pragmatic Point of View* (Kant 2006).

8. Carr 1986: 525, 532

9. As Searle has noted in reference to both boxing and chess, even competition is predicated on a more basic cooperative achievement [collective intention(s)], namely *our* accepting the rules of our competitive activity (Searle 1995: 23-24, 27-29).

10. There are also indirect references to others in our experiences as Gurwitsch (1979) has argued. Carr's arguments also anticipate Searle's theory of collective intentionality (Searle 1995) in important ways.

11. It is not the case, as I acknowledge at the start of chapter two, that metaphysics itself is inherently problematic. Rather, the problem is where one introduces metaphysical premises without sufficient evidential authority. In a sense, the complaint is that valid patterns of reasoning are touted as sound by some in respect of metaphysics; validity being necessary but not sufficient for soundness. One might accept validity alone in metaphysical argumentation on the assumption that a test for soundness is impossible. That assumption is one that phenomenological philosophy challenges. Phenomenology calls for rigor and evidence in phenomena in all cases. For example, if A is part of B, it does not follow thereby that B will have all the properties of A. Similarly, if B is analogous to A, we can't assume on the basis of analogy that B's constitution is closely similar in form to that of A's. Lastly, one cannot conclude on the basis that B appears to have a property that A possesses, that B thereby has other properties that A has. All three of these patterns of reasoning are deployed in arguments that groups possess consciousness or intentionality in an intrinsic or original fashion.

12. Carr 1986: 533

13. ibid.

14. ibid: 532; In agreement with Husserl, it is that strict adherence to experiential evidence that forms the bases for adequate ontological theory. That is, ontology is liable to phenomenological evidence, not the reverse. Also, none of this entails a rejection of realism, as I see Searle's realism and social ontology as largely consistent with the Husserlian project at hand. Rather, it only requires, as Husserl put it, bracketing those considerations for purposes of primary research.

15. If Mathiesen does not actually believe in a literal sense of collective consciousness, as her other writings would lend credence to, then she has a very odd way of expressing herself. Regardless, what's more important to me here is what her argument says and how that might be taken by those who believe she's offering an argument for a robust sense of collective consciousness, like the authors addressed earlier. Perhaps I'm flirting with Pandora's box by taking the notion of collective consciousness as a live possibility, but I believe it's more dangerous to ignore this possibility than to try to lock said box. I don't assume that nobody believes in collective consciousness, as there are plenty of examples of otherwise intelligent people believing all sorts of nonsense without evidence

or argument. If this is of no interest to philosophers as a serious matter I think they should entertain it more carefully. For example, if one denies a distinction between intrinsic intentionality and derived intentionality and holds that intentionality has a relation to consciousness of a particular kind, one could be *prima facie* committed to collective consciousness if they believe intentionality is latent in the world at large.

16. This distinction is derived from Searle, the distinction is outlined in the introduction.

17. Mathiesen 2005: 235; Mathiesen claims in another article: "I am starting from the presumption that some sort of ontological individualism is true; groups are composed of individual human beings and the properties of groups supervene on those of the members and the rules that govern their interaction" (Mathiesen 2006b: 162-163). While she concedes ontological primacy to individuals, as she does in the 2005 article at issue, she aims in the 2006b article to argue that groups can be said to have genuine knowledge on the ground of the "epistemic features of group views" as opposed to concerns over whether groups can possess "particular sorts of mental or cognitive properties characteristic of beliefs" (Mathiesen 2006b: 171). The phenomenologist, however, would hold the latter concern to be necessary for demonstration, regardless the demonstrations capable only on the basis of the former. Mathiesen's characteristics in question are "aiming at truth and being epistemically rational" (ibid: 161). The trouble with allowing such arguments is that they imply that this book itself has knowledge, that programs for statistical modeling of data have knowledge, etc. Those are conclusions I count as weaknesses, not merits, of such an argument for any who accept that only conscious beings have knowledge, strictly speaking.

Per the use of reference to modeling Mathiesen makes: she references views like Goldman 2006, or alternatively Nichols & Stich 2003. However, the integration of such views with phenomenology has been challenged (see Gallagher 2001 & Gallagher 2006a), and alternative models proposed (see Gallese 2001; LeGrande 2006; Lohmar 2006; and Gallagher & Zahavi 2008: Ch. 7-10). Per the issue of empathy that Mathiesen associates the modeling discussions with see also Thompson 2001 and Zahavi 2001b.

18. Mathiesen 2005: 247

19. ibid. Simulation here is to be understood in relation to simulation theory wherein one "simulates" the experience of others. On simulation theory see Goldman 2006. Simulation theory is often contrasted with theory-theory, wherein our experiences of others involve not simulations but theoretically based projections of others. Both theories arise in the analytical discussions of folk psychology. For excellent synopses of each theory see Gordon 2008 and Ravenscroft 2008. An alternative thesis, strongly grounded in evolutionary psychology, is presented in Nichols and Stitch 2003. I would also add that Mathiesen's use of simulation here is incoherent if she intends to refer to systems of mirror neurons as being implicated, as is suggested by her citation of Goldman. The neural mirroring activity in question is caused by the observa-

tions of other acting individuals, not in relation to the observing groups. For very strong phenomenological critiques of *both* theory-theory and simulation theory as inadequate see Gallagher 2001 and Gallagher 2006.

20. "Not only will I see my thinking as that of one thinking 'as a member of the collective,' but conceive of my experience as one that all other members do or would (if they thought about it) share" (Mathiesen 2005: 247). See also Mathiesen 2006a: 246-247

21. Mathiesen 2005: 248

22. ibid; Further discussion on why a shared conception or collective perspective is required for a plural subject, and how that sense of the nature of the collective can direct or inform one's individual action in relation to the collective interests, is presented in Mathiesen 2006a: 246-248

23. Assuming it is the same condition, as the essay of interest here discusses collective consciousness, the other essay moral agency.

24. Mathiesen 2006a: 249

25. ibid.

26. If Mathiesen is speaking only of modifications of individual consciousness, as is accepted as a real possibility, then all she would appear to be saying is that individuals need to be aware of their group participation. Again, given a lack of disambiguation, I entertain the possibility that she might also be speaking about the collective itself.

27. See Mathiesen 2005: 243-246. Compare also Searle 1995, Gilbert 1996, Tuomela 2000 and Tuomela 2003.

By using quotation marks in referencing "we," I do not suggest hesitation, but refer to the phenomenal experience as distinct from a reified object in the world. This is a convention found in writings of the phenomenological tradition, through which one denotes an avoidance of a specific metaphysical stance regarding the ontological status of that which is referenced.

28. See Smiley 2008: §3 & May 1987: Ch. 1-2

29. May 1987: 40

30. Smiley 2008: §3

31. To be clear, I am not denying that there is purpose or reason to refer to collectives as subjects of action or as subjects of moral evaluation. There is a wealth of literature on these questions that would be irresponsible to merely wave away (Bratman 1999, Petit 1993, Tollefsen 2006, Shockley 2004 and 2007 etc.). Rather, the argument is only against collectives as being thought of as conscious, experiencing subjects.

32. Human beings are instances of subjectivity. Subjectivity refers to the whole of a subject of experience, not an experienced subject but a subject who *experiences*. The claim is then that collectives don't have experiences. If collectives possessed consciousness, they would have experiences–the collective itself would have experiences–as distinct from the individuals. Given that consciousness has a dependence relation on certain physical systems, i.e. consciousness is part of the natural world even if not describable adequately in naturalistic terms

on the phenomenological view, it's reasonable to accept that consciousness can only be embodied in certain kinds of physical systems. That consciousness is embodied is another core belief of the phenomenological tradition. Claiming that plural subjects lack subjectivity is not to deny that they can be subjects *experienced* or subjects of moral evaluation, but only to deny that the plural subject itself *experiences* anything and to raise the question as to how it could be an *embodied* consciousness.

33. Husserl and all subsequent phenomenologists, *qua* phenomenologist, are against such approaches as a matter of principle. This represents what Husserl diagnoses as part of the speculative metaphysical tradition he rejects, and a return to Aristotelian principles of preserving the phenomenon by placing them first. Husserl 1999: §§60-62. See also, Merleau-Ponty 1958: Preface

34. Carr 1974: 87; see also Carr 1973: 18

35. Carr 1974: 87

36. Carr 1973: 18

37. Husserl 1999: 106/136

38. ibid: 105/135

39. One might express a concern here in line with the views of J. David Velleman. Velleman argues that it is possible that "distinct intentions held by different people can add up to a single token intention" (Velleman 1997: 31). However, Velleman means something different than I by 'intention.' Velleman states, "An intention, after all, is the state in virtue of which someone is said to have made up his mind" (ibid: 30). He comes to this view by following a distinction Michael Bratman previously argued for in Bratman 1984. The concern expressed here, as from the phenomenological tradition, is that something has gone wrong by conflating different senses of intention; namely, *Intentionalität* and *Absicht*. Intentionality is most basically consciousness' directedness at an object [*Intentionalität*]. All Carr and I are claiming is that the contents of consciousness are experienced as transcending one's own consciousness, i.e. as being something the verification of the intentional content to which must be sought *extrinsic* to one's consciousness itself. Whether this ultimately affects Velleman's view or those like is not argued for in the present work. Though, I suspect that he misunderstands Searle's view in the relevant paper, as Searle's view is not primarily oriented through *Absicht*, but *Intentionalität*. Some of the blame for this clearly lies with Searle, as his discussions of collective intentionality don't tend to distinguish carefully between the various senses of intentionality (e.g. Searle 1995).

40. Husserl 1999: 106/136

41. Carr 1986: 523

42. This does involve a rejection of causal theories of mental content. The details of that rejection are, however, beyond the scope of the present work. It does bear mention, however, that phenomenological theories, like most internalist theories in the analytic tradition, do not discount the role of causal processes in cognition entirely. What is rejected is the notion that cognition itself or con-

sciousness can be adequately described in purely causal terms or causally motivated terms. See Gallagher & Zahavi 2008: Chapter Six for discussion.

43. Carr 1986: 525

44. What kind of qualitative character is not obvious. However, I'm tempted to say that it is a cognitive qualitative character, as opposed to a non-
cognitive qualitative character of the sort that dominates discussions in analytic
philosophy of mind; perhaps it is a categorial element of one's experience. For
the distinction see Strawson 2005 and Gallagher & Zahavi 2008: Chapter Six.

45. Mathiesen 2005: 238; Carr also uses the body metaphor in his discussion (Carr 1986).

46. See also Gilbert 1992 and Gilbert 2000; Gilbert's view will be addressed directly in Chapter 5.

47. Carr 1986: 532-533

48. ibid: 532

49. ibid.

50. ibid.

51. Schmid 2003b: 205-206

52. Note that I am not arguing that one can't call a collective a plural subject or even treat it as a subject of moral responsibility. Rather, I'm only arguing
that it does not follow from such descriptions that the plural subject has subjectivity, i.e. that it is an experiencing (conscious) subject in its own right. As such,
my view here is consistent with positions like that presented in Shockley 2007.

53. I understand the term 'subjectivity' to refer to an entity with the power
of consciousness in its own right. There are, then, variant ways in which subjectivity can be particularly manifest, each with its own objective specifications.
This is why, for instance, Nagel's famous paper arguing that it is impossible for
humans to know what it's like to be a bat is so compelling. Different forms of
subjectivity make for different structures of experience whose internal possibilities are alien to those of another kind (Nagel 1974).

54. Here I purposely turn to a group one is not a member of as example–on
the view that it is more illustrative to the present concern. Groups one is a member of, I hold, won't function in a significantly different manner. Groups to
which one is party do guide, inform and impart meaning to those actions one
takes as party to that group. However, one doesn't experience the group itself as
something in itself conscious in the way one experiences other agents who comprise the group to be agents. While one experiences oneself as part of something
larger than oneself, one doesn't experience oneself as part of something itself
possessive of its own consciousness. In cases of collaborative problem solving,
we speak of the group's thinking something through together–whereby we attribute responsibility for the achievement(s) to the group. This doesn't mean,
however, that the group itself–as something distinct from the individuals–
thought through the puzzle and achieved the end result. Rather, it means only
that the work was engaged in by individuals acting *together*, wherein no individual accomplishment itself represents adequately what has been done and to

describe the accomplishment in reference to individuals alone loses the sense of the collaborative nature of the enterprise.

55. Mathiesen 2005: 248
56. ibid: 240
57. Husserl argues that the experience of another consciousness is always the product of apperceptive attribution. It is apperceived in that it is only ever indicated through experience(s), not itself perceived directly. Simple cases of apperceptive "filling" include experiencing two-dimensional profiles as parts of three-dimensional objects. The experience of a profile of something as opposed to the thing involves distinct apperceptive contents integral to the experiences themselves.
58. Mathiesen 2005: 235, 248-249
59. A similar line of argument–that derived intentionality does not imply the presence of consciousness–has been employed by Daniel Dennett (1987: Ch. 8-9). Dennett, however, argues that we are all instances of derived intentionality–the intentionality of Nature. Dennett's view is thoroughly eliminativist and naturalist about minds, intentionality, consciousness and meaning–the very antithesis of phenomenology. Dennett poses to one the following dilemma: "Either you must abandon meaning rationalism–the idea that you are unlike the fledgling cuckoo not only in having access, but also in having privileged access to your meanings–or you must abandon the naturalism that insists you are, after all, just a product of natural selection, whose intentionality is thus derivative and hence potentially indeterminate" (Dennett 1987: 313). The phenomenologist simply denies the latter; deny naturalism. "...whereas the majority of analytic philosophers today endorse some form of naturalism, phenomenologists have tended to adopt a non- or even anti-naturalistic approach" (Gallagher & Zahavi 2008: 4). That isn't to say that the phenomenologist must deny modern science, only that they understand philosophy to be engaged in a different sort of inquiry from that of natural science (ibid: 22). Nor would phenomenology deny Darwinian evolutionary theory. Dennett claims, after all, that Darwin was an eliminativist about mind (Dennett 1987: 314). Of course, Dennett's assertion is wildly controversial to anyone not committed to the dubious position of Ultra-Darwinism, indeed, there's little evidence that Darwin himself would have accepted Ultra-Darwinism. However, the dispute over meta-philosophical issues between phenomenology and Dennett's eliminativist naturalism is too large and historied to be engaged in here; as is the question as to what is denied under the term 'naturalism' in Husserl and phenomenology generally. (See Gallagher & Zahavi 2008: Ch. 2, esp. pgs. 28-41; Petitot et al. 1999; and Reynaert 2001.) Suffice to say that as a phenomenologically oriented philosopher I don't accept the framework Dennett operates in, nor the terms of the dilemma to which he believes alternative views are committed.

Chapter 2
A Metaphysical Critique of the Notion of Collective Consciousness

This chapter offers a systematic evaluation of and critique of three theses advocating in favor of the possibility of collective consciousness: the group mind thesis, the emergent mind thesis, and the socially embedded thesis. In Kay Mathiesen's case, she claimed to offer a phenomenologically motivated argument in favor of collective consciousness, in spite of the fact that her use of Husserl and reference to Alfred Schütz are tangential to her paper. To offer a more robust phenomenological account, this chapter reexamines the writings of Husserl in order to clarify his claims. Following this, the three theses on collective consciousness are submitted to critique. The aim is to motivate each thesis more fully, in order to better address their respective strengths and ultimate failures from the vantage of a robust phenomenological philosophy of mind.[1] The phenomenological tradition's systematic understanding of consciousness is marshaled against the idea of collective consciousness. Specifically of concern here are a couple of consciousness's essential components: the embodied or kinaesthetic dimensions of consciousness and consciousness's temporal dimensions, both of which represent distinct and essential kinds of intentionality operative in consciousness.[2] Both dimensions of consciousness are supported also by contemporary neuroscience. The embodied characteristics of social objects are clarified, as both Mathiesen's as well as John Searle's ways of speaking about how collective intentions are embodied are potentially problematic in ways that can be improved upon.

It is a common misconception that phenomenology is, or must be, wholly anti-metaphysical.[3] Such a view would be hard pressed to explain Husserl's and other phenomenologists' interest in and statements about ontology and other positive claims about metaphysics. What is more accurate is phenomenology insists that metaphysical discussions be grounded by having some discernable reference to phenomena. This constraint aims to eliminate metaphysical speculations that are purely theoretically motivated or that operate in abstract conceptual terrains with no discernable basis in relation to conscious experience. That is, one ought to reject views that have no discernable phenomenological origin that

one could uncover and identify.[4] By a theoretically motivated problem without
phenomenological basis, one counts conceptual puzzles that are motivated on
purely argumentative grounds where one has failed to critically examine the
definitions of their concepts. This chapter's examination of differences of emphases between a speculative metaphysical theory and a phenomenologically
grounded metaphysical theory is key to understanding a Husserlian theory of
intersubjectivity. Again, it is argued here that the conditions Mathiesen identified as conditions for collective consciousness are better understood as conditions for plural subjects–intersubjective unities of subjects. The work of this
chapter will be important to the chapters that follow.

In the previous chapter, it was noted that Mathiesen interpreted Husserl's
discussions of higher order pluralities or social subjectivities as representative of
concrete analyses directed at collective consciousness. She states, "Husserl provides an analogy between persons and 'personal unities' which suggests that
personal unities may have a kind of consciousness similar to that of individuals."[5] As evidence, she quotes the following passage from Husserl:

> In the case of a state, a people, a union, etc., there is a plurality of bodies,
> standing in physical relationships something required for intercommerce, either
> direct or indirect...Each Body has its spirit, but they all are bound together by
> the overarching *communal spirit* which is not something beside them, but is an
> encompassing "sense" or "spirit." This is a subjectivity [*sic!*] of a higher level.[6]

Unfortunately, this quote is misleading out of its context. In the section of *Ideas
II* from which it is drawn, Husserl is discussing the constitution of the "spiritual"
world, i.e. the social world, the world of human cultural objects. Husserl identifies all social objects as being unities of body and sense. He states:

> We have here a fundamental analysis *embracing all spiritual Objects, all uni-
> ties of Body and sense*, hence not only individual humans but also human
> communities, all cultural formations, all individual and social works, institu-
> tions, etc.[7]

Clarifying the distinction, he later states the point more generally. By 'body' one
refers to "that which is animated and which bears sense."[8] This is to claim that
social objects arise through the combination of some bearer of sense and a sense
(meaning). This is the same basic idea captured by how Searle treats the establishment of institutional facts through intersubjectively constituted meanings.
Institutional facts, for Searle, "...require human institutions for their existence."[9]
Institutional facts are facts that depend on collective intentionality, established
on the basis constitutive rules[10]–collective intentional attributions of status ascriptions distributed over social groups in a codified fashion which generates or
creates some new fact.[11] That is the vehicle by which Searle describes intersubjectively constituted meanings, i.e. meanings that have their origins and functionality only within a social context.

To emphasize the difference between a Husserlian and a Searlean view, take Barry Smith's objections to Searle's use of constitutive rules in making physical objects *count as* something else.[12] Searle's view is problematic in that he requires 1) reference to the physical world, and 2) that he uses a *counts as* relation without adequate clarification.[13] Smith states the problem:

> Moreover, even if a piece of paper, in a given case, truly does serve as the physical underpinning for the debt in the sense of Searle's formula, there are many other cases in which debts exist with no paper record at all. Searle would say, perhaps, that the physical underpinning here is provided by blips (memory traces, beliefs) in peoples' brains; but once again, it seems ontologically wrong to state that blips in brains may count as debts in certain contexts. (And it seems wrong, also, to suppose that, by destroying such blips we would thereby succeed in destroying the debt.)
> Relational social objects can exist even in the absence of all pieces of paper and in the absence of all blips (in brains or computers) and records of any form.[14]

Husserl's sense of body in relation to intersubjectively constituted unities of sense avoids the problem Searle has here in that it makes clearer that the 'bodied' component is "that which is animated and which bears sense" as opposed to some physical object which counts for the intersubjective meaning. It can be physical, but need not be. Searle's emphasis on language works fine for things like chess pieces. But, as Smith rightly points out, Searle has problems with social objects like property rights, works of music, fiat borders, etc. One can add things like flight paths, shipping lanes, and works of art more generally. Although Searle's modified position, that these function by socially constituted declarative acts, likely offsets concerns with some of the above, it notably does not help him with music or any other non-linguistic art forms. If Smith's criticisms are correct, Searle's account isn't sufficiently well equipped in its stated form to handle general cultural categories, what Husserl calls *ideal* spiritual Objects, for example drama, literature in general, works of arts, etc.[15] This is to say that Searle is not clearly able, if couching social reality in linguistic terms, to adequately address the general categories operative in the social world, especially where said categories are not themselves linguistic in nature.[16]

As Husserl notes, it's not appropriate to require a bodily dimension in relation to social categories themselves; the categories themselves, as ideal in form, are distinct from particular instances.[17] The problem is Searle's exclusive emphasis on objects, encumbered by his well-known view that everything is physical, in the sense of being part of the physical world; and that the physical world is entirely unified, even if not reductively physical.[18] Searle requires, it seems, treating a region of air as an object in order to bear the relative predicative characteristics, e.g. being a flight path. Husserl's view, which denies the naturalism permeating Searle and orients itself to experienced meanings whether signifying extra-conscious objects or not, can accommodate events and states of affairs better than Searle's object-oriented approach. As such, one can say that a given relative region of atmosphere over some land mass bears the sense of being a flight corridor, a no-fly zone, restricted air space, or make sense of claims about the state of literature or a given musical period, etc., in manners clearer than Searle. Phenomenologists avoid having to make the two major ontological commitments that contribute to the problems Searle faces, 1) that everything is physical and 2) that the social world is entirely founded through linguistic acts.[19]

That the object of Husserl's concern in the section of text Mathiesen quotes from is concerned with intersubjectively constituted meanings is important. Noted of her quote from Husserl above as an error is the word 'subjectivity.' This was noted because Husserl's text has been, for reasons unclear, modified in Mathiesen's use. In the actual translation of the text, Husserl ends that section by stating: "This is an *Objectivity* of a higher level."[20] The choice of 'Objectivity' as opposed to 'subjectivity' is vastly important and undermines significantly Mathiesen's use of Husserl's work. For one, Husserl in no way extends a sense of subjectivity to intersubjective groupings of subjects. Rather, he only refers to them as bearers of intersubjectively constituted meanings: ex. church, team, etc. Husserl only speaks of plural subjects, using the more recent terminology, as constituted by and bearing socially constituted meanings, and does not speak of them as subjectivities whatsoever.

Mathiesen is also quite clearly overextending the analogy of the unities between an individual subjectivity and social unities functioning in more complex forms of our intersubjective life. There being an analogy is insufficient for identity or sameness in kind or of attributes. For one, an individual subject's body has a lived dimension (*Lieb*). Even if there is a "body," or bodily dimension, to social objects, which includes institutions and social groups, it's not obvious that they have a lived-bodily dimension in a manner similar to the way individual subjects have a lived-bodily dimension. It's also not clear that Husserl would ever attribute consciousness to groups. Rather, he only acknowledges that some groupings of subjects also bear an intersubjectively constituted sense (meaning), ex. being Lutheran, being a football team, being *S*'s circle of friends, etc. While sense is dependent on consciousness or subjectivity, sense is not composed of consciousness or subjectivity; a fact glossed by the mistreatment of the text. Husserl's point is just that social objects involve intersubjectively constituted meaning impositions on objects, events or states of affairs that otherwise don't bear those meanings for individual subjects outside their socially conditioned context. As the previous chapter argued, it is not clear that socially constituted unities of persons are themselves conscious entities, or even why one should think they were. Husserl makes no claim that could be seen as suggestive of such in the text itself.[21] The aim here is to give a closer examination of the case for collective consciousness by looking not just at Mathiesen's arguments, but to consider potential cases by weighing their merits against the philosophy of mind, with reference to material from both phenomenological and analytical traditions.

The Three Theses Considered

As mentioned in the first chapter, Mathiesen rejects precedent theoretical models of consciousness functioning on a collective level. In particular she rejects the following three theses: group mind, emergent mind and socially embedded mind. They can be summarized thus:

> The *group mind thesis*: "Collective consciousness is a stream of consciousness that is literally shared by more than one conscious subject."
> The *emergent mind thesis*: "Collective consciousness is a kind of emergent consciousness dependent on a number of interacting individuals."
> The *thesis of the socially embedded mind*: "Collective consciousness describes the fact that all individual consciousness is dependent on social context."[22]

Each of the above theses involve, according to Mathiesen, a failure to meet the three conditions she argues are necessary for a theory of collective consciousness: collectivity, plurality, and awareness. Remember, it has been granted that these conditions can serve as conditions for plural subjects (subjects of we-intentions), but *not* as conditions for collective consciousness per se. The reason for this is that collectives can be spoken of as unified subjects of action and that in experience one can have intentions that are in the first person plural form (we-intentions). However, it is not the case that plural subjects or we-intentions are indicative in any way of a collective's having consciousness. Plural subjects, even if distinct from individual subjects and capable of having properties distinct from their individual members, are not themselves conscious. In that Mathiesen's treatment of Husserl does not differ in method from her treatment of the three rejected theses, we can reasonably conclude that a mistake is made in theoretical speculations detached from an experiential or phenomenological ground.[23] It becomes, then, a question of pushing concepts around without a clear sense of their phenomenological meanings. If true, any understanding of Husserl becomes hopeless. In reference to each of the three theses for collective consciousness, the aim is to find some example that may motivate such positions and submit them to a rigorous analysis.

Before proceeding, it is worth noting that discussions of collective consciousness tend to fail to disambiguate "collective consciousness." Discussions of collective consciousness tend to dangerously conflate modifications of individual consciousness associated with collective endeavors, and collective consciousness as a thing unto itself. The former is not denied; it is the latter notion that is under scrutiny.

The Group Mind Thesis

Mathiesen rejects the group mind thesis on the grounds that it is not really *collective* at all. This thesis represents "a single consciousness distributed across a number of brains."[24] As such, it fails to represent an actual plurality. As *one* consciousness it is not a *group* consciousness.[25] Despite multiple bodies being "tapped into" the consciousness, as in the case of the Borg of *Star Trek: The Next Generation*, there is only really a singular consciousness. The Borg are actually an imperfect example, as *Star Trek*'s writers appeared to struggle with the elimination of individual mind as distinct from the group's. One might argue that justice to this notion as generally conceived has not yet been done. The notion of a hive mind is popularly conceived as being a *shared* stream of consciousness wherein all individual participants contribute as individual "voices" in the group mind. The hive mind is thought of as having a strong controlling force over the thoughts of its membership, as, again, in the case of the Borg. That it is a *shared* stream of consciousness does not necessitate, however, that it is a *singular* stream of consciousness.

Mathiesen raises a strong objection to the notion of a single consciousness distributed over a group: "As Husserl, and other phenomenologists have noted, in order for there to be more than one mind, there must be something inaccessible about the minds of others."[26] It is thus argued that accessibility to a stream of consciousness requires that separate subjects cannot participate in one another's streams of consciousness directly. One wholeheartedly agrees with Husserl that separate consciousnesses must in principle have distinct streams of consciousness that are in principle not given to others in a direct and immediate fashion. As Husserl states, "if what belongs to the other's own essence were directly accessible, it would merely be a moment of my own essence, and ultimately he himself and I myself would be the same person."[27] Immediately before this Husserl states: "Properly speaking, neither the other Ego [*Ich*] himself, nor his subjective processes or his appearance to his own essence, becomes given in our experience originally."[28] What Husserl argues is that since the experience of the other's self and their *acts* of consciousness cannot be directly accessible, they cannot be given with the same first-personal givenness and immediacy that one experiences in one's own case. Mary cannot experience Tim as Tim himself does, nor experience Tim's acts of consciousness even if Tim and Mary can share intentional contents.

Neither Husserl nor Mathiesen has offered reasons as to why individual subjects could not be "tapped into" or participate in another stream of consciousness. Presentations of a group or hive mind thesis in fiction tend to represent it as being a sort of "telepathic party-line" akin to teleconferencing between multiple parties. There is a connection to which all parties are privy, yet this connection does not have to violate a participant's essential individuality, nor need it grant access to participants' subjective processes or awareness. This view appears to present a form of an emergence thesis. Either the "party-line" is itself an individual consciousness in its own right, with awareness and intentional acts and contents of its own independent of the participants, or it only is in virtue of the consciousnesses of those involved. That is, either a hive mind itself emerges as a new consciousness where there are subjects functioning in common, or is some other sort of emergent property or function of subjects in commerce with one another, like an operative internet connection between several linked computers. If the latter were the case, there's no necessity to its being a consciousness in its own right, as it's only necessary that it serve as a "meeting place" for distinct consciousnesses. To motivate the claim that it itself had to be a consciousness would require separate argument. If the former were the case, then one might ask where and what this supposed consciousness is. In this, one can appeal to Ned Block's China Nation objection to functionalism in order to raise doubts about its plausibility, especially if such a consciousness emerges out of any grouping of persons.[29] Additionally, one can raise the further question as to what manner of embodiment, as a condition for consciousness, is operating in cases of the Chinese nation qua consciousness or a hive mind.[30]

The relevant facet of Block's China Nation argument is his argument to the effect that a strictly functional definition of consciousness is too liberal. By a strictly functional definition of consciousness one means any articulation of a functionalist theory of consciousness wherein the only criteria for consciousness are its functional properties, i.e. that consciousness is no more than the expression of and execution of a machine table. Block argues that there are physiological conditions associated with neurological states of affairs in addition to whatever purely functionalist scheme is indicative of consciousness. If consciousness could be defined in only strictly functional terms, it would be possible for the population of China as a whole to realize the functionality of consciousness. The idea of the Chinese population, taken as a unified whole, being conscious strikes one as wildly implausible. If it is not a plausible candidate for consciousness, any definition of consciousness that would allow it would be faulty. That one thinks it is implausible is not a defeater, however. Block himself concedes that there is nothing ruling out that minds could extend across other subjects, at least if functionalism is a correct theory of mind.[31] Block claims that underlying our intuition is the suspicion that the Chinese Nation as a whole would not have qualia. That is, there would be no subjective feel or phenomenological character, no conscious experience, for the functional whole the Chinese Nation formed. There is nothing it is like for the Chinese Nation as a whole to be conscious. However, minds–at least consciousness–essentially require some phenomenology.[32] Absent qualia, there is a plausible case for the Chinese Nation not to be a mind, or, at least not to be a consciousness (if such a distinction is viable).

An additional point underlying the intuition that the Chinese Nation on the whole cannot possess consciousness could be the view that consciousness must be embodied.[33] This would require that each consciousness would have to be embodied in some manner.[34] If consciousness is essentially always an embodied consciousness, then the implausibly of a group mind thesis increases. What the embodiment of a group consciousness would be is not all that clear. Embodiment also factors into subject-specific kinaesthetic awareness, affecting the nature and structure of experience.[35] It is on this ground that Michael Tye denies that microphysical duplication constitutes a basis for the claim that microphysically identical subjects had identical experiences, or even remotely similar experiences.[36] What sort of kinaesthetic awareness does group consciousness have? What informs the structure of its experience? If group consciousness, as distinct from the individual subjects who compose it, is embodied somehow in the individuals who compose it, couldn't its kinaesthetic awareness be that of those subjects or at least available to them? If that is the case, how it is a *distinct* consciousness beyond being summative of its parts is unclear.[37] If the group does have its own distinct consciousness, then its kinaesthetic dimension, by informing and delimiting possibilities of sense for that consciousness, radically differs from individuals in virtue of radically distinct embodied states of affairs. These would differ so radically, that it is not clear how individual psychological descriptions could be appropriately used, let alone be even remotely functionally analogous, to descriptions of a group consciousness' phenomenology.[38]

A group mind thesis may also require our accepting an actual or possible consciousness for every combination of subjects ever co-existent. Every pairing, every classroom, every combinatorial set of persons, could represent the formative parts of another unique consciousness. This would mean populating the world with a whole host of odd entities. For instance, one may ask *when* such consciousnesses come into being and go out of being, or as to the temporal structure of their experience (what that consciousness protends or retains, especially as groups have fluid memberships).[39] Does changing members constitute a change of the identity of the whole (a Ship of Theseus concern)? In what sense would these types of consciousness have unity or intentionality (acts and contents of their own)? If unity is requisite for consciousness, then this cannot be a consciousness in its own right were it to exhibit a principled plurality on these fronts.[40]

A given consciousness must also exhibit a uniform structure of horizons.[41] A non-unified set of horizons or background structure would rule this out as an instance of consciousness. The problems with such a thesis, while perhaps not making it logically impossible, appear to make it at least wildly implausible, in addition to being a problem-ridden view that risks the possibility of its not offering any meaningful theory of consciousness whatsoever.

In order to motivate a group mind hypothesis, one might reference the behaviors of insect populations, such as ants, or schools of fish.[42] While the capacity of certain animals to act as a social whole can be very interesting to observe, it does not clearly represent evidence for collective consciousness; it does nothing to increase its plausibility. Though, such cases do not obviously decrease the plausibility of a claim to collective consciousness either. That individual animals act in groups doesn't imply a group mind, regardless of how efficiently they function, or appear to function, together. An equally plausible understanding of such phenomena is that there are only individual consciousnesses, and that one takes it as evidence that cooperation is a relatively basic feature in the lives of conscious organisms. Such a view has the added benefit of not postulating any additional metaphysical entities. In addition, the view is supported by research in a number of other fields as well.[43] If one is skeptical as to the attribution of consciousness in any capacity to such beings at all, one would have to allow that what is observed is just an expression of mechanistic causal activities, in relation to which we postulate teleological explanations.

Second, at the very least, these animals don't seem to have sophisticated forms of consciousness to begin with. One could just as well argue that the group manifestations of behavior are more an evolutionary function, increasing their fitness, than representative of anything relating to a group consciousness. That is, given the apparently relatively low level of sophistication to what, if any, consciousness these creatures have, it is advantageous to them to be very responsive to physical conditions in highly regular, highly regimented fashion. And these cases represent more the sophisticated range of physical possibilities than any novel case for a new form of phenomenology, despite our folk psychological musings.[44]

It is important to reiterate that consciousness, while a necessary condition for subjectivity does not encapsulate the whole of subjectivity. Subjectivity is a broader notion, with perhaps a more narrow extension than conscious being. Subjectivity represents the whole, of which consciousness is an essential part. As such, when one lays an embodiment condition on consciousness, the body-consciousness pairing is part of subjectivity, and represents more than consciousness alone. One might say that there is not ant-subjectivity even if there is some rudimentary form of ant consciousness. V.S. Ramachandran speculates, for instance, that a recursive mirror neuron network may be a necessary condition for the experience of a self.[45] Alternatively one might argue consciousness was dependent on the larger set of conditions for subjectivity in order to be. That is, that consciousness and subjectivity might be in co-dependent ontological relation. There may well be more conditions that can be specified, each of which undermines the claim that a group mind could represent a subject in its own right, even if it's possible that there be consciousness of a hive form. If such cases exist, one may have to concede to ants and fish some rudimentary sense of subjectivity, but that would not commit one to a group mind thesis.

These metaphysical questions aside, the types of experiences the group mind thesis would implicate are hard to discern. One would have to be able to experience one's stream of consciousness in unison with another's. Not even the strongest descriptions of empathy speak of cases where two or more streams of consciousness are as one. The best that can be said in appeal to phenomena is that we experience things with others, we model other's experiences, we act in concert with others, we act in parallel with others, etc. None of these represents a merging of experiences in an immediate sense wherein there is a uniformity of experience, an unrestricted access to another's kinaesthetic or temporal dimensions of consciousness, etc. Though some discussions of mirror neuron research claim one experiences the other's action, pain, or emotion, it's not clear yet how one should describe these cases. Surely the neurological events in one's brain are not identical to that of the other's. At best, one can say only that one can and does model the other's behavior for oneself at a neurological level that is nonconscious. But that is far from experiencing the other's state of affairs.

The Emergent Mind Thesis

The emergent mind thesis of collective consciousness suggests a second-order consciousness, "it is the society or group as a whole that is the subject of these states of consciousness, not the individual members of the society or group."[46] Mathiesen identifies at least three problems with this kind of view. First, epistemologically, there is a problem determining what are the intentions of the collective consciousness (intentional system as she calls it in this section), especially in distinction from individual member intentions. Second, there is the problem that an emergentist view has difficulties distinguishing first order beings with intentionality from higher order beings with intentionality, that is, systems composed of parts having the power of intentionality. The individual writ large, group as analog to individual, is composed of different proper parts than individuals themselves. Hence there is a worry about committing the fallacy of composition and having vague criteria for identifying instances of consciousness. Third, ascriptions of consciousness in this way are the result of metaphorical or analogical ascriptions of language.[47] That one can use intentional language in description of a phenomenon in no way implies the presence of consciousness or intentionality. That is, one may commit a version of the homuncular fallacy. For example, children speak of the thoughts and intentions of their toys and of fictional characters like the Muppets. However, this does not mean that Kermit the Frog or their teddy bear have consciousness. Rather, they can bear such descriptions in virtue of metaphorical transfer or analogously through the intentionality derivatively ascribed them via their Muppeteer. Mathiesen rightly argues such views make collective consciousness a trivial or promiscuous category. "If one wants to give up the view that consciousness is a phenomenon that crucially includes such features as awareness, and call all self-organizing entities conscious, then there are multiple collective consciousnesses in a very trivial sense."[48] To identify anything responsive to its environment as actually exhibiting intentionality, not merely metaphorically, "is to deprive the concept of intentionality of its special link to conscious awareness."[49] If intentionality is an essential defining characteristic of consciousness, as phenomenologists argue, and intentionality requires some basic awareness of experience as integral to experience itself, as phenomenologists also argue, then any second-order consciousness lacking awareness could not constitute a *bona fide* instance of consciousness.[50]

Is this really a good argument against the notion that a collective consciousness could emerge from a collective as something new? There is nothing here establishing why a new consciousness couldn't emerge–especially if we are to take this as parallel to more general theories of emergence in philosophy of mind. This would require of Mathiesen that she offer some principled argument against cases of iterative emergence,[51] or argument against emergentist theories of mind more generally. She offers neither. Of course, Mathiesen's express concern is supposed to be the phenomenological case, not the ontology or metaphysics of mind. If that's true, it's puzzling how an emergent theory–an overtly metaphysical theory–is supposed to enter into the discussion in the first place. On phenomenological grounds, one would have to conceive of a consciousness raised in and through our interactions with others, as something *experienced*. No plausible case is given to motivate such a case *phenomenologically*.

Perhaps, one argues, the experience of being in a crowd that takes on "a life of its own," such as a mob, would serve as counter-example to the claim at the end of the previous paragraph. Certainly the phenomena of flash mobs or crowds at sporting events suddenly turning violent represent cases where the will of the mob has to be recognized as both unifying and informing the actions and states of mind of the individuals in them.[52] It is not here denied that mobs or crowds might represent plural subjects, if anything the phenomenological view wants to capture such instances as cases of collective action. What is argued is that the apparent loss of self-control is not genuine, that individuals being swept up in the moment and acting as-if they had anonymity, license or the cover of the group is not sufficient as a basis to argue to the conclusion that groups have consciousness of their own. Where Larry May has argued that mobs can take on a will of their own and endorses Sartre's claim "that there was a common will and something like a common person manifested by the actions of the members of the mob [that stormed the Bastille],"[53] one only disagrees partially. The analogy drawn in relation to individual action is good to a point. But if the claim is that there is actually a common will which might be taken as evidence for a common consciousness, then the claim has overextended the limits of an otherwise useful analogy. Rather, such events can be understood as manifestations of the force of the anonymity involved in being one of many can have.[54] In virtue of an indeterminate foundation of solidarity, a sense of collectivity emerges, motivating we-intentions in the minds of individuals. Sometimes the "we" is taken by the individual as affording one a sense of license. The lack of determinateness to the collective's basis, however, leaves individuals to their own devices, and through a sort of monkey-see-monkey-do or process of trial and error, individuals develop and act within a dynamic, fluctuating sense of group "license." Crowds don't immediately turn violent; a process of escalation unfolds, wherein individuals formulate expectations, sense similar expectations in others, until small acts turn to larger ones and one lets their self get carried away in the dynamism of this spontaneous order.

What's more, mobs appear to form their identities through solidarity formed in opposition to something else, another group, an institution, an authority, a disagreeable state of affairs, etc. Individual expectations of what will happen, what ought to happen, what has just happened, etc., all develop a sufficient match in addition to some shared sense of awareness across individuals. Add the opposition to something in common to focus and give determination to the solidarity and the anticipations as to the negative consequences of resistance, and one has a basis for understanding mob action without accepting collective consciousness. The challenge of mobs is that they are fluid, short-lived, spontaneous networks of intentionality formed across sets of individuals who might not otherwise organize. But the genesis of "mob-mentality" should be consistent with the formation of other groups–just operating faster and due to the disorder internal to the mob subject to more rapid changes and internal fractions.[55]

More benignly, one might contend that something like the emergence of cliques and fractions in groups serves as some form of an experiential basis for an emergentist view. These cases, however, don't clearly resemble the types of emergence general spoken of by emergentists in the philosophy of mind. An emergentist thesis involves the claim that consciousness is an emergent property, contingent upon certain physical states of affairs presenting in the certain relations with appropriate causal histories so as to give rise to the new property of consciousness at a higher-order. Certainly the fluidity of social groups and their respective allegiances is analogous to something like emergence in this sense. Groups themselves could very plausibly be thought of as emergent phenomena, but the case for the emergence of a new consciousness ranging over the group itself does not follow from this. Of course, an individual could be aware of shifting allegiances or clique formations and changes. The political maneuvering in bodies like the U.S. Congress strongly support that such awareness can occur. What's not clear is how a group, like the U.S. Congress, is supposed to be accompanied by the emergence of a new consciousness, Congress' consciousness. Even if the U.S. Congress takes positions on things that not all of its members agree to, this does not entail the presence of a super-consciousness at a higher-order than the individual subjectivities. There is insufficient evidence to support the claim that there is a new consciousness present in such groups. Certainly an individual's memberships or associations with collectives can affect their frame of reference. The positions of and actions taken by groups like the U.S. Congress could just as well be counted as derived capabilities, contingent upon systematic sets or networks of collective intentions, expressed and tacit, which support such groupings or institutions and are themselves subject to the particular form the given group takes. In addition to concerns raised in relation to the group mind hypothesis, one can add that the emergentist theory would require a rather liberal version of the multiple-realizability thesis to be true and deny attempts to add further conditions to limit realization possibilities.[56]

The Socially-Embedded Thesis

The socially-embedded thesis frames matters differently, claiming: "we should not be asking how individuals can form a collective subject, but how individuals are formed by the collectivities in which they inhere."[57] Instead this view claims, "each of us is a 'collective subject' in some sense, because our consciousnesses are inextricably tied up with and dependent on the social collectives in which we are born and live."[58] This view is traditionally argued for in one of two ways. First, there is the Hegelian argument according to which self-consciousness is only possible in an intersubjective context. Our individuated consciousness is dependent on others to be self-conscious.[59] Second, there is a

Wittgensteinian line of argument according to which a social context is necessary for the contents of one's thoughts to have meaning. Mathiesen concedes the importance of a social dimension in conscious life, but denies the presence of any notion of collective consciousness operative here.

It is true that there is no notion of *collective consciousness* appealed to in either the Hegelian or Wittgensteinian chain of reasoning. That is because to engage either line of argument in a discussion of collective consciousness is a non sequitur. These are theories about how social factors function as conditions for consciousness or specific forms of consciousness. The Hegelian line of reasoning argues only that there is a social condition for one's identification of oneself as conscious agent–the basis of his theory of recognition.[60] The Wittgensteinian theory only argues for social conditions for communicable meanings, it is certainly persuasive for linguistic meanings, but does not obviously address phenomenological meanings.[61]

Neither line of argument directly invokes collective consciousness, unless one assumes that any reference to sociality implies reference to collective consciousness. It is not clear that the Hegelian view assumes this in any meaningful sense. One could claim that the Wittgensteinian view does implicitly require a notion of collective consciousness, but only if one assumes that socially constituted meanings depend on collective intentionality *and* collective intentionality presupposes collective consciousness. Neither is an unproblematic position. That socially constituted meanings depend on collective intentionality is a less problematic view. That collective intentionality presupposes collective consciousness, however, is fraught with the very vagaries that seem to motivate claims about collective consciousness in the first place. This also assumes a position to the effect that collective intentions are *collective,* or collectively achieved, objects, as opposed to being *intentional* objects. By that one means only that it is not clear that collective intentions require the *intending* of a collective–whatever that would amount to.[62] Individuals can intend as parts of a collective, on behalf of a collective, or in accord with a collectively construed interest. But collectives are not things that themselves intend in the sense of consciousness. One might speak of a collective's intent to act [*Absicht*], but that doesn't require the collective itself has consciousness–only that its members have consciousness. The collective's intent could be nothing more than the result of the intersubjective exchange of its members, not something originating from a super-agent.

An alternative argument for the socially embedded thesis is suggested by Evan Thompson: "Individual consciousness is formed in the dynamic interrelation of self and other, and therefore is inherently inter-subjective."[63] Contemporary analytic philosophers may note the similarity here with debates over wide and narrow mental content. "Narrow mental content is a kind of mental content that does not depend on an individual's environment. Narrow mental content contrasts with 'broad' or 'wide' content, which depends on features of the individual's environment as well as on features of the individual."[64] As some analytic philosophers are careful to note, however, there are really two different types of wide content.[65] First, there is what I will call causal content. By 'causal content' I refer to those contents, like perceptual mental contents, that depend exclusively on some causal connection between subject and the external world. I have in mind what Husserl sometimes referred to as hyletic data. I further stipulate that this type of content involves an *immediate* or unmediated interaction between subject and world. However, as in Thompson's case, and Putnam and Burge elsewhere, often the argument is made for socially contexted or socially conditioned contents.[66] I shall call these 'intersubjective contents.' Intersubjective contents, in distinction from causal contents, are those contents that are dependent on a given *social* context. A classic example of intersubjective contents is language. One can add that socially constituted objects and their related meanings also involve intersubjective contents.[67]

The difference between causal and intersubjective contents can be underscored by considering the example of a painting. When one views Picasso's *Guernica* they experience perceptual content of the colors, shapes, contours, etc. However, one also views it *as* a work of art, a painting, i.e. as a social object with meanings that are not exhausted by causal explanations. Alternatively, take for example a J.S. Bach cello suite: there are the sounds, pitches, timbre, harmonies, melodies, etc. And, there is *that* it is a work of music, that it is a cello suite, etc. It is the phenomena itself that matter phenomenologically.

Thompson's position could be articulated by the following argument. Consciousness depends on content. Without wide content, specifically intersubjective content, there cannot be any content. That is, narrow content, uniquely individual mental contents, cannot arise without precedent intersubjective content. At its face, the argument is not implausible. However, if intersubjective content is formed by and functions in virtue of collective intentionality,[68] one can understand this as claiming that individual intentionality (and its respective individual contents) is dependent on collective intentionality (and its respective social contents). And, if one claims that collective intentionality requires a notion of collective consciousness, one could add that this implied that individual consciousness was dependent on collective consciousness. In such a fashion, one could offer an actual argument for a socially-embedded thesis. Such a position also would be predicated upon a notion of collective consciousness.[69]

If that is the argument, one could respond to it by questioning the claim that individual intentionality and individual consciousness are respectively dependent on collective intentionality and collective consciousness. This is not to deny that there are socially constituted meanings that are important. Nor is it to claim that socially constituted meanings are reducible to individual or subjective meanings. Rather, it is to claim that if there are socially constituted meanings that are based on a mechanism of collective intentionality, they are dependent on individual intentionality, even if not reducible to I-intentions. If there were not individuals who were conscious, individuals with intentionality, there could not be *socially* constituted meanings. To be inter-subjective there must first be a subjective in relation to which the intersubjective is constituted.[70] If socially constituted meanings are to be dependent on a plurality of individuals, the individuals in question must first be capable of intending meanings. This does not require a notion of collective consciousness. Mathiesen herself appears to agree, "...collective consciousness and the intentionality of the collective is derived from that of its members."[71] Collective intentionality is not the intentionality of a collective consciousness, not some collective entities' cognitive achievement, but a mode of individual consciousness, or extension thereof, through which individual subjects interact with others to formulate and codify more complex intentional achievements than isolated subjects would otherwise be incapable of. If groups or collectives are dependent on their constitutive individual members for intentionality, then a strong claim for social-embeddedness is not a workable position in favor of collective consciousness. A weaker claim, that individuals are social beings, embedded in social contexts, or that specific genetic developments pertaining to individual consciousness requires social embeddedness is still plausible.

Earlier it was noted that something Husserl claimed might be used to justify a claim for a version of the socially-embedded thesis. Specifically, where Husserl claims:

> We have here a fundamental analysis *embracing all spiritual Objects, all unities of Body and sense*, hence not only individual humans but also human communities, all cultural formations, all individual and social works, institutions, etc.[72]

In that Husserl counts the individual human as constituted in a similar fashion, one might take his meaning to be that the individual is constituted as a cultural or social object. Evan Thompson relies on what Husserl calls open intersubjectivity to justify a thesis like this. By open intersubjectivity one means that our consciousness is open to others. That is, "consciousness is not solipsistically closed in upon itself."[73] Taking this further, Thompson argues that culture, concrete intersubjective systems, are part of an individual's cognitive make-up in a very strong fashion. He states:

> Culture is no mere external addition or support to cognition; it is woven into the very fabric of each human mind from the beginning. Symbolic culture in particular shapes the "cognitive architecture" of the human mind. Stripped of culture, we simply would not have the cognitive capacities that make us human.[74]

Thompson uses the term enculturation to describe the "constitutive power of culture" over human cognition.[75] Particularly efficacious is the effect of language, as a symbolic means by which to codify and efficiently communicate joint attentional information. "The enculturation of mind in language fundamentally transforms the nature of human cognition."[76] As such, one may press the matter by arguing that, in being enculturated, the sense of our socially-embedded nature importantly affects consciousness. Thompson brings the argument around:

In phenomenological terms, this power of culture and language to shape human subjectivity and experience belongs not simply to the genetic constitution of the individual, but to the generative constitution of the intersubjective community. Individual subjectivity is from the outset intersubjectivity, as a result of the communally handed down norms, conventions, symbolic artifacts, and cultural traditions in which the individual is always already embedded.[77]

What does any of this have to do with collective consciousness one might ask? If one interprets the claim that subjectivity is intersubjectivity as a claim of material equivalence, one may be tempted to argue that the precedence of the cultural environment over one's conscious life implied the precedence of the collective over the individual. Doing so, however, clearly overreaches by ignoring an ambiguity in what sense of precedence one speaks. Having developmental precedence does not necessarily equate to an ontological precedence. As Kathleen Haney has argued: "Empathy and the knowledge of the other it makes possible motivates language development and the multifarious human possibilities, including the enculturation of culture and values and the development of the sense of personhood which depends on it."[78] The individual subjective achievement of experiencing others as others represents a condition for the very possibility of the place wherein enculturation can happen. When one holds there to be a strong reciprocal relation between individual consciousness and its social environment, one need not deny the ontological priority of individual conscious as a necessary constitutive component of the social environment in the first. This is an alternative interpretation of the claim that subjectivity is intersubjectivity, interpreting the claim to mean that individuated subjectivity bears social intentional horizons, but that subjectivity is not materially equivalent to intersubjectivity.

Dan Zahavi offers further support for this interpretation by distinguishing two senses of intersubjectivity in Husserl, two directions of cognitive achievements: the constitution of intersubjectivity and the constituting intersubjectivity.[79] Intersubjectivity is constituted in and through the intentional achievements of individuals, individuals are, in turn, affected and influenced by those intersubjective achievements. Even if the constitution of an individual's consciousness is importantly influenced and conditioned by an intersubjectively rich environment, this does not mean that said environment itself is conscious or non-dependent on consciousness. One ought resist any urge to reify intersubjective wholes and present them as subjectivities in their own right.

Hans Bernhard Schmid, borrowing a phrase from Annette Baier, probably would object that this position falls under the sway of a "Cartesian brainwash," and that we are committed to the erroneous Cartesian way of understanding the subject as *ego cogito*. Schmid would argue that the motivation to reject collective consciousness, or more specifically, to maintain subjective individualism—the position that only individual subjects have intrinsic intentionality - is a by-product of the Cartesian understanding of the ego. The culprit, according to Schmid, is that: "Where there is intentionality, it is said, there has to be somebody who 'has' it–the good old subject."[80] Against this background, it should not be surprising that a prevalent attitude toward a group mind or collective consciousness is that "the specter of the group mind (or collective subject) has to be exorcised...."[81] For Schmid, the solution is relatively simple: "Collective intentions are not intentions of the kind anybody '*has*'–not single individuals, and not some super-agent. For collective intentionality is not subjective. It is relational."[82] Certainly one does not object to the claim that there is no super-agent involved. However, that individuals don't have intentions is a point of disagreement. The import of this disagreement can be further clarified. In another article, Schmid clarifies what he takes it to mean:

> But luckily, the alternative between the collectivist conception of the group (as an ontological primitive by virtue of which our intentionality can be collective) and Searle's *atomist* view (that the collective is a psychological primitive by virtue of which individuals can form a group) is not exhaustive. If we conceive of collective intentionality in a non-atomistic way, I think it becomes clear that the question about the relation between collective intentionality and the group is futile since *collective intentionality* is *the group*. Thus the ontological status of groups is neither prior nor secondary to we-intentions, because groups are neither a lower-order precondition of we-intentions (such as the brain), nor are they something that exists independently of our we-intending (like the existence of a tree that makes my belief true that there is a tree). The existence of the group is no truth condition of our individual we-intentions, nor are our individual we-intentions independently existing preconditions for the existence of the group. And neither is the group an ontological primitive that has collective intentionality as one of its higher-order features, nor is collective intentionality a psychological primitive in the heads of individuals.[83]

When Schmid states that groups are not a pre-condition for we-intentions, this only seems to confirm that we-intentions manifest in individuals' consciousness. All that he appears to be adding, taken from the final sentence of the quoted passage, is that the very capacity for collective intentionality is dependent on there being relations between subjects in the first place. That is not something I take to be all that controversial. To Schmid, however, the problem for the position of subjective individualism would be that one has simply been duped by a Cartesian view–that intentions are "had" by anyone–and that this is the right way to speak about intentionality and consciousness.[84] Despite this difference, it is telling that Schmid, a self-proclaimed collectivist who has characterized Margaret Gilbert's theory of plural subjects as insufficiently collectivistic, doesn't appear to accept a notion of collective consciousness; expressly seeming to deny such a view makes sense. What this shows is that even those who adhere to more collectivistic positions on collective intentionality aren't forced to accept that there is collective consciousness.

Emphasizing more common ground with Schmid, for instance, while characterizing a Husserlian position Kathleen Haney argues:

The intersubjective community, the *Lebenswelt*, is no kind of amalgam but is, for Husserl, created by the dialectical commerce among persons. The communication of values and meanings, from the most difficult and personal to the most ordinary and denotative, rest on language, which itself can be communicated through empathic effort. The lived cultural world is an empathic agreement and communication in its essential aspects, although its constitution is not exhausted by the efficacy of consciousness alone.[85]

The collective frame of reference Schmid seeks to isolate could be viewed as something that emerges out of, or is enacted through, subjective achievements, but is not itself something reducible to subjective achievements.[86] Schmid's argument appears to conclude that: 1) there is no collective consciousness in the sense of some super-agent; and, 2) relations between subjects count as a necessary condition for collective intentionality in general. If the claim is that an immediate concrete relation between subjects in the present moment is a necessary condition for a given formation of a collective intention, then one objects, as that puts the cart before the horse.[87] Further differences with Schmid's view will be returned to in a later chapter and include a more detailed critical appraisal of his position.

Returning to Mathiesen, it is perplexing that she asserts, "I will not argue it exists and we experience it–I think this needs no argument."[88] She claims this because she believes collective consciousness is a common part of our experience of the world. Elaborating, she states, "Collective consciousness, as I will define it, is a familiar and ubiquitous part of our world. It is as common as families, clubs, tribes, churches, states and ethnic groups."[89] While it is not clear if a definition of collective consciousness is offered in her work, it is clear that collective consciousness is a far more controversial subject matter than she admits. And no discussion of collective consciousness offered in her other papers is helpful toward clarifying the concern.[90] It is not obvious what the common thread across the groupings she mentions is, let alone whether each entails an operative notion of collective consciousness. Mathiesen is not unaware of opposition, though she discounts it as an ontological worry, not a phenomenological one. She believes ontological fear of collectivity is ultimately unwarranted. As argued in the previous chapter, it is not at all clear that phenomenology supports a claim in favor of collective *consciousness*, as opposed to collective entities or subjects. Nor is it clear that the ontological worry is unwarranted. This last point is especially important to Husserlian phenomenologists, as Husserl firmly believed phenomenological inquiry done right establishes an ontology.

To end on an historical point, consider that Leibniz readily admitted of unities of phenomena, while denying they represented substances. Leibniz argued that such complex phenomenal unities bear uniform references as a convention, not by anything in their essence; for example: "The Army of the United States," "The New York Philharmonic Orchestra," "The Minnesota Vikings," "The College Faculty," "The Obama Campaign," etc. While these might bear uniformity of reference, and a great amount of coordination between their members, there is no clear evidence for their exhibiting consciousness. Either dealing with such groups or organization from outside or in participation, there is no sense of consciousness beyond that of the individual members. Certainly one might experience an inefficient bureaucracy, programmed responses, strict message control, etc. But these represent facets of the organizational relations between members of said organizations, not consciousness on the organization's or group's part. That is, one can and does experience first hand the entrenched collective intentional structures and relations of this or that group–even to the point of frustration at times, owed perhaps to the behaviors of complicit or unreflective members–but none of this involves the experience of consciousness beyond that of individual subjects. There are apperceptive transfers and analogical apperceptions involved in case of individuals, where one experiences them as subjects in the full sense. But experiences of groups don't bear out that sort of transfer or hold the same apperceptive contents.

What differs? Individuals are experienced as subjects in the phenomenological sense, as being *experiencing* beings themselves. Phenomenologically, groups are only experienced in manners consistent with "subject" in a grammatical or semantic sense, as unities of sense and reference; however, it's not the case that groups themselves are experienced as the metaphysical bearers of consciousness, i.e. subjectivities in their own right. Moves to make metaphysical attributions of properties require yet further argument than those examined here. Experience doesn't warrant the additive ascription's literal sense, even if such metaphorical ascriptions or analogies–when taken as metaphor and analogy and nothing more–aren't intrinsically problematic. Experiences are had by the individuals participant to such groups. And one can experience others as, in specifiable contexts, being constituted in relation to either determinate or indeterminate collectivities. This can alter the meaning of a given person's presence by changing their role, one's anticipations in respect to their future actions, etc.[91] Analysis of each case in cognition will bear out the difference.

As argued in this and the previous chapter, the viability of collective consciousness appears to both lack phenomenological basis and rest on shaky metaphysical ground. It is reasonable to claim that the thesis of collective consciousness is motivated by a chain of reasoning along the following lines: Groups can have attributes and beliefs that differ from those of their members. In order to have beliefs one must possess consciousness. Since groups have beliefs unique to themselves and that can differ from those of their members, groups must have consciousness that is unique to themselves as well. Additionally, since groups can have attributes or properties that are distinct from that of their members, there is no principled reason to deny them consciousness that is distinct from that of their members.

What one can see, however, is that there are good reasons to withhold consciousness from being attributable to or predicated of groups. And having distinct group-specific properties and beliefs can be seen as no more than a derived capacity of their collective intentional foundations. Group-specific capacities and properties are functions of the iterative levels of intentionality individuals acting in concert with one another either informally or formally attribute to the constitution of a given group through the thoughts and actions of persons internal and external to those groups in dynamic networks of interrelations. Given that, there is little warrant in postulating a new subjectivity or new consciousness over the individuals that contribute to the composition of groups. That groups represent something distinct from individuals and can be interacted with as such does not imply that they are themselves something conscious. That only necessitates that groups can have structures to which their offices or functional roles are independent of specific individuals; for example, the office of the President of the United States or the position of CEO of a corporation. Who fills a given office, role, position in a formalized institutional structure is variable. Even which roles, the numbers of persons who can fill that role at a given time, and the duties and powers pertaining to the role-bearer are variable. This only underscores the great range of variability social interactions are susceptible to, not that a group can be conscious independent of those subjectivities (conscious subjects) who compose its material membership.

Notes

1. These are Mathiesen's terms. Insofar as one might want to distinguish between mind and consciousness, the complaint of confusion in terminology ought to be directed to her usage, which I adapt for simplicity's sake. Read each case in this context as referring to consciousness where a distinction between mind and consciousness would be important. But note that the appeals to the same patterns of argumentation are what seem to motivate the terminological shift.

2. For discussion of the effects of embodiment on consciousness, see Merleau-Ponty 1958, Gallagher 2006b, LeGrande 2006, Ratcliffe 2008a, and Stawarska 2006a as a small list of examples. For Husserl's discussions of time consciousness see Husserl 2008

3. An excellent analysis of phenomenology's relation to metaphysics is Zahavi 2003b.

4. For examples of this sort of constraint I count Husserl's *Crisis* and "Origin of Geometry" (Husserl 1970).

5. Mathiesen 2005: 242

6. Husserl as quoted in Mathiesen 2005: 242. The noted emphasis is mine. The reason for this will be made clear shortly.

7. Husserl 1989: 255

8. ibid

9. Searle 1995: 2; see also p. 27, 31-37, 79-126

10. Searle's initial formulation for constitutive rules is "X counts as Y" or "X counts as Y in context C" (Searle 1995: 28). However, Searle's view is now that "all of institutional reality (with the one crucially important class of exceptions: language itself) is created by speech acts that have the logical form of Declarations…and indeed are maintained in existence by speech acts and other

sorts of representations that have the logical form of Declarations" (Searle 2008: 48). Of Declarations, Searle claims: "By definition, Declarations change reality by representing it as being so changed" (ibid: 49). As such, Searle modifies his formulation to read: "By Declaration we create the Y status function" (ibid: 50), of which the previous formulation is now counted as a specialized form.

11. The final clause is owed to Searle's distinguishing not just brute facts from institutional facts, but he also comes to distinguish social facts: "any fact involving two or more agents who have collective intentionality" (Searle 1998: 121). Institutional facts and constitutive rules involve collective intentional acts of status attributions, where social facts don't necessitate a status attribution or the larger scale collaboration of subjects.

12. Smith & Searle 2003: 285-291

13. I doubt that Searle's modifications, noted above, are satisfactory modifications for B. Smith.

14. Smith & Searle 2003: 289

15. Husserl 1989: 255

16. Avoiding such quandaries is a major benefit of an ontological neutralism of the sort functioning in phenomenological method and also Jorge Gracia's metaphysics (Gracia 1999).

17. Husserl 1989: 255

18. For example, Searle 1995: xi-xiii; Searle 1992: Ch. 1-5

19. It is true that Searle has criticized phenomenology in an attempt to dissociate his views from that tradition (Searle 2005, which is also Ch. 6 of Searle 2008). Addressing Searle's misconceptions about phenomenology, however, and his subsequent overstatements regarding the distinctions between his views and phenomenology, is a task beyond the scope of the present work.

20. Husserl 1989: 255, emphasis added

21. There is a sense in which the second indented quoted passage from Husserl above may bolster the case for a socially embedded theory of mind. More on that below.

22. Mathiesen 2005: 236

23. I suspect that Mathiesen is generally more influenced by Margaret Gilbert, despite couching her abstract in terms of Husserl and Alfred Schütz–both of whom are considered only in passing in a section that is not really integral to her overall thesis. Gilbert herself cites Emile Durkheim and David Lewis as two of her influences, both of whom are in Mathiesen's bibliography.

24. Mathiesen 2005: 237

25. I suspect that an analogous argument is highly problematic to homuncular theories of mind like those offered by William Lycan and Daniel Dennett.

26. Mathiesen 2005: 237

27. Husserl 1999: 109/139 as in Mathiesen 2005: 237

28. Husserl 1999: 109/139

29. Block 2006

30. As stated in earlier sections of the work, I am only interested in cases where minds and consciousnesses come together with reference to the term

mind. If those two categories come apart, cases of minds without consciousness are of no importance to me. As a work oriented through phenomenological philosophy, one might also argue that minds without consciousness were an absurdity born of detached theoretical speculations. However, such an argument is beyond the scope of the present inquiry.

The term hive mind is something established independent from the present work, and which is in fiction. It is a more elegant expression than 'hive consciousness,' which is the intended meaning.

31. He does so by arguing against a provision of Hilary Putnam's (2006) against minded-entities being part of another minded-entity (Block 2006: 115-117).

32. See Nagel 1974 for a case to phenomenology's irreducibility in the narrow sense the term phenomenology has in analytic philosophy of mind. See Tye 2008a for summary of qualia as an issue in analytic philosophy of mind.

33. This is by no means a new idea, ancient Buddhist thought held that consciousness and pyschophysicality formed a co-dependent whole. That is, that consciousness cannot be disembodied. See for example the discourses in Holder 2006. In more recent literature, see for example Varela et al 1992.

34. Here we set aside the question as to whether or not there are specific physical structures on which consciousness is dependent. In doing so, we set aside the multiple realizabilty arguments that affect functionalism and other matters in analytic philosophy of mind.

It is also worth acknowledging that Lycan has made reasonable criticisms of Block's argument. Lycan's gestalt failure point is particularly notable (Lycan 2006: §IV). However, if the embodiment thesis–that all consciousness must be embodied–holds, then it poses an awkward and potentially insurmountable challenge to his and Dennett's homuncular theories of consciousness.

35. See for instance, Husserl 1970, Nagel 1974, Thompson 2007, Gallagher 2006

36. Tye 2008b: §§4-5

37. Summative theories of collective intentionality are generally not held on the ground that groups can and do have properties or predicates not attributable to their members individually.

38. See Tye's examples of XP1 and Lolita in Tye 2008b: §§4-5

39. Time consciousness is fundamental to the structure of consciousness in the Husserlian tradition. Protentive intentions are futurally oriented anticipations located within the experience of the given moment, and affect the sense constitution of the present experience. Retentive intentions are the retained intentional achievements of the just past as they are operative on the sense constitution of the present. See Husserl 2008.

40. See Husserl 1998: §118

41. See Husserl 1998: §83. Note Husserl's footnote equivocating the meanings here of "horizon" with "halo" and "background" (197/166 n.28). In contemporary Searlean terms, then, one might claim that a uniformity of background conditions must apply.

42. David Midgley actually counts insect populations as a meaningful analog for human interactions (Midgley 2006: 107). These types of cases are fraught with behaviorist assumptions. Behaviorism is no longer counted as a credible theory of mind or consciousness. Unfortunately, behaviorism's influence persists.

43. See, for instance, de Waal 2007, de Waal 2009, de Waal 2010, Wilson 2012

44. Combs & Krippner 2008 attempt to offer an alternative case. One objection to their work is the failure to argue that the experience is identical across a plurality of subjects, which would be necessary for *bona fide* collective consciousness. Even arguing that shared experiences are qualitatively identical would be a hard task. I don't deny that one can assume a point of view associated with a group. If one means only that by the phrase 'collective consciousness' then my concern is chiefly that the connotations of the phrase used to pick out the noted type of act are at best misleading if not entirely inappropriate. More critically, however, adopting the point of view of a plural subject is an *abstraction*. Such an act is an *analogical* extension of something one does in relation to other conscious beings as well, the capacity of which certainly does not entail or require the presence of an actual consciousness. One can just as well adopt the point of view of a rock, a stream or a planet. Albert Einstein famously indulged in a thought-experiment about the point of view of a beam of light, which eventually helped him conceptualize the physical theories of general and special relativity. None of that necessitates *actual* consciousness in the object whose point of view is considered in virtue of analogical judgment. A formal analogy between two things is not evidence that those things share material properties. Nor do formal analogies between two things constitute a ground for material analogies. I might, for instance say that the arrangement of a few marks on a whiteboard are formally analogous to the spatial relations between the Scandinavian countries, that doesn't imply any further similitude or identity between the analogs themselves.

Analogical similarities being mistaken for more substantive identity claims appear to be a surprisingly common mistake. My suspicion is that this is mostly predicated on a misunderstanding about the limited import of teleological judgments. My suspicion is based on arguments found on teleology in Spinoza (1992: Book I, Appendix) and Kant (1987), and more recently Searle (1992: Ch. 4); in addition to the treatment of analogy in Husserl (1999), Langer (1996 & 1953), and Wittgenstein (1958 & 1980); as well as Nietzsche's related criticisms of regular failures to think about causation with any clarity (1997: "The Four Great Errors").

45. Ramachandran 2012. Unfortunately, this most recent book of Ramachandran's is not nearly as well written or argued as his previous.

46. Mathiesen 2005: 237

47. ibid: 239-240

48. ibid: 240

49. ibid.

50. See also Shoemaker 1996, D.W. Smith 2005 and Thomasson 2005. Additionally, the issue of awareness relates to contemporary debates over higher-order and same-order monitoring theories of consciousness, i.e. whether experiencing that one is experiencing is an additive component of an act of consciousness or part of it, that have their origins in Brentano's views on inner perception or inner consciousness, adapted by Husserl and others. See Brentano 1995: Book II, §II.8-12, §III; Husserl 2001b: Investigation V. See discussions in Zahavi 1999, 2005 and Gallagher and Zahavi 2007, and 2008: Ch. 5

51. Lycan 2006 includes arguments for the possibility of such iterations, albeit on a homunculist model of consciousness that is itself not without serious problems.

52. See Chapter 2 of May 1987 for descriptions of this sort with analysis.

53. May 1987: 36

54. Arguably May and I disagree over how to interpret Sartre, as Sartre appealed to the alterity in the mob as part of its cohesion and basis for its solidarity. That is, Sartre appeals to the alterity of the subjects who compose the mob.

55. While I don't believe mobs have a unified will in any literal sense, I don't deny that collective responsibility might be able to be attributed to mobs (See May 1987 and Shockley 2007). However, I do want to deny that the sense of agency applicable to groups is distinct from that of individuals. Individuals possess their agency, at least in part, on the basis of their having consciousness. Groups have a derived sense of agency that is dependent on extensions of their members' consciousnesses. Such is beyond the scope of the present project itself. I do see fertile ground, however, for expanding this discussion and developing more the moral side of things in relation to discussions of the effects of the bureaucratic mindset. (See, for instance, Jones, Parker and ten Bos 2005: Ch. 7)

56. The Multiple Realization Thesis: "Psychological states are 'multiply realizable;' i.e. capable of 'realization,' 'instantiation,' 'implementation' in various structures and organisms" (Kim 2006: 179). And, for example, the Structure Restricted Correlation Thesis: "If anything has mental property M at time t, there is some physical structure type T and physical property P such that it is a system of type T at t and has P at t, and it holds as a matter of law that all systems of type T have M at a time just in case they have P at the time" (ibid: 181).

57. Mathiesen 2005: 240

58. ibid: 241

59. This argument often takes its starting point from Hegel's treatment of the master-slave dialectic presented in the section entitled "Self-Consciousness" of *Phenomenology of Spirit* (Hegel 1977: §B).

60. More recently, Paul Ricouer has developed the Hegelian argument's implications within a hermeneutic phenomenological vein. (Ricoeur 1992 & Ricoeur 2005). See also Honneth 1996.

61. One could argue that the beetle box thought experiment (Wittgenstein 2001: §293) does address phenomenological meanings. Such an argument would be analogous to how Tyler Burge extends Hilary Putnam's arguments from "The Meaning of 'Meaning'" from linguistic to mental contents (Burge 1979). I am

not very sympathetic to views that end up equivocating between language and thought or counting thought as a species of language–as Jerry Fodor tends to do, and arguably also in the later works of Martin Heidegger. My view is that Wittgenstein's argument only demonstrates the possibility of public confusion owed to indeterminate nature of the manner of publicly communicable reference. It does not definitively show that there is no private phenomenologically meaningful experience of one's beetle, only the inability to overtly communicate what that is like in determinate fashion to others. And, this failure is due to a lack of a shared experiential basis or shared frame of reference. That is, Wittgenstein's argument actually could be seen as supportive of the position that language is dependent upon collective intentional foundations.

If one's experience is *directed at* their beetle, in virtue of this one's experience is *about* something, as such it is phenomenologically meaningful. That it is hard to describe phenomena adequately, especially where the phenomenon in question is foreign to one's audience is really not remarkable. It's no different than saying that the word "red" is meaningless to one born blind because they have no phenomenological correlate to relate to. It is no more interesting than recognizing that monolingual Chinese speakers don't understand the monolingual English speaker in their midst. The blind individual, Chinese speaker and English speaker each still have *experiences*, even if those experiences differ in nature or fail to have the relevant shared elements to facilitate communication or publicly available meaning and cannot be communicated readily. The theory of collective intentionality, and language's dependence on collective intentionality in Searle's account seems to adequately encapsulate Wittgenstein's concern. This is not to say that subjective phenomenological meanings are not a tricky and potentially problematic matter in their own right.

62. For instance, Searle's theory of collective intentionality emphatically rejects the notion that *intending* (performance of an intentional act) is done by anything other than individuals (Searle 1995).

63. Thompson in Mathiesen 2005: 241

64. Brown 2007

65. David Chalmers has tried to get around or bolster the distinction between narrow and wide content with a distinction between notional content and representational content. See Chalmers 2002 & 2003.

66. See also Putnam 1975 and Burge 1979. As stated in an earlier note, Putnam's argument only bears on *linguistic* content, not mental content. Burge's contribution was to extend Putnam's argument to mental content. One can hold that linguistic content, linguistic meanings, are dependent on extrinsic conditions without having to hold that mental contents are too. One could also hold, as is reasonable, that not all mental contents are wide, even if some are. However, this issue is beyond the scope of the present project.

67. Searle's theory of collective intentionality actually makes any and all social meanings and social objects dependent on language. See Searle 1995.

68. This is a claim that is potentially controversial. Given collective intentionality's strength in offering a theory of social meanings, and the lack of strong alternatives, the claim will not be challenged here.

69. In Schmid 2006 §V much the same argument is outlined.

70. The hyphenated form is used for emphasis–a common practice in the continental traditions; I am not introducing a terminological distinction.

71. Mathiesen 2005: 248

72. Husserl 1989: 255

73. Thompson 2007: 383

74. ibid: 403

75. ibid: 403

76. ibid: 407

77. ibid: 409

78. Haney 1994: 136

79. Zahavi 2001a; see also Donohoe 2004

80 Schmid 2003b: 203

81. ibid: 204

82. ibid: 214

83. Schmid 2003a: 93

84. See also §V of Schmid 2006

85. Haney 1994: 139

86. There are interesting parallels here both with what a defensible non-reductive materialist metaphysics of mind advocates for and how Searle speaks of the emergence of non-reducible systems from arrangements of lower-order phenomena. In the case of Searle, I don't take this to be accidental, as Thompson's position in Thompson 2007 is very much a detailed statement of what Searle has needed as justification for something akin to what he terms "biological naturalism."

87. (*a*) That is, it is the same problem with most causal theories of intentionality. They put the condition for satisfaction of the intention as the condition for the intention, thereby inverting things and would seem to make error and projections in principle impossible barring some non-externalist content.

(*b*) On another point, one might object that really now the debate is over what calling collective intentionality relational means. Certainly that discussion could be had. I suspect that where we differ is thus. I count the individual subject as intersubjectively constituted, and thereby already in some sense "relational." Naturally, an extension of this to collective intentionality is then of little worry as I count this sense of relationality to be relatively trivial in that it just points out what we already know to be true. Schmid seems to pack something more into the notion of being relational, sometimes calling it something "between" subjects. To my mind, a failure of Schmid's is accepting such a spatial metaphor, which amounts to smuggling in the objected to "Cartesian" position anyway.

88. Mathiesen 2005: 235

89. ibid.

90. Mathiesen 2006a & 2006b are not about collective consciousness, and don't appear to use that phrase at all.

91. This is probably why the "turn-coat" political members bear any significance each electoral season, where one party trots out members of the opposition in support of their candidate as evidence of "bi-partisanship."

Chapter 3
Plural Subjects: Phenomenology and Collective Intentionality

In this chapter, I turn to what sort of stance Husserlian phenomenology can outline on plural subjects. The view presented takes David Carr's initial sketches of plural subjects and expands upon it.[1] Carr's view is that the experience of a 'we' not reducible to conjunctive sets of reciprocated I-intentions, and the source of that irreducibility, lies in the experiences of togetherness. While Carr remains staunchly neutral on ontological questions, contra-Carr, I agree with Dan Zahavi that the ontological neutrality of Husserl's phenomenology is a methodological precept about where one starts one's inquiry, not an all-encompassing theoretical prohibition against ontology.[2] Husserl's *Logical Investigations*, particularly the *Third* and *Fourth Investigations*, and other core writings are harder to understand if there is a proscription to eschew ontology all together. Especially difficult for Carr are assertions of Husserl's 1927 *Encyclopedia Britannica* entry on phenomenology that phenomenology is ontology.[3] Also problematic are Husserl's sense of region in his ontology, presented in *Ideas*.[4]

Informative for present purposes is an argument about the dependence relations between different material regions Husserl was attempting to work out. For Husserl, there are three material regions: Nature, Consciousness, and the Cultural World [*Geist*].[5] Each region has its own essence, and the investigation into what is essential to one region is not necessarily the same as that for another. Hence, one ought not treat consciousness as a natural object or a cultural object, and so on. To stress the distinctness of essences is not to deny that consciousness is dependently related to the natural world in some way. After all, it's quite clear that the Cultural World [*Geist*] is dependently related to both Nature and Consciousness. The social world, the world of human cultural achievements, is dependently situated in relation to consciousness and the natural world. It is neither a domain of natural objects nor a domain of pure consciousness, but a domain whose presence is dependent on both.

I argue that the phenomenology of plural subject experiences and collective intentionality more broadly support a formally collectivist and subjectively individualist ontology, the same basic structure found in John Searle's social ontol-

77

ogy.[6] Formal collectivism is the position that we-intentions are basic kinds of intentional states and not reducible to conjunctive sets of reciprocal I-intentions. Subjective individualism is the view that the intentional states themselves are always and only ever situated or manifest in individual consciousness, not in some additional consciousness or super-agent.

The similarities in kind with Searle's account of collective intentionality thus make the position outlined in this chapter susceptible to similar lines of criticism as those made against Searle. This chapter offers only the initial statement of my phenomenologically informed view. The next chapter will defend the view from criticisms, and further extension and discussion will take place in the chapter following the next.

This chapter ends by returning to direct consideration of Carr's account, with a section critically expanding upon a surprising and significant lacuna residual in Carr's view. In his paper, Carr never addressed the question of the sort of evidence plural subject intentions had available to them. This is a very surprising omission given Husserl's emphases on evidence associated with most of his extant materials on or associated with questions concerning intersubjectivity. Thus, I supply an account of evidence consistent with Husserl's writings.

Preparatory Considerations about Phenomenology and the Phenomenological Approach

Carr begins his paper with a brief recounting of the broad trends in how analytic philosophy has dealt with intentionality. The point of his remarks is to draw out the differences between starting from an ontology or latent set of ontological commitments–as a kind of exercise in philosophical apologetics–and phenomenology's approach of taking the phenomena and their characteristics independent of specific pre-commitments of an ontological nature.

I will briefly recount Carr's statements, leaving criticism to others, as the point here is only to sketch in broad strokes the trend lines underlying the differences between traditions. First, Carr notes there are those who treated intentionality "as a kind of ghost-in-the-machine redivivus, come back to haunt them."[7] Specifically, he names Gilbert Ryle and Ludwig Wittgenstein and their apparent commitments to materialist ontology. Following these figures, and reacting to the more trenchant types of phenomena that the early behavioristic theories of intentionality and mind had problems handling, one finds a set of clearly reactionary attitudes:

> Reaction among this group has ranged from a disdainful refusal to admit the problem–intentionality is declared without argument to be appearance, not reality (e.g. Quine)–to elaborate arguments designed to reduce the intentional to the causal (e.g., Dennett). The latter resemble nothing more than the gymnastics of theologians attempting to explain the presence of evil in a universe whose uniform goodness they are convinced of in advance.[8]

Alternatively, one also finds approaches like Searle's that assert that intentionality is part of the natural world, while maintaining a robust and independent role for intentionality.

In stark contrast to these approaches, which aim at their root to defend or make defensible a particular ontological commitment or set thereof, one finds in phenomenology those

> who have a taste for the variety and even the irrepressible untidiness of things. For them intentionality is a tool for getting at and describing some of this variety. These are the true phenomenologists and even the true descendants of Husserl, I would argue, especially if one considers the *Logical Investigations* and the manuscripts (veritable models of untidiness) rather than the programmatic texts.[9]

This neutrality, or disposition to start analysis rather than merely defend a pre-given account because of its argumentative elegance despite the cost to the phenomena, is born out in Husserl's methodological prescripts: the *epoché* and reduction. Husserl asks one to bracket out existential considerations in order to isolate and identify the phenomena subject to investigation. Once the phenomena in question are isolated, one systematically analyzes their characteristics by modulating the characteristics thereof one by one until one isolates the *eidos* of the phenomena. To strip anything away from the *eidos* is to destroy the phenomena in question. The variant genera and species one finds can then be placed in an adequate taxonomic framework. The *epoché* sets the ontological status of the object of consciousness aside, in order to focus on it as object of consciousness.

The point of all this is to stress an important difference in orientation that analytic readers might not appreciate at face value.

> Thus we could say that the analytic approach tries to fit intentionality into an ontology of the real world, while the phenomenological approach explores the realm of intentions themselves, and the real world only *as* it is mentally intended. Each is interested thus in both the mind *and* the real world, but they approach their relation with different methods and different priorities.[10]

This is not, to my mind, to decry analytic philosophy as a method or tradition at all, regardless of Carr's tone. Rather, it is to emphasize a deep-seated difference in approaches. Where analytic philosophers tend to focus on rigors of argumentation, and seek elegant argumentative positions, phenomenologists tend to focus on rigor of description and accuracy in respect of the phenomena at issue. Again, these are only broad strokes characterizations. I find merit in both approaches. However, I am firmly of the mind that the phenomena must take precedence. Phenomenology stresses making sense of what is experienced as it is experienced first, ontological commitments are secondary.[11]

Carr's Account of Plural Subjects

Everyday experience is intersubjectively situated; one encounters others *as* conscious experiencing subjects in their own right. One has experiences *of* others as well as experiences *with* others. Some experiences are in a *we*-mode, where an accurate description of them requires use of the first person plural, *we* did or experienced such and such. Some experiences with others are such that one cannot describe them adequately if one's description is in the form of you did *x* and I did *x*, in distinction from describing them in the manner of *we x*. Some experiences described in the first person plural cannot be reduced to conjunctions of first person singular intentional descriptions without a loss of meaning, they are not reducible to what *I* experience *and* you experience as individuals. Individually oriented descriptions leave open coincidental experiences, and sometimes one uses "we" to describe cases of coincidental individual experiences, experiences that are more congruent with one another, as distinct from being experienced as *together*. Experiencing something as part of a whole, e.g. as a member of a team or in partnership with another, cannot be adequately described without regarding the we-mode.[12] It is those cases where "we" is necessary for accurate description that are the phenomena of plural subjects.

In an experience that is essentially in a we-mode, i.e. a plural subject experience, one's acts of consciousness directly reference others:

> The establishment of the *we* in common perception is the simplest form of what Husserl calls the *Vergemeinschaftung der Monaden*:[13] when two subjects confront one another and stand in relation to the same objects they form, to that extent, a rudimentary community that can itself be considered as performing an act (*cogitamus*) through 'its' diverse (and in this case simultaneous) presentations.[14]

Collective intentional or intersubjective moments of experience, instances where there is a non-reducible *we*, can be understood as foundational for higher order intersubjective meanings. The broader social world and the meanings constituted in it are based in *shared* experiential foundations. This does not imply that there is strong collectivity, i.e. that collectives themselves are subjectivities. The 'we' as subject of experience, the "rudimentary community," is often referred to in contemporary literature as the plural subject. Carr states, "The community is a *'community of monads*, which we designate as *transcendental intersubjectivity.'* It is transcendental because it makes 'transcendentally possible the being of a world,' in this case the intersubjective world."[15] "The 'communities' of which Husserl speaks, beginning with the simplest perceptual encounter between two persons, are available to *me* only insofar as I participate in them through my communication with other persons."[16] For Husserlian phenomenology intentionality's socially constitutive role is what differentiates the cultural or social dimensions of the world from the natural world and their respective categories of meaning. It is clear that an individual subject alone is inadequate for those meanings that are fundamentally *social* in nature. Adequate analyses of specific social objects ought to reference those communities constituting of the object with the meaning that it bears in experience. "It is, as we have seen, the *cogitamus* which is the starting point of intersubjective phenomenology."[17] The intersubjective world is not premised on "I's," but "we's."[18] Intersubjectively situated meanings are only intelligible in relation to pluralities of subjects, that is, they receive their sense constitutions through intersubjective exchange or in intersubjective contexts, not by an individual alone.[19] Collective intentionality need not be understood as substantively different than intentionality in the singular; "it is based on the *cogitamus* in just the same way that individual phenomenology is based in the *cogito*."[20] Given the locus and limitation of consciousness per se to the individual subject of experience and intentionality's intrinsic origin in consciousness, it is individuals who perform the *act* of intentionality with reference to the *cogitamus*, the plural subject, and not the *cogitamus* itself. The grammatical subject (the subject of syntax) does not properly speaking intend anything itself. The *intending* subject, the conscious subject, is not equivalent to the *subject of intention* or subject matter of acts of consciousness, i.e. it is not the syntactical subject referenced in and through an intentional act.

Phenomenology's emphasis on the experience of a plural subject, an experienced "we," is such that it does not initially concern itself with the existence of a specific correlate to that experience in actuality, nor does it prejudge what the subject-term "we" might range over. An experience of a plural subject intention, an experience that is about *our* experience, not just *my* experience, any experience in the we-mode, is inclusive of what the "we" ranged over. To this point, it is important that one not conflate satisfaction conditions with intentional possibilities. Acts of intentionality are liable to evidence themselves in fulfillment, but are not constrained for their possibilities by what may be achieved in actuality. One can think "there's a unicorn on the lawn" whether or not there is a unicorn on the lawn. However, one's intention is not evidenced or fulfilled unless there is actually a unicorn on the lawn.[21] Propositions, complex syntactically articulated wholes constituted by the arrangement of more basic meanings, arise only in the interrelation of consciousness and objects articulable to it in the world. This is why it is meaningless in some sense to ask of those blind from birth to think about how "the balloon is red." They can know in the abstract that red is a color and that one is predicating it as a property of the balloon's of a certain sort, but *redness* itself is a null category to them. The range of possible meanings is dependent on the constitution of the intending subject herself.[22] The import here is that who, or even what, "we" is inclusive in respect to is determined by the specific intentional achievement of the individual for whom the experience is manifest, irrespective of whether that is capable of evidentiary fulfillment. If one experiences taking in a sunset *as together with* their horse, their imaginary friend, God, their pet rock, what have one, the key point is that the intentionality of the experience itself is in a *plural* form. It is that plural-mode intentionality which establishes the criteria according to which one checks as to the evidentiary merit or lack thereof in respect to what was experienced and how it was experienced. Importantly, the individual's experience, evidenced or not, has the specific sense-structure regardless of questions of a corresponding state of affairs in the world "outside" their experience or the epistemological merit of their report.

To linger on this last point a moment, phenomenologists are not claiming that anything one claims to experience is *real*. Rather, anything one claims to experience–so long as one's description is accurate–is what and how one *experienced*. When one says, for instance that they dreamt of *x*, hallucinated of *x* or thought that *x* happened or another was party to what was experienced, that's true to what the individual reports of their experience. As a description of experience, it is accurate; again, so long as the reporting is accurate and reliable. A similar precept has been adopted by V.S. Ramachandran in his neurological research. Arguably, that precept has enabled him and his colleagues to make enormous strides in neurology and clinical applications. There the reports of subjects help researchers determine what might be going on in the brain. In either case, subjective reports are not infallible and need to be corroborated with additional evidence. But in either case to eliminate subjective reports is to miss something integral to the phenomena being investigated. This does not mean that anything goes, far from it actually. It is to emphasize our finitude and the fact that experience does not always match reality. After all, what sense could an appearance-reality distinction bear if there is no difference? And why care about epistemological questions if what is experienced by an individual or set of individuals might not reflect what is the case, or possibly refer to what is available to be experienced in a more public sense?

Many analytic and phenomenological philosophers agree that the I or *individual* subject is the locus of intentionality. This individualism of intentionality is often paired with or seen as an obvious conclusion of definitions of intentionality. For instance, Galen Strawson's view is that the concrete phenomenon of intentionality is "essentially mental and indeed essentially experiential (conscious) phenomenon."[23] That is, "we can think about things. We can target, hit, refer to, mean, intend an object, present or absent, concrete or not, in thought."[24] Take also Searle's claim that: "Intentionality is that feature of the mind by which mental states are directed at, or are about or of, or refer to, or aim at, states of affairs in the world."[25] What is not clear is how this connects to individuals. This might seem to preclude by fiat other possibilities. Shaun Gallagher and Dan Zahavi illuminate why it is that phenomenologists connect these two things. "To the extent that phenomenology stays with experience, it is said to take a first-person approach. That is, the phenomenologist is concerned to understand the perception in terms of the meaning it has for the subject."[26] "Intentionality is a ubiquitous character of consciousness, and as the phenomenologists put it, it means that all consciousness is *about* or *of something*."[27] Phenomenology studies meanings from the first-personal perspective or as they are experienced, and all experience is *someone's* experience. Phenomenology's focus on experience thus directs its analyses to examinations of the intentionality of consciousness. Phenomenology appeals to consciousness as individually situated in embodied cognition; each consciousness is some*one's* consciousness.[28] And, as Carr notes, even if it is not controversial to refer to pluralities or groups as *objects*, it is rather unclear how one can consider them to be *subjects*.[29] Nonetheless, Carr points out that we do make attributions of *perceptual experiences and actions* to both individuals and groups. More importantly for phenomenology is that one can have experiences that are strongly identified with or attributed to a *we*, experiences that are said to be *ours*, not just *mine* or mine and yours.[30] For example, one speaks of *our* travels as distinct from *their own* individual travels, or of *our* nuptials, *our* battlefield maneuvers, *our* chess match, etc. In such experiences one does not leave behind a first-personal point of view, only shifts from a singular to a plural form or plural mode of experiencing. This works both, as Carr notes, for common *perceptual experiences* as well as common *action*.[31]

This distinction is not unimportant. Carr establishes that there are at least two distinct ways in which plural subjects are found in experience: the plural subject of experience and the plural subject of action. In the case of common experience, one has an *object* in common. In the case of common action, one has an *objective* in common. "In both cases there is reference back to a common *subject*, a *we*."[32] This is not to claim that they function identically, as the difference in act-types of intentionality bear distinctly different evidentiary conditions.

> ...There is of course the difference in what Searle calls the 'direction of fit.' We can express this difference by saying that in perception the experience is called forth by and tailored to the object, which exists independently of it; while in the case of action the object (or objective) is literally brought forth or produced by the action itself.[33]

This means that the object in common represents the basis for the plural subject of experience, whereas the we-subject must be prior to common action in that it establishes the common action. This means that plural subjects of experience are prior to plural subjects of action. In order for there to be common action there must be a plural subject, and some experiential common ground is necessary for the formation of the plural subject itself.

If some common basis is necessary for the experience of a plural subject that means plural subject experiences are grounded in stable and persistent phenomena extended through time. "To be a genuine or full-fledged subject, the *we* must, like the I, persist throughout a multiplicity of experiences *and* actions spread out over time."[34] Indeed, temporal extension and stability over time are necessary for the plural subject's concretization. As Carr notes, one can't just have an experience with others as parts, but the experience must be such that one can come to recognize those others and oneself as participant in a unity of some sort. "The sense of common experience has to endure long enough and be diverse enough to establish an enduring group of persons who mutually acknowledge their membership in something common."[35]

One might take the just quoted passage as contradictory to what I've said earlier about the emphasis of phenomenology being on the individual and independent of the specific extrinsic conditions or evidentiary merits. I attribute the apparent contradiction to Carr's language. He is stressing that there be a narrative structure to the plural subject experiences and actions, just as there is to an individual's experiences and actions. The sense-constitution associated with a given experience or action is not such that it forms in a vacuum, but always within an ever-changing contextual horizon. Carr stresses that, like an individual, the narrative structure of the group is subject to disagreement and division. Such disagreement and division would be problematic were there a shift away from the first-personal experience and if the sense of an individual's experience were determined from outside. The coherence of group narratives is such that they are never settled, but always in a process of "reciprocal narration, persuasion, negotiation, revision."[36] One need only think about how in recounting an experience or action had with another, how easily disagreement can arise between participants, how individuals' descriptions tend to differ in emphasis and character. Since each individual is experiencing what they do from their unique lived-embodied position, it stands to reason that such differences are persistent in and operative in common experience and the common actions predicated on the more basic experiential foundation. Univocal third-personal unity is likely a fiction; a range of first-person differences that underlay and function as part of plural subject unities is more the reality. The apparent contradiction is resolved in that there is no shift away from the first-personal stance; rather Carr is slipping from first-personal experience to the passive or active collaborative narrative construction of a group extended over time. That narrative can be differently inflected for each individual, reconciling those differences across individual subjects is something separated from the individual's conscious experience itself. Plural subject experiences are not necessarily experiences of univocal or strictly identical experiences; individual experiences within or in relation to the plural subject experience still may diverge.

To distinguish the robust sense of "we" from coincidental cases, Carr refers to bona fide plural subjects as communities. He stresses that plural subjects, communities, are in some manner "intentional subjects, analogues in some ways to individual subjects. This means first of all simply that intentional properties–beliefs, perceptions, actions, desires–are ascribed to them."[37] The key term here being *analogues*, as some are wont to take that they are intentional subjects of some kind and ascribe identity in kind with individual subjects.

This does not mean that any or all common bases are sufficient for founding a community. For example, the group of all persons who are 5'6" is probably not a socially significant grouping. Though, often non-intentional properties do contribute to or play a role in how a plural subject is constituted. As such, "communities, like individuals, we might say, have bodies as well as minds."[38] It is because of this that "the community is *primarily* or *essentially* an intentional subject."[39] Here "intentional subject" refers to a subject intended and not the subject doing the intending, that is, a *part* of an act of consciousness not the *agent* of consciousness as such.

That one can speak of something as embodied is not a necessary indicator that it is embodied. While I accept the principle that to be conscious is to be embodied, that all consciousness is embodied, it does not follow that anything one can speak of *as if* embodied is thereby conscious. This holds in the case of plural subjects. While one can refer to a plural subject as a unity and can speak of them as embodied, reference in such cases does not necessarily pick out an embodied consciousness. Plural subjects may be "embodied" in the metaphorical sense, but it would not be accurate if by "embodied" one means to say that it is an individuated conscious entity in its own right. As such, the embodiment that plural subjects have is an *as if* or derived form of embodiment, not primary embodiment. This is to be expected if one accepts that consciousness is embodied and is intrinsically intentional. Just as the intentionality of plural subjects is an *as if* or derived intentionality and not intrinsic intentionality, the plural subject is both subject intended and intended bodily without being either an intending or embodied subject, or subjectivity proper.

The idea of an "intentional subject" can be fraught with ambiguity and deserves more critical attention. For one, speaking thus is potentially misleading as it makes use of a rather seductive metaphor. Carr is right to acknowledge how some non-intentional properties can be part of plural subjects. However, this is entirely a function of his own criterion for shared or common experience as foundational to the formation of any such group. Non-intentional properties can become the basis for shared experiences that can give rise to the strong sense of we necessary for plural subjects. There are a number of examples one can cite: race, sex, and economic class, all of which under certain circumstances can ground common experiences.[40] It is these non-intentional properties, in addition to the shared intentional elements, that form the "body" of the plural subject. The question that must be addressed is to what this account requires us to commit.

My suspicion is that there is yet no experiential or phenomenological basis to count plural subjects as more than the subject of someone's or several someone's experiences and that they are embodied only in a strictly *metaphorical* sense, i.e. they are not psycho-physical unities of their own right like an individual human being. Searle too acknowledges a role to be played in collective intentionality by non-intentional components, what he calls brute facts. For Searle, these "embody" the collective intention. But this is not embodiment in the same sense as how a conscious subject is embodied. There is no kinesthetic awareness, no motility, etc. What is missing in discussions of embodiment is a sufficiently careful set of distinctions surrounding what is meant by something's being embodied.

There are at least four different things that one might mean when they speak of embodiment. First, one might speak of something's being embodied in the sense that it has physical parts. If those parts are only accidentally associated with the thing in question, what Husserl calls pieces, e.g. my shoes relative to me, then they are of no interesting consequence.[41] If those parts are essential, what Husserl calls moments, e.g. my heart or brain, then one makes an interesting observation. Second, one might use talk of embodiment to refer to something's having a dependence on physical parts. That is, for something's being the thing it is there must be a physical part(s) of a certain kind or arranged in a certain non-arbitrary relationship for its being; for example, one's heart must stand in a functional relation to one's cardiovascular system in order that one be a living organism, it cannot merely stand in a proximate spatial relation. Thirdly, one could use talk of embodiment to refer to something's being a physical thing. For instance, a rock is a physical thing, and in that sense, it might be said that it is embodied. Lastly and principally important for phenomenologically oriented discussions, one is embodied in the sense of being a psycho-physical unity, that one is an embodied consciousness. Interestingly, this final sense is not precisely co-extensive with one's physical body and has somewhat fluid boundaries, as supplements to one's physical being of certain sorts are often constitutive contributing elements to one's embodied experience. For instance, the clothes one wears, glasses if one wears them, well functioning tools or weapons in use by proficient parties and so on, all supplement one's embodied experience. However, there is a basic limitation to those embodied experiences extended beyond one's physical body in that they only include those elements which are part of the conscious subject's experience, their being part of *my* experienced embodied dimension is a necessary ingredient in their contribution to embodied consciousness.

Given these distinctions, what can be said about the sense in which plural subjects are embodied? Since plural subjects include at least one subject, the intending subject, e.g. a human being, there is a sense in which they have physical parts, and some of those physical parts are important to the possibility of plural subjects. Further, the sense of a plural subject as a whole could very well be said to have dependencies relations on certain physical parts and their arrangements in systems. For instance, a set of corpses is not a plural subject–they lack the contribution of consciousness or intentional systems necessary in addition to the physical elements, not to mention their physical parts are not systemically functional in the appropriate sorts of ways. Plural subjects are most certainly not, however, physical things in their own right like rocks. The interesting question remaining is whether or not plural subjects are embodied psycho-physical unities like individual subjects, like an individual human person. What complicates matters for some is 1) plural subjects include at least one psycho-physical unity (subjectivity), often more, in their composition and 2) there are certain intentional properties that one can predicate of plural subjects (beliefs, attitudes, etc.) that are not predicable of their constituent member-parts. Neither of these is definitive or compelling evidence for identifying plural subjects as embodied as psycho-physical unities of their own right in the same way as an individual human being is an instance of an embodied subject. To use the first element as evidence that plural subjects *are* an embodied consciousness in virtue of the fact that at least one such being is a part of their constitution is a rather obvious instance of the fallacy of composition.

As per the second element, it should not surprise one that in virtue of their cognitive capabilities one can attribute intentional properties to things without consciousness. Words, pictures, symbols like stop signs, and so on, exhibit some form of intentionality, but they are not conscious in virtue of their intentional characteristics. Searle is correct to argue that, "We need to distinguish the type of intentionality humans and animals have intrinsically from the sort of derived intentionality of words and sentences, pictures, diagrams, and graphs."[42] Intrinsic intentionality is the intentionality of consciousness itself. As such "Intrinsic intentionality is observer-independent–I have my state of hunger regardless of what any observer thinks."[43] On the other hand, one can attribute intentionality to non-conscious things, for example, a German word, a billboard, a date on the calendar counted as having a specific significance, etc. Such cases are instances of derived intentionality. "Derived intentionality is observer-dependent–it is only in relation to observers, users, and so on, that, for example, a sentence of French has the meaning that it has."[44] Given that derived intentionality is not immediately tied to a consciousness, "all derived intentionality is derived from the intrinsic."[45] How this bears on the question of plural subjects is that their intentionality could be explained entirely in terms of derived intentionality. This view is bolstered by the dependence of derived intentionality on intrinsic intentionality as well as the intuition captured by the analogy of a collective with an individual, namely that plural subjects can do similar things in comparison to individual subjects in virtue of their dependence on individual subjectivity.

One benefit of counting the intentionality of plural subjects as derived intentionality is that one maintains the underlying intuitions that lead to the preceding concern without falling subject to the fallacy of composition. By withholding intrinsic intentionality from plural subjects, one thereby withholds the possibility of their being embodied in the sense of being psycho-physical unities in their own right. Second, this view retains a ground for individual contributions to plural subjects whereby a ground for individual responsibility or complicity is maintained. Since a plural subject can't exhibit intentionality without some subjectivity's contribution of intrinsic intentionality, the idea of a metaphysically real "group mind" is entirely avoided. One can experience groups *as if* they have minds, none of which requires one to commit to their metaphysical reality. Further, the sometimes counter-intuitive behaviors of groups can be explained in virtue of the complex network of collective intentionality that individuals fluidly maintain and revise in dynamic systems of relations with one another. The non-identity of their individual narratives, or interpretations of an accepted narrative's meaning, accounts for difference of beliefs and actions taken by individual participating individuals.

Perhaps one thinks something suspect has transpired here, in that this talk of intentional subjects in relation to plural subjects might appear to be contradicting what has been stated and argued for earlier. I aim to now dissolve such worries. To say from the first-personal orientation of phenomenological inquiry "that a community is primarily or essentially an intentional subject is to say that, whatever else it might be, it exists primarily through its intentional properties–its experiences and actions–which gives it the character of being *of*."[46] This is to say plural subjects, or communities, embody orientations to the world, things in the world, and other communities and individuals in the world as well. In short, communities might be understood as communally held sets of comportments. Crucially, however,

> to use the third-person 'it' in such descriptions is highly artificial and mislead-
> ing. Better to say: for any such community of which I am a member, it is *we*
> who experience, believe, feel and act; it is in and through such intentional rela-
> tions, and through the narrational form of reflection and self-constitution...that
> *we* exist and maintain our existence as a community.[47]

Carr denies making any ontological commitments as to the status of the community itself, a view to be critiqued shortly. Key to present purposes is the assertion that communities, plural subjects, are intentional achievements of the individuals who compose them, which in turn affect and inform their members' perceptions or actions. "As a *world* they make up not a collection of objects and objective relations but a complex of meaning which is not detachable from the community intentionality which constitutes it."[48] Even if a plural subject has an independent set of characteristics that are not reducible to those of their individual members, there is no plural subject independent of those members. To clarify: plural subjects are ontologically dependent on individuals, as conscious, beings capable of setting up a world, and imbuing intentionality in a derived form beyond themselves–e.g. through the formation of symbols, language, artworks, etc. However, it is not the case that what is true of the plural subject can be distributed across its members. Plural subjects thus have some measure of independence from their constituent members.

Carr turns expressly against the notion of the "group mind" and Sartre's example of storming the Bastille.[49] Carr charges those who reason to the notion of strong collectivity or a group as a consciousness in its own right with *post hoc ergo propter hoc* reasoning.[50] The Sartrean model is not adequate as a paradigm of social reality, even if cases like that Sartre describes are genuine and dangerous.[51] Such views fail: "by abandoning and subverting the individual subjectivity they take us from the I not to the *we* but simply to a putative large-scale I."[52] Groups are not subjectivities in their own right, but depend for their powers–intentional or otherwise–on subjectivities proper. None of this means that groups can't have intentionality, only the intentionality in question is derived and not intrinsic in nature.

Identifying the intentionality of plural subjects as an instance of derived intentionality and their sense of embodiment as the less robust sense of being dependent on physical parts doesn't diminish the status or minimize the power of complex plural subjects formalized by conventional systems of intentional agreements or acceptances like corporations or nation-states, nor eliminates their bearing meanings whatsoever (a metaphorical sense is still sense).[53] What it does is to clarify the conditions for fulfillment regarding these subjects, as intended in experience, which are plausibly verifiable. Metaphorical senses have conditions for fulfillment that are complex, untidy, and that can mask their more direct descriptive elements in virtue of their distance and historical derivations from intrinsic intentionality.

Critique of Carr's Neutrality and his Flirtations with Collectivistic Descriptions

Carr insists that a strength of the phenomenological approach, as he understands it, is that it remains "ontologically indifferent,"[54] or that of the plural subject "their ontological status, in any absolute sense of that term, need not concern us,"[55] and that he is concerned with more the question of *how* we experience plural subjects, *we* experiences and actions, than with *what* the plural subject is.[56] This comes to a head in Carr's final paragraph:

> The reality of the intentional subject–singular or plural–may seem a pale thing to those whose notion of reality is tailored to the hard physical world. And it may be difficult for them to fit such ephemera into their seamless ontology. But that is their *theoretical* problem. For all of us, outside the constructed worlds of our theories, selves, our own and others, and the communities to which we belong, are as real as anything we know.[57]

As such, one may be left with the impression that ontology and theoretical systematization of one's understanding of the world is somehow contrary to phenomenology, or a fool's game. I argue that, first, this is not what Carr means, and second, while he is correct to assert that the ontological neutrality of Husserl's methodology is a benefit, he overextends its application.

One can assert that Carr's use of "ontology" and "ontological" would be more correct if they were to read "metaphysics" and "metaphysical." Placing Husserl in context, Dan Zahavi reminds us that for Husserl, metaphysics is understood to be the examination of the presuppositions of sciences that deal with *reality*, and that it is this that Husserl denies phenomenology is oriented towards.[58] In virtue of comments Husserl makes throughout *Logical Investigations*, "it is not difficult to establish a solid link between the descriptive nature of phenomenology and its metaphysical neutrality."[59] Illuminating some of the above, "it is in part this metaphysical neutrality that is behind Husserl's repeated claim that the difference between a veridical perception and a non-veridical perception (say, an illusion or a hallucination) is irrelevant to phenomenology."[60] Phenomenology is concerned with descriptions of experience from the first-personal perspective, not with something *beyond* or *outside* or *external* to consciousness. This is what is intended by the bracketing of the question of the object of experience's *existence*.

Zahavi lays out three ways one might appraise Husserl's call for metaphysical, or ontological, neutrality:

> 1) To embrace the rejection of metaphysics as liberating one from pseudo-problems.
> 2) To embrace a distinction between metaphysics and phenomenology, and to hold that while phenomenology might lay a ground for metaphysics, it itself is not metaphysics and should not try to answer such questions.
> 3) To regret the rejection of metaphysics and the limitation from attempting to answer metaphysical questions as an "unnecessary straightjacket."[61]

In what is quickly becoming indicative of a pattern in Zahavi's thought, his own view is that these are not three obviously opposed positions. Instead, he argues that they are only incompatible positions where one assumes metaphysical questions form a homogenous whole.

> Thus, it could very well be argued that there is a variety of metaphysical questions, and that some might fall into the first category, some in the second and some in the third–i.e., there might be metaphysical pseudoproblems that phenomenology is wise to abandon, metaphysical questions that are beyond its reach, and metaphysical questions that it is capable of addressing.[62]

In other words, since metaphysical issues form a heterogeneous set, phenomenology helps us understand some issues as being ultimately vacuous or only apparent problems, others are out of its reach and yet other issues pose questions suited for fruitful analysis through phenomenology's methods.

One may worry about equivocating between ontology and metaphysics. Clarification is necessary. If "ontology aims at articulating the essential structures of different ontological regions," then Husserl's phenomenology is consistent with ontology.[63] And since ontology can remain neutral about existence claims, where metaphysics focuses on "what it means for an object to be real, actual to exist," metaphysics is just a different enterprise.[64] If this is correct, Carr might be guilty of equivocating between ontology and metaphysics. Yet, as Zahavi reminds us, phenomenology is not neutral on all questions of existence; Husserl expressly addressed questions of existence and reality, his inquiries and concerns with intersubjectivity being motivated principally out of such concern.[65]

Carr clearly overextends the neutrality at work in phenomenological method. What in phenomenology is a methodological proscription about where to begin analysis–by not assuming a particular theoretical framework and thereby presupposing its assumptions about reality–is not a totalizing prohibition. Rather, one is cautioned to avoid starting from a set of ontological or metaphysical givens, thus potentially arguing from a position with uncritical presupposition; doing so is more likely to plumb the implications of what one's assumed more than to reveal what is, what is actual, or what is real. In such cases, one effectively only ever accomplishes conditional analysis: if $q_1...q_n$ are true, then x, y, z follow.

One can illuminate this by considering Merleau-Ponty's reflections on the painter Paul Cézanne. Merleau-Ponty cast Cézanne as a phenomenological exemplar, offering an indirect argumentation to the effect that Cézanne thought as a phenomenologist does or ought to: as one who sees past the inherited dichotomies latent in the tradition, to the phenomena themselves.[66] The difference between a Platonist or Aristotelian and Plato or Aristotle is that the latter initiate a path to thinking, the former operate within the confines of what has been given.[67] As such, there is merit to Zahavi's way of thinking about phenomenology's relation to metaphysical questions, which is effectively a way to assert that the relation is complicated. If the apparently widespread view that social reality is dependent on consciousness and intentionality is accurate, then phenomenology is perfectly suited as a rigorously established method for investigating intersubjectivity and social reality.

One important consequence of this break with Carr is that I disagree with some of his descriptions of plural subjects. This is to say that as phenomenological analysis progresses, and clarity of the basic phenomena is better established, certain descriptions of particular phenomena will lose sense and require reevaluation. In this case, my position is that the basic structure of intentionality is unnecessarily problematized by subjectively collectivistic descriptions of plural subjects. Where Carr's descriptions bear collectivistic connotations at times, I resist those connotations on the basis that they do not adequately reflect the basic nature of intentionality and are not open to being phenomenologically evidenced, unlike the nature of intentionality itself. Rigor of description requires that one redraw their descriptions to better reflect the phenomena. It is here that the ontological import of phenomenological analysis hits home. Where the basic nature of phenomena comes into focus, certain descriptions and descriptive strategies lose sense or are revealed to fail to reflect what is. The manner of description one takes in relation to a phenomenon determines the evidentiary criteria for that description, i.e. determines the criteria in accordance with which one assesses its adequacy in relation to that which it describes. Hence, the importance of the question of evidence, addressed at the end of this chapter.

Pairing Phenomenology with Searle

In spite of Searle's awkward attempt to criticize phenomenology, those who are familiar with *both* Searle's and Husserl's theories of intentionality recognize significant overlap.[68] Searle himself remarks that this should be unsurprising, given an object of study in common.[69] The particular basis for my conjoining of Searle and Husserlian phenomenology in the domain of collective intentionality is the *basic* similarities in their theories of intentionality and how their views on intentionality inform the respective approaches to collective intentionality.[70] I stress that I am not counting these as equivalent views, nor even views that are in agreement on all points.[71] Rather, given the similarities, my position is that both views can benefit from such an exchange.

Particularly helpful, given her familiarity with both traditions, is Amie Thomasson. Of the works on social ontology in Husserl and Searle, Thomasson observes, "While the [phenomenological] tradition is separate from Searle's and guided by different motivations, the key findings from the two sides are strikingly in agreement."[72] Further, Thomasson argues that where differences emerge, the phenomenological tradition has the upper hand "since it enables us to offer a broader and more adequate ontology of the everyday world."[73] As such, she argues that the contemporary discussion can benefit from the older tradition. I would add that the crux of this rests around the classical theory of intentionality in distinction from the more limited notions operating presently.[74] This is consistent with where Thomasson concludes:

> Broadening the account of the social world in this way [accepting the sense of intentional objects *vis-à-vis* Husserl and Roman Ingarden] enables us to offer a far better understanding of the social world, for it enables us to include such abstract features as governments, universities, works of art, and computer programs *without* requiring that all apparent talk about such things be paraphrased into talk about activities or rights of certain kinds.[75]

Phenomenology enables us to discuss intentionality [*Intentionalität*] without reducing it to or equivocating it with intent [*Absicht*]. Further, by having a framework in which to discussion intentional objects, without the constraints of overriding metaphysical commitments one is better able to discuss the objects as they are actually experienced.

Thomasson herself chalks this strength up to the notion of dependence operating in phenomenology.[76] I do not object to her arguments on this matter, counting the role of intentionality in phenomenology as also central to the difference. Likely she would point out that Husserl's views of intentionality and intentional constitution are steeped in this language of dependence, the *Third* and *Fourth Logical Investigations* (ontology) preceding the *Fifth Logical Investigation* (intentionality of consciousness) for a reason.[77] Granted, all that is correct, but this is to lay emphasis on a complementary view: intentionality in the phenomenological tradition operates in a more flexible and well-defined ontological framework, one that is not directed at offering an apologetics for any particular metaphysical view. With this, then, I turn to Searle in order to supplement and fill out details of the Husserlian view outlined above.

For Searle, collective intentions (we-intentions) have at least three essential characteristics: irreducibility, being individually manifest, and fallibility. He states:

> No set of "I-intend"s, even supplemented with beliefs about other "I-intend"s, is sufficient to get to the "we-intend." Intuitively, in the collective case the individual intentionality, expressed by "I am doing act A," is derivative from the collective intentionality "We are doing act A."[78]

All consciousness is in individual minds, in individual brains.[79]

[An account of collective intentionality] must be consistent with the fact that the *structure* of any individual's rationality has to be independent of the fact of whether or not he is getting things right, whether or not he is radically mistaken about what is actually occurring. ...[it] must be consistent with the fact that all intentionality, whether collective or individual, could be had by a brain in a vat or a set of brains in vats.[80]

As such, collective intentions are intentions for or about collectivities, not intentions had by collectives. Since consciousness is only manifest in individual minds, intentions regarding collective action must also be manifest only in individual minds. In other words, the intention of an individual about a collective action is essentially perspectivally situated, something a phenomenological account also accepts. The content of said intention, even if the *act* itself is "situated" in an individual consciousness, is directed at or *about* the collective experience or action. The individual experiences herself as party to the collective experience or action. As Searle puts it, "*I* am doing something only as part of *our* doing something."[81] That is what one does or believes in relation to the group's action or belief, that which is intrinsically intersubjective in scope, is subsumed under and dependent on the primary collective intention(s) in question. This doesn't eliminate individual thoughts or actions about the same subject matter. Rather one needs to distinguish between individual intentions that are either independent or dependent on a collective intention. That some individual actions or beliefs depend for their sense on the prior or background collective intentional framework is nothing spooky. Consider, for example, how great hitters in baseball sometimes purposefully fly out or bunt so as to sacrifice oneself with the purposes of advancing the runners as part of the team's strategy.[82] Looking ahead, if one's analysis were formally individualistic, sacrifice bunts and sacrifice flies will probably have to appear quixotic and senseless; or, one would be forced to accept a rather lengthy description of such phenomena where a simpler less burdensome one is readily available as an alternative.

On the one hand, intentions always and only arise in individuals' minds. On the other hand, intentions of a collective nature are distinct from those of a singular or individual nature. "We" represents a distinct set of concerns from the individual subjects that compose it. A necessary condition for a collective intention is that its content refer to the plurality or collectivity who represents its subject, the *who* of one's "we." It cannot be a *collective* intention unless it is *about* a collective. The "we" itself is not something that has any intentions itself as only individuals have intentions. Rather the "we" represents a projection whereby one extends their intention over some range of subjects in a (seemingly) nonarbitrary way.

While some theorists focus on making sense of one's participation in a collective and therefore how the collective state of affairs affects one's individual intentions [*Absicht*], it is important to distinguish between constitutive collective intentions and collective informed intentions. Constitutive collective intentions

[*Intentionalität*] are had by individuals and are formative of the collective state of affairs itself. Collective informed intentions [usually *Absicht,* but *Intentionalität* are possible as well] are those intentions formed in response to or in lieu of one's participation in a collective state of affairs. Unfortunately, these are sometimes confused with one another. In both Searle's and my own case, the emphasis is primarily on the former, constitutive collective intentions. As such, the view is that individual intentional achievements are necessary enabling conditions for collective states of affairs. While collective states of affairs in turn affect individuals' beliefs and actions, they do not come first in order of analysis. And beginning one's analysis with collectively informed intentions can be misleading, in that it may gloss the role of individuals' collective intentional achievements in forming the very state of affairs under investigation.

Because of our finite natures, that consciousness and intentionality have essentially perspectival characters, and that one does not ever have immediate access to another's consciousness, there remains a possibility of one's being radically mistaken in relation to what others' intentions actually are. That is, one's collective intentions might fail to garner fulfillment. The possibility of being radically mistaken just allows that an individual could be mistaken about a collective intention. There are at least three ways in which this could occur. First, one could be in error as to the entirety of the collective action one has intended. For example, one believes that we are throwing a party this Friday, where no such plan has in fact been made. Second, one could be in error as to an individual part of the collective action intended. For example, one believes they are to bring a dish to our party, where one is supposed to have brought drinks. Third, one could be mistaken about the composition of the plurality one counts as subject of one's intention. For example, one might mistakenly attribute to a set of individuals collectivity of intention. One might believe that there is a group of people intending to meet to discuss a book, where no one else shares that belief.

For epistemic reasons that arise from the subjective ontology of intentionality and consciousness, it is only appropriate to maintain an individualist position. This is particularly important in being able to account for the possibility of error. I could be of the mind that "we intend p" is an accurate descriptive expression of *our* intent to act in a particular manner, when in fact "we intend q" is what the majority are operating on the basis of, and p is not identical with q. Insofar as I intend that "we intend p" I have a collective intention. That I am wrong does not change the nature of my intention, unless one collapses the distinction between constitutive collective intentions and collective informed intentions. The truth status or justificatory status, related to one's intentions does not affect their formal properties or sense per se. The inclusion of a plurality of individual subjects in something together is the relevant formal criteria for an intention being a collective intention. Whether or not others related to what is intended of the plural subject in an individual's particular collective intentional act share that content is a separate matter in relation to its formal syntactic properties. Even if the structure of intention limits possibilities for sense, it does not reduce the range of possibilities so much as to eliminate the possibilities of error or disagreement.

For instance, on a given down on the football field, each player will have an assignment in relation to the action intended for the team's execution, represented by the play called. Sometimes an individual fails to execute the play as called. An individual receiver might run their route as a curl to the inside instead of a deep out pattern. If the quarterback were to look that way, they would recognize a failure to execute the called play. Can one accurately describe the receiver's situation as absent of a collective intention? That is, in virtue of their failure to act on the actual collective intention, do they thereby only have an individual intention? Clearly that can't be the case. Their action is intended as *collective* action, they did not act so as an individual without regard to others. Despite the receiver's having had a collective intention, he was mistaken as to the nature of the intention necessary for action consistent with the interests of the other members of the collective with which action had been intended. It is not correct to claim that because they were mistaken they were not intending collective action.[83] The receiver has succeeded in having an intention in the form of a collective intention, one potentially constitutive of collective action. However, the receiver has failed to have a collectively informed intention consistent with the play called and with the sub-plans of the other individuals constituting the collective in this instance.

What the example illustrates is that Searle's fallibility condition is not as odd as its many critics make it out to be. For instance, Anthonie Meijers has expressed concern that, "[Searle's] position allows for the possibility of a *single* person having the *collective* intention,"[84] or that a brain in a vat could plausibly be said to have a collective intention. *Prima facie* it may sound strange to think of a brain in a vat having a collective intention. If one accepts an envatted brain thought experiment, however, one accepts that brain as having conscious experiences such that there is a phenomenology to its experience that is unfulfillable in relation to the actuality. While the envatted brain might be radically mistaken as to the truth of its experiences, nonetheless, it *has experiences*. If it has experiences that are intentionally structured as to be together with others, it would have collective intentions. Again, there is confusion between constitutive collective intentions and collectively informed intentions.

Consider the individual case for clarification. One does not fail to have singular individual intentions just because one is mistaken. I might have an intention of a barn in barn county in virtue of what is experienced, even if there is no barn but only a façade. Where problems occur is in the attempt to fulfill my intention. I cannot bring to evidence the matter intended because there fails to be a truthmaker correspondent to my intention. Regardless of whether one accepts that we-intentions manifest only in individual minds, one ought to accept that similar types of failures can occur with we-intentions as with individual intentions. I might intend that we are meeting for our reading group at 6 p.m. on Saturday. That does not cease to be an intention regarding what *we* are to do if I am wrong about the time, location, or fail to recall that we agreed not to meet this week. My being mistaken does not change the formal characteristics of the intention itself, only raises questions as to a precedent failure of adequate justification for maintaining belief related to the intention's content.[85]

One thing disqualified as a candidate for collective action or plural subject and thereby for collective intentionality is accidentally synchronized actions. Searle's examples of people in the park running to get out of the rain[86] and two violinists practicing in synch with one another unbeknownst to each other[87] illustrate that for a collective intention one's intention must involve others. Individual actions of the same type, directed at the same objects, manifest at the same time do not themselves constitute collective activity.[88] The intention underlying the behavior must include intent to act collectively, to do so together. Collective intentions are not a matter of the status of a state of affairs in the phenomenally available public world, they are a matter of states of consciousness. One might object by claiming that "we intend to get out of the rain" is an accurate description of the behavior of the people in the park. Searle is correct, however, what really is going on is that there are a great number of intentions of the form, "I intend to get out of the rain," not an intent on the part of the persons in the park to get out of the rain as a matter of *collective* action. It is not that all persons in the park are working *together*, even if their goals are similar.[89] The individuals could opt to align their intentions and work together, but they don't do so simply in virtue of being caught in the rain at the same time as one another.

If collective actions depend on a shared experiential basis one might ask why a collection of individuals running to get out of the rain in the park could not be considered a plural subject.[90] Recall Carr's position on plural subjects requires that shared experiences can be narratively or intersubjectively put together in a way that constitutes a plural subject, and that certain events allow constitution of the plural subject after the fact. Two things are of note here. First, it is not right to identify individuals fleeing from the rain at the same time as *collectively* acting. The experience in common, of having fled from the rain, might *after* the individual actions count as a base of common experience around which to, at least temporally, form a plural subject. However, that plural subject formation would be *posterior* to the action in question, not constitutive of the action. Second, if shared experiences and intersubjective constitution is a prerequisite for plural subjects, then plural subjects are dependent on collective intentions, not the reverse, "collective intentionality gives rise to the collective and not the other way around."[91] Otherwise, one would have to accept the possibility of collectives and social institutions that could exist absent any individual subject whatsoever. One might ask, if collective intentions are intentions had by *individuals,* are plural subjects genuine subjects with their own *acts* of intending or do they involve only intersubjectively constituted shared intentional *contents*? This poses something of a false dilemma, especially if one accepts Aron Gurwitsch's notion of co-intentional reference as constitutive in relation to any socially contexted experience.[92]

Gurwitsch roundly criticizes traditional ways of describing our experiences of others, whereby those experiences become philosophically problematic. In response to the philosophical motivations to recognize a problem of other minds framed in terms of access, Gurwitsch rejects formal individualism. The problem for formal individualism is that it conflates the singularity inherent in consciousness' always being someone's, the *mineness* of experience, with consciousness' being singular in the form of its intentional act: "As a result, however, the 'mental processes appertinent to We' ['*Wir-Erlebnisse*'] become unintelligible."[93] Gurwitsch offers the following alternative:

> Included in the sense of every mental process, in the effecting of which we know judgmentally, let us say, that other people also effect similar mental processes, there is also the co-presence of those others which is co-apprehended through the "we" (and, more particularly, co-apprehended as effecting these mental processes together with me). On the basis of the immanental co-presence of others pertaining to the sense of these mental processes–others together with whom I effect the mental processes in question–these mental processes are determined specifically as *ours* and are distinguished from those that are specifically mine.[94]

And subjective individualism is not in jeopardy in that "the ego is a constitutive moment in each mental process as mental process, [thus] it is then impossible that other people should effect the identically same mental process as I do."[95] Since consciousness is always an individual's, and essentially so, there is not identity between the *acts* with others, but with the *contents* as intended in some fashion or other.[96]

Diagnosing the problem with traditional approaches to our experiences of others, Gurwitsch notes that a major contributing factor to how philosophy has erred so consistently is it has traditionally carried an operating assumption that all meaning is homogeneous, primarily, I would add, through how we tend to think about propositions. Gurwitsch suggests: "We should rather ask *if human encounters have indeed many different senses, if they do not occur, as it were, in many different dimensions and that the sense of a particular human encounter is determined according to that dimension in which it happens.*"[97] His answer is affirmative. "Human encounter" is a very general category; as such it is not terribly informative, but neither is it terribly restrictive in terms of its possible fulfillments. There is a plentifully variegated set of experiential kinds and modes operating under this heading, not a singularity. Put another way, there are an indeterminate number of acts of consciousness and contents of consciousness that could be paired in the range of human experiences. The language of plural subjects and collective intentionality attempts to offer some general framework for speaking about that range of experiences.[98]

Here the main point is that there are varied ways in which others can be co-present to one's experiences. Through the constituting intersubjectivity, the co-presence of others operates in a tacit set of background conditions coloring one's context and one's way(s) of understanding it. In collective actions others are co-present as implicit or explicit actors in common, recipients of action, or potential observers. In constituting a collective state of affairs, others are co-present in each individual's intentions pertaining to that state of affairs. "We intend *x*" establishes not only the "we" in question, which others are co-present as actors, but also the experience, belief, or action in question. The dependence of the collective state of affairs requires the acts of individuals–whether expressly conscious or tacitly complicit–to be established in the first place. The individual understandings of the collective state of affairs can diverge some, but in order to succeed must have sufficient commonality to establish said state of affairs. In virtue of success, the individuals can act on collectively informed intentions to achieve new ends in common. The resultant action and corresponding responsibility might be predicated of the collective, but the action is not the same as the individuated acts of consciousness necessary for its being.

Carr and the Question of Evidence

There is a final concern specific to Husserlian phenomenology, one it is surprising that Carr did not address. One could respond to Carr's analysis by pointing out that he neglected to provide any consideration as to what constitutes evidence in relation to plural subject intentions. Further, one can point to where Husserl argues as to the impossibility of evidencing intentional contents directed toward other subjectivities,[99] and argue that plural subject intentions, in that they include references to others and others' intentional states must thereby be a species of empty intention–intentions incapable of being evidenced, fulfilled, or that have impossible satisfaction conditions. Husserl himself says the following:

> Even the possibility of a vaguest, emptiest intending of something alien is problematic, if it is true that, essentially, every such mode of consciousness involves its possibilities of an uncovering of what is intended, its possibilities of becoming converted into either fulfilling or disillusioning experiences of what is meant, and moreover (as regards the genesis of the consciousness) points back to such experiences of the same intended object or a similar one.[100]

One is left, then, with a puzzle as to how intentions whose contents implicate that which is alien to what is available through experience can be verified. It should be stressed that is a problem for analysis, since in everyday experience such concerns rarely occur to one or vex one at all.

Initially, it is worth pointing out that, in a marginal note to his edition of *Cartesian Meditations,* Husserl identified the first-person singular form of intention as being inadequate, and an exclusive reliance on it as containing the potential to lead one into unjustifiably restricting phenomenological insights and investigations.[101] Moving beyond that concern, one must recall that, for Husserl, the experience of the other involves appresentational contents. Appresentational contents are nothing peculiar to the experience of others, but are present in mundane experiences. For instance, that one experiences a house and not a house-façade, despite only having a singular experiential profile available to one at a given moment, is on the basis of an appresentational filling out of the content.

One's anticipations and projections of possibilities, manifest in everyday experience (that objects have other profiles, a back, for example) are appresented in the experience of objects.[102] The experience of another subject involves appresentational contents as well, e.g. that they have a backside, but most importantly the other's consciousness–as *other*–is essentially appresentational in character. By extension, plural subject intentions, collective intentions appresent the other's state of affairs in relation to that which is intended.

It is important to make the distinction between what is present in the experience as such and that which is appresented in that the standard of evidence, what constitutes fulfillment of the intentional content differs in the two cases. Appresentational contents are verified or subject to fulfillment in relation to the harmonious character of the continuously revised series of appresentations in accord with the object. For instance, if in experience one sees a red beach ball and one's experience is of that beach ball from one profile, one is liable to experience it as a red beach ball. One projects forth similar characteristics as pertaining to the unavailable profiles. Those unavailable profiles, however, are appresented in experience, not presented proper. Now, one's appresented redness of the beach ball is verified if, in continued experience of the ball and its further profiles, the experiences retain a harmonious appresentative structure–that one never finds a green panel on a further profile of the ball, one never comes to expect of the ball that its characteristics violate one's projections. In the specific case of the other, this means:

> …it is clear that its fulfillingly verifying continuation can ensue *only by means of new appresentations that proceed in a synthetically harmonious fashion,* and only by virtue of the manner in which *these appresentations owe their existence-value to their motivational connexion with the* changing *presentations proper, within my ownness,* that continually appertain to them.[103]

That is to say, intentions about or directed at others, including plural subject intentions, are evidenced in relation to continuity in respect of expectations in the appresentational structures of experience. The object of one's intention and its "indicated system of appearances are indeed *analogically adapted* to the analogous appearance."[104] In the case of a shared action, this is realized through the action itself. In the case of shared belief, this is realized through one's not being presented with disruptions as to the continuity of the beliefs being shared. With respect to shared convictions, that the continuity of one's anticipations with regard to the other(s) that they continue to hold that conviction is not disrupted. And in the case of the basic sharing of an experience with another, that one's appresentational manifold of experiential projections not be disrupted, e.g. that one hears snoring emanating from the other, one hears the other engaged in some other activity, or one sees them moving away in the periphery of one's vision, etc. In all such cases, the basis for the continuity of evidence in respect of the intentional content is maintained only through continuity of that which is available through appresentational harmony being maintained in experience.

One might object that this is not a very strong form of evidence or that it leaves much of our social intercourse with others to be rather indeterminate in nature.[105] On reflection, however, this is precisely how we should think of such experiences. For one, it is unreasonable of us to expect apodictic evidence as to the experience of the other or experiences involving others, let alone in respect of many physical objects.[106] Second, the properly considered evidentiary standards associated with experiences of others would have to preserve the alterity of others. Were apodictic evidence possible in our social interactions with others, the very otherness of others would be rendered impossible. This is why, in summarizing his findings in the *Fifth Meditation*, Husserl says:

> ...the concretely apprehended transcendental ego (who first becomes aware of himself, with his undetermined horizon, when he effects the transcendental reduction) grasps himself in his own primordial being, and likewise (in the form of his transcendental experience of what is alien) grasps others: *other transcendental egos*, though they are given, not originaliter and in unqualifiedly apodictic evidence, but only in an evidence belonging to "external" experience. "In" myself I experience and know the Other; in me he becomes constituted–appresentatitvely mirrored, not constituted as the original.[107]

Since other consciousnesses are essentially "exterior" to one's own, any and all experiences involving other subjectivities cannot be open to apodictic standards of evidence.[108] Rather, the adequacy of the evidence available is, as we've already noted, sometimes entirely restricted to individuals' appresentational manifolds of anticipations and projections.[109]

Conclusion

In summation, what can one say about plural subjects? First, they are intentional subjects in the sense that they are parts of the contents of intentional acts, we-intentions or collective intentionality. These contents help establish the conditions for fulfillment while establishing a sense or meaning to our experiences that cannot be reduced to the singular: *our* and *we* aren't reducible in meaning to *my* and *I*. Plural subjects are embodied in the sense that they have physical component parts upon which they are dependent, that is one can't meaningfully experience a plural subject without there being some physicality that is part of what the plural subject is. However, plural subjects are not embodied in the same sense that one might speak of consciousness' being embodied. Finally, some shared experiential basis is necessary for plural subjects to be formed, and this must be maintained over time for a plural subject's continuance. Basically, in everyday experience one is part of a fluid and changing set of plural subjects (differentiated "*we's*"), and as interest or one's underlying shared experiential basis grounding one's *we* dissipates or dissolves, those specific bonds pass into a meaningfulness as past and no longer presently "live." Finally, it was shown how a phenomenological view, inspired heavily by Husserl, can be understood to be an approach similar to Searle's.

Notes

1. Carr 1973 and Carr 1986
2. Zahavi 2003b
3. Husserl in McCormick & Elliston 1981: §III
4. Husserl 1998: §9-10, 33, 45f., Husserl 1989; D.W. Smith in B. Smith & D.W. Smith 1995, D.W. Smith in Petitot et al. 1999, D.W. Smith 2007: Ch. 4
5. D.W. Smith 2007: 144, B. Smith & D.W. Smith 1995: 327-338; see also Petitot et al 1999: 25-32
6. Searle 1995; Formal collectivism and subjective individualism are distinctions borrowed from Hans Bernhard Schmid, see Schmid 2003a.
7. Carr 1986: 521
8. ibid.
9. ibid: 521-522
10. ibid: 522-523
11. Some, like Carr, appear to argue that ontological commitments are not important at all. As stated previously, I disagree if taken too broadly. If the point is that ontological pre-commitments are potentially damaging to the adequacy of one's theory in relation to the world it intends to represent, then I have only minor reservations dependent upon how that is understood in greater specificity. That is, if one can never maintain that which one previously garnered phenomenological evidence for, then I'm leery of agreement. If it's only to say that one should not pre-figure their conclusions prior to having phenomenological evidence substantiate a conclusion, then I heartily affirm.
12. It is less that something is assumed here, and more that one is focused on how the phenomena are to be described, if given rich and adequate description to more than a superficial gloss. An example presents itself to me as I am working. Outside my window, the park across the way, there are three individuals playing Frisbee. One cannot play Frisbee by oneself, as it is a game that requires more than one subject. One could certainly throw a Frisbee alone, and chase after it herself, but one is not playing at Frisbee at all if that is the case, much as one is not playing tennis if one practices against a backboard or playing baseball if one takes batting practice in a batting cage. At best, one is isolating an individual component of the larger activity, one that requires others. One might say even that such practice is best when it can simulate the presence of another in absence: when the deflection off the backboard lacks predictability, simulating another's return to some extent or the pitching machine's delivery varies based upon how the seams of the ball hit the spinning wheel, leaving indeterminate the specific behavior of the pitch one faces. While on one level, it would be to commit no violence to say the three are each individually tossing the Frisbee back and forth, this ignores the larger phenomena by reducing it to its participants and their individual acts. In other words, playing Frisbee, that

which binds their actions *together* falls away. In more complex cases, one might point out that a corporation has powers and characteristics that none of its individual members alone has, and that the activities of the corporation require and are constituted through the working *together* of the individual members and the explicitly and implicitly codified practices that inform or direct their individual activities as *part* of that whole.

13. Reference is to the title of §55 of *Cartesian Meditations* (Husserl 1999): Cairns renders this "Establishment of the community of monads." Carr is clearly not happy with how Cairns renders *Vergemeinschaftung,* opting likely for something more like: "Monads effecting (entering into and thereby constituting) community." Carr's right to emphasize the active nature of this "community." A further alternative could be to think of Husserl's discussion of the *communalization* of subjects or subject entering into *community* or *commerce* with one another as the establishment of *common* ground. Italicization of those terms with shared root sense in the previous sentence is for purposeful emphasis.

14. Carr 1973: 30

15. ibid; Carr quoting from Husserl 1999: 129-130/157-158

16. Carr 1973: 33

17. ibid.

18. To assuage my realist readers who may worry about an odd multiplication of the world, allow me to offer a disambiguation. There is but *one* world in the physical sense of that term, that sense of world is what is often used in the natural sciences. When I use 'world' or 'worlds' where the plural use makes sense, I refer to world in the phenomenological sense: a system or network of meanings. This is the sense used when one says of someone that "they are in their own world" or of a culture distinct from one's own that "it is a whole other world." Given that there are subjectively and culturally idiosyncratic meanings, it is only natural that one can speak of world*s* in this sense. I do not take the plurality of phenomenological worlds to entail anything about the metaphysics of the natural world, though I do take it to have implications relating to the socially constituted objects, categories, meanings, what have you.

19. What was argued in Chapters One and Two was that one need not reify intersubjective wholes, i.e. make them into subjectivities in their own right, in order for this to happen. The systemic interactions between individual subjects proper is what gives rise to these types of phenomena. As such, I argue Schmid's emphasis on relationality (Schmid 2003a, 2003b, 2006) is correct, though I find his way of thinking about and framing the consequences of the relationality of subjects with one another and the intentional achievements expressed in and through such interactions to be problematic.

20. Carr 1973: 34

21. Contemporary externalist theories of content tend to collapse this distinction. That is why some externalists, or causal theorists, sometimes affirm to the conclusion that one can't actually have the thought that "there's a unicorn on the lawn." To address causal theories of content is well beyond the scope of the present discussion. Phenomenology counts as non-sensical any theory that col-

lapses the distinction between conditions of satisfaction for what is thought with what is thought itself. Whether that means we reject all contemporary causal theories functioning in analytic philosophical circles is left an open question, though I doubt very much that all causal theories fail in this respect.

22. By this I understand, for instance, that the nature of one's embodied state of affairs and its history is determinative of the range of possible objects or meanings one has available to them in experience. Searle would add that one's biology is constitutive of one's embodied state of affairs. This is part of his "biological naturalism": "Mental phenomena are caused by neurophysiological processes in the brain and are themselves features of the brain. …Mental events and processes are as much a part of our biological natural history as digestion, mitosis, meiosis, or enzyme secretion" (Searle 1992: 1). I reserve judgment as to whether one's biology is the whole of one's embodied consciousness, as Searle believes, or a part. Michael Tye plies similar intuitions, arguing that since one's physical state and the history of one's physical states are constitutive elements of one's experiences, the *what* of experience is dependently related to the *how* of experience, and the how of experience is dependent on *what* physical constitution one possesses and has possessed (Tye 2008b: §5).

23. Strawson 2005: 44

24. ibid: 43-44

25. Searle 1998: 64-65

26. Gallagher and Zahavi 2008: 7

27. ibid: 7

28. One recalls that these were problems for the case of collective consciousness, as discussed in Chapters One and Two. The idea is that even if we *can* describe experiences a certain way, that's not license to believe that reality is a certain way. Getting clear on the basic structure of intentionality–arguably the central issue of phenomenology as a whole–reveals, however, that descriptions of experience involving collective consciousness either are without coherent sense-structures, doing violence to the basic natures of intentionality and consciousness, or function on the basis of unclear or metaphorical descriptions of phenomena in question.

29. Carr 1986: 524

30. ibid: 525

31. ibid: 525-527; The distinction is important, insofar as it gets at both intentionality proper [*Intentionalität*] and the sense of intent associated with goal-directed action [*Absicht*].

32. Carr 1986: 526-527

33. ibid: 527

34. ibid: 527

35. ibid.

36. ibid: 529

37. ibid.

38. ibid: 530

39. ibid.

40. ibid.

41. Primary discussion is in Husserl's ontology (Husserl 2001b: Investigations III-IV), but use of the terminology also appears earlier in *Logical Investigations* (Husserl 2000a: Investigation II, §1, 14, 36, 38-40).

42. Searle 1998: 92

43. ibid: 94

44. ibid.

45. ibid.

46. Carr 1986: 531

47. ibid.

48. ibid.

49. ibid; the example from Sartre figures in Larry May's treatment of groups (May 1987).

50. Carr 1988: 532

51. ibid.

52. ibid.

53. As one moves into these more formalized intentional systems one invokes and attributes deontic powers derived from the collective intentional achievements of those involved. Searle's original account evoked constitutive rules (X counts as Y in context C) as the mechanism for this. Searle revised his position. He now counts constitutive rules as types of performative declarative acts (by Declaration we create the Y status function), and that it is the declarative act that is the more basic species of intentional act pertinent to these powers (Searle 2008: Addendum to Chapter 2, 48-51). This is clearly a response to the vast set of criticism surrounding constitutive rules since Searle's original formulation of his social ontology. I suspect it only pushes any problems back a step instead of resolving criticisms.

54. Carr 1986: 522

55. ibid: 531

56. ibid: 532, see also Carr 1999

57. Carr 1986: 533

58. Zahavi 2003b: 5

59. ibid: 6

60. ibid: 7

61. ibid: 7-8

62. ibid: 18

63. ibid: 16

64. ibid: 17

65. ibid.

66. Merleau-Ponty 1964: 13-16

67. A similar complaint is made by Heidegger regarding the "schools" of thought, i.e. those who restrict their thinking to being directed by a given framework instead of thinking about the framework and what it intends to provide itself. This spirit of thinking in a way that is not operating within a competitive enterprise between camps or schools of thought is instructive for our under-

standing of the pettiness often displayed in regard to and inabilities to communicate from one camp to the other within the analytic-Continental dispute. See Heidegger 1995 for example. The germs of this are clear also in Husserl's 1913 essay, "Philosophy as a Rigorous Science" (Husserl in McCormick & Elliston 1981: 166-196).

68. Searle 2008: Ch. 6. While there are certain points of agreement and acknowledgements of there being value to phenomenology, Searle's criticisms of Husserl in particular amount to a straw man responding to a straw man. This is owed to Searle's mostly relying on the testimony of colleagues, and Searle's particular interest to respond to Hubert Dreyfus's conjoined criticism of Husserl and Searle (Dreyfus 1993 and Dreyfus 2000). Dreyfus' caricature of Husserl as a Cartesian, a polemic he thinks can be found in Merleau-Ponty and Heidegger, amounts to a straw man criticism of both Searle and Husserl, as neither is at all a Cartesian in a substantive manner. Granted, later phenomenologists find Cartesian elements in Husserl's thought that are worth critique, but don't count him as a Cartesian in full. Searle's response to Dreyfus' published criticisms and those offered in their personal interactions, amounts to a straw man reply, only making matters worse. This is owed to Searle's near complete ignorance of Husserl's writings: including his admission of not having read enough of *Logical Investigations* to have reached the theory of intentionality. (Searle 2008: 111) More measured and informed comparisons, with the appropriate contrasts, can be found in Meixner 2006, Johansson 2003, and Thomasson 1997.

69. Searle 2008: 112

70. "Searle's analysis of intentionality is very similar to that of Husserl" (Johansson 2003: 235). And, "Searle's philosophy, I want to stress, is very different from…Husserl's" (ibid.). Most importantly, as Johansson notes, where Searle locates intentionality spatially, in the brain, Husserl staunchly refused to answer such a question, counting the notion of consciousness' spatial location as a category mistake (ibid: 240). See also Johansson 2003: 253, note 23.

71. Meixner 2006 presents a very well put contrast between the classical theory of intentionality and modern theories of intentionality, specifically functionalist views and representationalist views. Searle's view is treated by Meixner as an instance of the latter.

72. Thomasson 1997: 109

73. ibid. See §II of that work for the full argument.

74. Again, Meixner 2006 is instructive

75. Thomasson 1997: 123, emphasis mine. It is worth stressing that the work of art is a perfect sort of example of the sometimes too narrow focus in the collective intentionality literature. One might retort that there are uses of the example of a jazz ensemble in this literature as well. However, such examples tend to focus on *obligations* and *moral* valuation, not the *aesthetic* values or *musical* nature of jazz that is what is important in the experience of jazz musicians. In fact, some uses of this example feel odd to one with experience in the practice of playing in jazz ensembles, that there's not a proper appreciation as to what this type of group practice involves for the musicians who actually experi-

ence it. This isn't to criticize the specifically moral interests that drive treatment of the example or their findings, only to point out that morality is not the principal interest, often not even an express interest, of the musician in such cases and to point out that a violence is done to the phenomena and practice of musicians if obligation structures are the sole point of discussion. Wynton Marsalis gave an interview once that is instructive, however, I have long since forgotten where that was published.

76. Thomasson 1997: 123

77. Husserl 2001a and Husserl 2001b. Intentionality of language is addressed in the *Second Logical Investigation*.

78. Searle 2002: 92.

79. ibid: 96.

80. ibid. (Emphasis mine)

81. Searle 1995: 23.

82. See also Bratman 1999

83. My example is similar to one presented by Nenad Miscevic (Miscevic 2003: 262-264), though, I believe my example is superior in that it does not rely on differences of attitudes about collective actions at the outset. Miscevic's example involves a team as a whole being persuaded to throw a match, except that "Honest John," due to his incorruptible nature is not included in the decision or discussion pertaining to the shift in intent. As such, Miscevic is building in differences of attitude towards the collective action that has been arranged and manufactured. Miscevic's example is thus of one individual who is not privy to his team's not sharing his intent or attitudes about their action. My example relies only on an honest mistake, where all team members do actually share in a common goal, but fail to realize it in sufficient unity with one another as to achieve it, they fail to actualize the shared intent.

84. Meijers 2003: 174

85. "Perhaps an uncomfortable feature of the analysis is that it allows for a form of mistake that is not simply a failure to achieve the conditions of satisfaction of an intentional state and is not simply a breakdown in the Background. It allows that I may be mistaken in taking it that the 'we' in the 'we intend' actually refers to a we; that is, it allows for the fact that my presupposition that my intentionality is collective may be mistaken in ways that go beyond the fact that I have a mistaken belief' (Searle 2002: 97).

86. Searle 2002: 92.

87. Searle 1995: 25.

88. This could conflict with some of what Tuomela allows as weak collective intentions (Tuomela 2000). If there is disagreement, I side with Searle–disqualifying those things that too liberal a position on collective intentionality might include.

89. There may be, however, a problem for Searle in providing a criterion of acknowledgement for genuine collective behavior. As his account stands, there can be no such thing as mob mentality. When riots occur, it appears to make sense to claim that a number of individuals are acting as individuals, not a col-

lective. There is no overarching "we intend to riot," only numerous cases of "I intend to riot." Precisely when is it that we are justified in saying that the rioters are acting collectively?

In both the park example and the mob cases, there is nothing barring the possibility of smaller groups acting together. For example, a family may work together to get out of the rain or a gang to loot together. The point of the examples is to show that a collection of persons acting to similar ends does not itself constitute an instance of collective intentionality. A *collection* of persons is not a guarantor of *collective* activity or behavior.

90. The example comes from Searle 2002: 92

91. Searle 1997: 449

92. Something like Gurwitsch's notion is also functioning in Husserl's *Crisis*. Husserl uses the term *kompräsent* (co-present) to refer to how others are present in one's conscious experience as other in §54b (Husserl 1970: 185). It is not clear to whether Gurwitsch or Husserl was the originator of the notion.

93. Gurwitsch 1979: 28

94. ibid.

95. ibid.

96. Consider also: "It is a world of culture because, from the outset, the life-world is a universe of significations [*Bedeutsamkeiten*] to us, i.e., a framework of meaning [*Sinnzusammenhang*] which we have to interpret, and of interrelations of meaning which we institute only through our action in this life-world. It is a world of culture also because we are always conscious of its historicity, which we encounter in tradition and habituality, and which is capable of being examined because the 'already-given' refers back to one's own activity or to the activity of Others, of which it is the sediment" (Schutz 1962: 133).

97. Gurwitsch 1979: 33

98. Gurwitsch's view will be discussed more in Chapter 5.

99. "Properly speaking, neither the other Ego [*Ich*] himself, nor his subjective processes or his appearance to his own essence, becomes given in our experience originally. If it were, if what belongs to the other's own essence were directly accessible, it would be merely a moment of my own essence, and ultimately he himself and I myself would be the same" (Husserl 1999:109/139). And, "...in the case of that appresentation which would lead over into the other original sphere, such verification must be excluded a priori" (ibid.).

100. Husserl 1999: 105-106/135-136

101. "The dangerous first person singular! This should be expanded terminologically" (Husserl 1999: §42, 90/122, n2). This is underscored by reference to Husserl's *Ideas I*. In section 121 of *Ideas I*, Husserl asserts: "Undoubtedly there is such a thing as a collective gladness, a collective liking, a collective willing, etc" (Husserl 1998: 289/251). Though, Husserl's examples–particularly loving a group of children as distinguished from loving the children individually–reveal that he's more concerned with how to address one's intentional acts where distributed over a collective, and how to address the polythetic syntax of

the act, which is addressed in the sections before. Nonetheless, Husserl was not blind to the plural

102. "Every experience points to further experiences that would fulfill and verify the appresented horizons, which include, in the form of non-intuitive anticipations, potentially verifiable syntheses of harmonious further experience" (Husserl 1999:114/144).

103. Husserl 1999: 114/144

104. ibid: 118/147. For example, if an experience of what is in fact a blood orange doesn't itself undergo change, nor in how it is experienced if analogically perceived as "tangerine." Rather the "tangerine" sense is appended to the perceptual sense system. And, one might very well go so far as experiencing this as tangerine up to tasting it. Indeed, one might even continue to experience it as tangerine through eating it, especially if one doesn't know what tangerine is or how it differs from blood orange. Until some disruption occurs that gives one reason to modify the sense of one's experience, the harmony of one's array of sense-profiles in correlation with the objects of experience will maintain the given sense-structure in relation to that which is experienced.

105. In *Ideas I*, Husserl identifies, at least, the following categories in relation to evidence: assertoric evidence, apodictic evidence, pure or impure evidence, purely formal or material evidence, adequate or inadequate evidence, and immediate or mediate evidence (Husserl 1998: §§137, 138, 141).

106. Husserl 1998: §138, 331/286

107. Husserl 1999:149/175

108. This part of Husserl seems very well to embody the concerns critics, like Levinas, have as to phenomenology's treatment of others. They are experienced as objects of one's experience, yes. However, that does not entail that they are experienced as mere objects. Nor does this entail that one objectivize the other in the normatively laden sense of that term. The intentional contents constitutive of the experience of alterity are such that the evidential possibilities associated with our experiences of others are, for the most part, distinct in form from those associated with mere objects; though, clearly distinct in the material evidences associated with the respective contents.

109. Using Husserl's distinctions from *Ideas I*, it is more precise to say that the evidence of others is either adequate or inadequate. *Adequate* evidence, he defines as being "of essential necessity incapable of being further 'strengthened' or 'weakened,' thus *without degrees of weight*" (Husserl 1998: 333/288). Naturally, then, *inadequate* evidence is such that it is "*capable of being increased or decreased*" (ibid.). In relation to others, we can achieve adequate evidence, e.g. they perform the action indicated or they assert their belief directly, what have one. Though, it's reasonable to observe that our social interactions are sometimes guided on the basis of inadequate evidence, sometimes on the basis of adequate evidence. What's key to preserving the other as other, however, is to maintain the impossibility of apodictic evidence. The asymmetry of the experience of others is integral and essential to the experience of *other* as other.

Chapter 4
Responding to Criticisms: Phenomenological Evidence and Horizon Intentionality

In this chapter, I defend a subjective individualist approach of collective intentionality. The view is coupled with a denial of an atomistic conception of the subject. The specific form of subjective individualism argued for claims that only individual subjects, conscious beings capable of having experiences, have the capacity for intrinsic intentionality. The position is informed by the classical theory of intentionality, found in the phenomenological tradition. First, subjective individualism will be distinguished from formal individualism. Second, I respond to criticisms of subjective individualism offered by Hans Bernhard Schmid. Schmid contends that subjective individualism is unable to account for relations between subjects and social norms.[1] After responding to Schmid's concerns, it is argued that a subjective individualist position is able to account for the largely passive constitutional maintenance and attendance of the social world in a manner consistent with experience. Schmid's view is then criticized for failing to adequately account for the nature of intentionality by not adequately addressing the concepts of evidence and horizon intentionality.

Throughout, the chapter relies on a background of early phenomenological philosophers, namely Husserl, Aron Gurwitsch and Alfred Schütz, and their analyses of the intentionality manifest in intersubjective life, in support of a ground for social ontology consistent with subjective individualism. Specifically, addressed in the later sections of the chapter are the concepts of evidence and horizon as they relate to the general theory of intentionality; it is argued that they contribute to a robust subjective individualist position.

Two claims are germane to the argument. 1) Intersubjective experiences bear specific types of evidentiary, or fulfillment, conditions that are more favorable to subjective individualism. The second claim is 2) that experience's being richly intersubjective and socially contexted is a constitutive feature of consciousness associated with its horizon structure. In virtue of this horizon structure, others are related to one's experience on a basic manner, without requiring one to postulate intentionality in an intrinsic sense anywhere other than in the case of individual consciousness.

Even if intentionality is intrinsic only to individuals this does not present a problem relating to other persons anymore than to other beings generally. Relationality–one of Schmid's express problems for subjective individualist theories–is thereby not a problem unique to or specific to intersubjective experiences whereby one is bound to adopt a solipsistic or atomistic view of the subject on the phenomenological model. This is owed to the appresentational dimensions inherent in the experience of phenomena. For instance, that one experiences a house and not a house-façade, despite only having a singular experiential profile available to one at a given moment, is because of appresentational filling out of the experiential content. One's anticipations and projections of possibilities, manifest in everyday experience (that objects have other profiles, e.g. a back) are appresented in the experiences of objects.[2] One's experience of another subject *as* subject necessarily involves appresentational contents, most importantly the other's consciousness and their conscious states, as consciousness that is *other* must be essentially appresentational in nature. By extension, collective intentions involve appresented states of affairs involving other subjects' states of consciousness and the others' relations to whatever is intended in the mode specific to the act-content correlation of the intentional state itself.

Why not Formal Individualism?

To describe the plural form of experience in relation to the individually situated acts of intentionality, as I have been doing, is to assert a form of individualism relative to the ontology of mind. In the collective intentionality literature, Hans Bernhard Schmid distinguishes between two separate senses of individualism: formal and subjective. Formal individualism is that view where the *form* of one's intentionality is individualistic. It is the view that all intentions can only be in singular form, in the form of an 'I intend' this or that, never in a plural form of a "we intend." Schmid identifies Descartes' view of intentionality as a formal individualist account.

> Descartes' account is individualistic in that it restricts intentionality to the form "I intend," "I think." It does not seem to have crossed Descartes' mind that there could be intentionality in the first person plural form, too. I shall refer to this version of individualism with the term 'formal individualism,' for what is at stake here is the form of intentionality.[3]

The historical question as to whether or not this is a fair interpretation of Descartes or not is here ignored. More contemporaneously, Schmid identifies Michael Bratman's theory of collective intentionality as being a formal individualist view.[4] For Bratman, the form of relevant intentions is "I intend that we *J*."[5]

Subjective individualism is the position that intentionality of any form, collective intentionality in particular, "is exclusively in the minds of individuals and independent of anything external."[6] "As opposed to formal individualism, subjective individualism does not limit intentionality to the singular *form*, but restricts the class of possible *subjects* or 'bearers' of intentions to single individuals."[7] Husserl could be seen to be criticizing formal individualism where he states: "...that I can become aware of someone else, presupposes that *not all my own modes of consciousness are modes of my self-consciousness.*"[8]

For a formal individualist, like Bratman, there are approximately three conditions to be met for something's being a *shared* intention: 1) mutual responsiveness, 2) commitment to joint activity, and 3) commitment to mutual support.[9] One of Bratman's motivations for his individualism is that: "a shared intention is not an attitude in the mind of some superagent consisting literally of some fusion of the two agents. There is no single mind which is the fusion of your mind and mine."[10] However, Bratman's view departs from Searle's on the issue of reductionism. Bratman's view is that *qua* individualism, any collective or group intending must be reducible to the intentions of individuals. The reductive stance that results in formal individualism is reached on the grounds that *shared activity* requires a plurality of participants, each required to be in a given range of mental states relative to that activity.

Searle, on the other hand, is against reducibility on the grounds that the mental state that is a collective intention is not reducible to further individual mental states.[11] A collective intention is singular, not compound or composite. Collective intentions are not built up out of other individual mental states. The non-reducibility of the intentional or mental state itself does not have to preclude the co-presence of others whatsoever. With respect to conditions for realization of action, shared intentions, and perhaps other species of collective intentions more generally, are not satisfied simply on the grounds that the activity itself is engaged in by a plurality of individual subjects. Rather, those implicated and involved must share a proper comportment towards the intended action in order for the fulfillment of that intention. The evidentiary requirements for the action(s) are relative to the content specified by a collective intention that is reducible to the actions of individuals, but each individual's intentional achievement requires its own evidencing.[12] It is always possible that some individuals participating in a collective state of affairs have their intentions about that state of affairs fulfilled with greater adequacy, while others do not.

It is in virtue of the claim that collective intentions are decomposable or reducible to the intentions of individuals that Schmid understands formal individualism to be a reductive thesis.[13] Formal individualism offers a reductive explanation for collective behaviors on the basis of a bias against collectivity. More to the point, it is committed to the position that all intentional states are in the first-person singular. That simply does not match experience; the experience of the first-person plural is both genuine and non-trivial. Granted, formal individualists would argue that they are not denying the phenomenology, but asserting that on analysis these types of experiences can be accounted for as sets of singularly stated intentions. But one asks what basis the formal individualist has for this revision. If the more basic phenomena in question that the formal individualist points to is that all experience is *someone's* experience, I fail to see why that commits one to formal individualism. There is nothing here that denies an individual could intend in the first person plural. An inability to do so would seem more problematic, as then relations with others truly would be hard to understand. Again, why would all experience or action be reducible to the singular form, especially if one finds oneself operating in *plural* contexts throughout one's life? I agree with Schmid that collective intentionality, plural subject experiences and actions, should not be reductively construed.

One readily concedes that little is lost in capturing what is experienced, if of a common object of experience, one substitutes a "we saw" for "I saw and you saw." However, something is lost where one tries the same substitution in cases where "we saw" is part of "we saw *together*." "We saw together" is not equivalent to "I saw" and "you saw." "If we see it *together*, something essential to the experience is lost when that substitution is made, since in this case each of us saw the tower and was aware that the other was seeing it too."[14] In other words, a shared experience evokes a strong sense of "we." The strong sense of "we" is not intended in cases where you and I each see the same object, but on separate occasions. That element of shared experiences is one of the essential qualities of a plural subject or bona fide "we."[15] The intuitions of the formal individualist, then, are partially correct: some instances of a "we intend" are not significantly different from the form "I intend and you intend." However, formal individualism is not adequate for detailing the stronger sense of "we together." Formal individualism reduces all experience to mine and yours and can't adequately account for experiences that are primarily *ours*.

A final problem with formal individualism is that it equivocates between two things in its descriptions of experience. There is a switch from first-person to third-person description at root in the manner of description one finds in formal individualist theories of collective intentionality and plural subjects. Carr argues,

> It may be argued that collective experience and action can still always be broken down into the perceptions or activities of the individuals involved, and that their "plurality" can be accounted for simply by referring to the way in which each individual includes the others in his individual understanding of what is going on. This may be true, but it would involve a third-person, external description of the scene. Our procedure, however, to repeat, is to consult our first-person experience of participating in experience or action. And what we maintain is that in using 'we' (in this special way) each of us construes the action or experience in question such that its proper subject is not I but we.[16]

In other words, cashing out "we *x*" by reducing it to "I *x,* and you *x*" does not adequately represent the intentionality manifest in collective experiences or collective actions. Formal individualism replaces what is experienced with an abstraction that is extrinsic to the experience itself.

Defense of Subjective Individualism vis-à-vis Hans Bernhard Schmid's Critique of Searle

Subjective individualism is the position that intentionality of any form, collective intentionality in particular, "is exclusively in the minds of individuals and independent of anything external."[17] Schmid understands subjective individualism to be a non-relational thesis.[18] He rejects subjective individualism on the grounds that "Collective intentionality is *relational*. An adequate account is incompatible with *subjective* individualism."[19] Schmid has, at least, two specific claims that motivate his position: 1) that an individual could have a collective intention with no relation to another subject;[20] and 2) that a subjective individualist account may not be adequate to account for social normativity.[21]

Schmid believes that subjective individualists miss something crucial by leaving open the possibility for envatted brains to have collective intentions. Schmid claims that even if sharedness is part of the *content* of an envatted brain's experience, it is not a *shared* experience. "It is obvious (and trivially true) that the sharedness of intentionality is not a matter of the form or content of one single individual's intentionality alone."[22] Instead, Schmid claims, "in order for (we-) intentionality to be shared, *all* participants have to have the appropriate (we-) intentions."[23] Schmid believes that a certain palpable relation must hold *in fact* in order that there really be *shared intentions*.[24] As argued above, it is not necessary that reality *be* how one is experiencing in advance or even at all in order that one intends that some state of affairs is so, i.e. satisfaction conditions for evidencing an intentional content need not be met *before* an experience have sense, as opposed to the satisfaction conditions being *determined by* the sense in question. Schmid appears to invert the order of intentional constitution and intentional fulfillment in evidence.

The possibility one could be in error or fail to fulfill one's collective intention is consistent with a characteristic of intentionality more generally. In cases of collectively pursued actions, intentions are not always realized through action, for example winning a baseball game. The intention to act itself is formulated *before* action, not *as a result* of action. Otherwise, it would always be correct to say of a losing sports team that they *intended* to lose. That represents a clear problem in explaining action. This is a far greater problem than if they intended to win and failed to bring to evidence their intended goal. If satisfaction conditions, like an action's actually happening, serve as genuine pre-conditions for intentionality and not the other way around, as Schmid's view appears to require, genuinely *collective* actions would be impossible.[25] If true, collective actions would require a prior collective intention that could not be formed without the world's *already* matching its form and content. Fiction, dreams, memories and anticipations could never involve intentions inclusive of others, given the lack of a real-world relation. Watson and Holmes could never solve a case *together*. Don Quixote and Sancho Panza could never set out for adventure *together*. One could never imagine or dream about going on vacation *together* with others.

Even the very protentive intentions constitutive of the wider "now" of the temporality of experience would be impossible, given the future's inexistence and the past's no longer being existent. Instead of requiring prefigured relations as a necessary condition for collective intentions themselves, one can appeal to a shared experiential basis as grounding phenomena for intentionality in the we-mode. The sense of *we* or *our* or *together* requires some commonality at its basis, but that commonality is what's necessary for the sense bestowal constitutive of a *plural subject* not what is intended of or in relation to that plural subject as Schmid holds.

In order to better understand how the intention itself is not affected, one can turn to a distinction made by David Woodruff Smith between an intentional character and intentional relation. Intentional character is the correlation between the *content* intended and the subject's intending. Intentional relation is the relation between the *object* intended and the content intended.[26] The former is an epistemic relation, the latter an ontological relation. The content of one's intentions can fail to correlate to an object. That is, there is no object standing in relation to the content of the subject's intentional act so as to fulfill the intention, i.e. evidence is lacking. What's more, one can emptily intend what is not present. For instance, I can now direct my thoughts towards a unicorn. That intention is of something, namely the content "unicorn" which has a sense, but fails to represent any real object in the world. Error, then, can occur when a subject forms a judgment, the underlying intentional content of which has no object in correlation. The same applies in relation to collective intentions. For instance, one could intend that we all flap our arms and fly to Australia to have tea with the Queen of England. That is in the form of a collective intention, but its content represents an impossibility (our flying without technological aid) and an implausibility (our having tea with the Queen of England in Australia). Simply because the *object* intended is not satisfiable does not change that the content of the intention is of a specific sort–an intention for *collective* action.

Critics of subjective individualism conflate intentional character and intentional relation, attempting to reduce the former into the latter. They do so by counting the collective intentional domain in terms of its *object*, through counting intentional contents as dependent on the objects in question. But socially constituted objects are *constituted* by the very contents in question. With emphasis on the *object*, they thus consider the subject's *act* of intending in relation to *what* is in the world and not the content manifest in consciousness. As such, the role of the individual is effectively nullified, given the emphasis on the ontological relations, where the epistemic relations are determined in lieu of the ontology. The mistake lies in that social objects get their being *through* the epistemic relations. In other words, since epistemic relations intersubjectively extended constitute social objects, it is erroneous to count those as posterior to that which they constitute.

Regarding the first concern of Schmid's noted above, he states: "Collective intentions, however, are not intentions of the kind anybody *has* for herself–not single individuals, and not some group mind. Rather, it is something individuals *share.*"[27] I am sympathetic to Schmid's refusal to understand intentional acts as being like paper in a wastebasket: being located "in" something. However, the question of an intentional act's spatial location amounts to a category mistake and therefore non sequitur. When one refers to a spatial location at all, for example neurological events in one's brain, one is changing the subject. Even if identity theories of mind are true, this holds: qua intentional act, it is nonsense to speak in spatial terms, even if qua neurological correlate there is sense to asking, in rough terms, about spatial extension and location. Schmid is wrong, however, to think that intentional acts could happen without a subject. While he is correct that the strong form of a "we" intends something shared, Schmid is collapsing the distinction between the intentional content and its conditions for satisfaction. He's collapsing what is intended with its correlate in the world. Doing so has the absurd effect of eliminating the possibility of any person's ever being mistaken about what is shared.

If Søren thinks to himself: "we are going to the zoo" where "we" ranges over himself, his parents and his teddy bear, Søren's not failing to have a collective intention because either a) his teddy bear can't have intentions or b) his parents have not formed any intention regarding the family's going to the zoo together. Søren can project forth something that is not yet *actually* shared, but which is *potentially* shared. Searle rebukes non-subjectively-individualist theories on the ground that they have trouble accounting for motivations pertaining to an individual's action. One notes, on the one hand, that Søren's intention could be used by him as a motivator to get his parents to conform their plans regarding the day's activities to his. More to the point, however, Søren's intentional state alone doesn't in any clear way direct his parents' motivations. Anyone who's ever been around children can attest to the fact that children and parents often have divergent intentions regarding the family's plans for a given day(s). To say they are intending what the family does, that the individuals involved don't have collective intentions, leaves us with a very commonplace phenomena now being needlessly perplexing. Similar behavior appears to underlie many political campaigns. When a campaign states "we will win the election" they aren't failing to identify a shared expectation just because the voters have not yet determined the fact of the matter regarding the electoral results. Political campaigns seem to operate on the notion that confidence in projection of the potentiality concerning their victory is part of what comes to constitute the basis for the eventual actuality. That's probably part of why one rarely sees a political candidate or their campaign say, "I think we might win in November" or "with a bit of luck I might just win this contest."

Turning to Schmid's second concern, that social normativity cannot be adequately accounted for on a subjective individualist view of collective intentionality, Schmid specifically targets Searle's view as being "normativity free." Schmid prefers to think that: "If the sharedness of intentionality is not necessarily *in itself* socially normative, it has *socially normative consequences.*"[28] I agree with Schmid that collective intentions can have socially normative consequences, as does Searle actually. For instance, Searle speaks clearly about the deontic

powers of collective intentional achievements when they coalesce to found institutional facts throughout his writings on social reality.[29] Searle's classic essay,
"How to Derive 'Ought' From 'Is'" demonstrates fairly straightforwardly, for
instance, how the act of uttering a promise generates a norm by which one's
success or failure to keep one's promise can be evaluated.[30] Arguably what
Searle is examining in his work on social ontology is how human acts generate
normative structures and norms. Indeed, in that classic essay, Searle introduced
the notions of institutional facts and constitutive rules, both key elements of his
more recent works.[31] Specifically, Searle points out that there is not merely one
kind of descriptive statement, counting at least the classically paradigmatic empirical descriptive statements and those that are indexed to some supporting fact
of human institutions.

> Though both kinds of statements state matters of fact, the statements containing
> words such as "married," "promise," "home run," and "five dollars" state facts
> whose existence presupposes certain institutions: a man has five dollars, given
> the institution of money. Take away the institution and all he has is a rectangu-
> lar bit of paper with green ink on it.[32]

What Schmid presents one with are two false dilemmas. Schmid's first false
choice is that one must either choose to deny an adequate view of social normativity or deny subjective individualism. Normativity can arise out of intentional
relations extended intersubjectively, and indeed there are such cases of codified
normative systems such as law or institutional rule.[33] Schmid's second false
choice originates where he claims that accepting subjective individualism requires denying the relational nature of collective intentionality. It is plausible to
think that for Schmid, the former disjunction is motivated by the latter. Yet implicating others in one's intentional life, through the "we" form of intention,
seems to rather clearly and expressly reference one's relatedness to others.

In speaking of this second concern, Schmid again appeals to the forced spatial metaphor of tradition: "Collective intentions are not intentions of the kind
anybody '*has*'–not single individuals, and not some super-agent. For collective
intentionality is not subjective. It is relational."[34] While it is true that no super-
agent is necessary and that collective intentionality is not merely subjective in
the sense of being whatever an individual fancies being true, Schmid evades
offering an argument as to why being relational means not being subjectively
individualist, i.e. why relationality implies that collective intentional states are
not states of consciousness. One appreciates wanting to avoid reifying or hypos-
tatizing intersubjective relations or reducing all reality to predicates and subjects.
One can further appreciate the desire to emphasize the dynamic nature of our
inter-relatedness with one another. However, one mustn't forget the simple point
that relations require *relata*. There are no free-floating relations. One doesn't
need to assume that one's relata are static in nature. If, for instance, one's sub-
jects-in-relation with one another are dynamic beings, it would only stand to
reason that the nature of their relations would be fluid and dynamic as well.

Schmid, like many contemporary reactionaries to the Modern philosophical tradition, overplays his hand. "Subject" does not entail "static," "without relation,"
"essentially preconfigured *in toto*," such that relations become superfluous or
non-essential to our ontology, or whatever Modern conclusion Schmid seeks to
draw regarding the nature of subjectivity.

Distinguishing Dependence Relations

Before moving on to the next section, it is necessary to briefly state distinctions in dependence relations. In specifying types of dependence relations, I will
make use of definitions offered by Amie Thomasson. Thomasson's distinctions
are informed by Husserl's philosophy and the work of Roman Ingarden, both of
which she appeals to in her criticisms of Searle's social ontology. Thomasson
distinguishes between the following kinds of dependence relations:

1. *(General) Dependence*: Necessarily, if a exists, then b exists.
2. *Historical Dependence*: Necessarily, for any time t at which a exists, b exists
at t or at some earlier time.
3. *Constant Dependence:* Necessarily, for any time t at which a exists, b exists
at t, which dependence may be:
Rigid–dependence on a particular individual; or
Generic–dependence on there being *something* or other of a certain kind.[35]

One can also make note of foundation relations, as many of the intentional
achievements manifest in everyday experience are complex in nature, involving
iterated layers of intentional achievements. This is to say that one intentional
state might be founded on another, and that systems of intentional states might
thereby be ordered in dependence relations relative to other intentional achievements. Quoting John Drummond:

> To say that an act is founded upon another means that it (a) presupposes that
> other act as necessary and (b) builds itself upon that act's matter or noematic
> sense so as to form a unity with it. Founded acts can also be objectifiying; judg-
> ing a state of affairs would be an example of a higher-order objectifying act.[36]

This is also of importance moving forward in that concerns with collective intentionality implicate certain axiological or practical considerations. Note also
that this undermines Schmid's claim that normativity is something the subjective
individualist cannot account for. Again, Drummond:

> Practical or axiological intentions, for example, when their specifically practi-
> cal and axiological moments are abstracted and isolated, are "non-objectifying,"
> since they present only an aspect of an object but do not present that object in
> its own right. However, practical and axiological intentions are necessarily
> founded on objectifying acts.[37]

As such, what is discussed in the collective intentionality literature, whether in terms of objectifying or non-objectifying acts, represents primarily founded intentional acts. For instance, the rules of chess are a systematically ordered set of declarative prescriptions *about* the pieces' individual capabilities and powers and also *about* how the game is to be conducted. Collective intentional achievements about the rule-properties of a given chess piece are dependent on some sense of reference to the piece in question or the sense of what such an object might represent in a more abstract sense. Other examples of dependent and iterated or founded intentional achievements include social institutions and higher order mathematical proofs. The latter are dependent on more primitive intentional achievements having to do with the properties and functions associated with numbers and their operators, the former founded on individual acceptances on some level. To the phenomenologist, these foundation relations always are traceable back to some ground in the praxis of lived experiences of individuals. In short, any instance of derived intentionality will ultimately be founded on some instance or complex of intrinsic intentional achievements. Any instance of derived intentionality, then, must have a founded nature. This does not prevent derived intentional states from serving as a ground for further founded derived intentional formations–as is clear in an analysis of social institutions. However, it does demonstrate that more primitive intentional achievements ground such states. This means that any description of founded intentional states that are presented in such a manner whereby they stand in contradiction to or with incoherence in respect to that which they are founded upon are inherently problematic descriptions of said intentional states.[38]

Arguments in Defense of Subjective Individualism

I begin by asserting a claim that most will concede the truth of: that only individual subjects possess consciousness, groups do not have consciousness. Borrowing a phrase from Annette Baier, Schmid believes that subjective individualists have fallen under the spell of the "Cartesian brainwash," and that such a view is committed to the erroneous Cartesian way of understanding the subject as *ego cogito*. Hence Schmid's view is that subjective individualism–the position that only individual subjects have intrinsic intentionality–is a by-product of the Cartesian understanding of the ego. The error, according to Schmid, is that: "Where there is intentionality, it is said, there has to be somebody who 'has' it– the good old subject."[39] To Schmid, the alternative is clear: "Collective intentions are not intentions of the kind anybody '*has*'–not single individuals, and not some super-agent. For collective intentionality is not subjective. It is relational."[40] Leaving aside the question of a super-agent, it is not clear what sense of "have" is implicated in the claim that individuals don't have intentions. This may have to do with the potential conflation of subjective individualism with atomism addressed in the conclusion.

The phenomenological tradition is critical of Descartes' conception of subjectivity, yet clearly accepts that consciousness and thereby intentionality in its intrinsic sense is always *someone's*. Take the examples of Schütz and Gurwitsch. For Schütz, the "subjective interpretation of meaning" is an essential feature of one's experience generally, but most importantly is essential to experiences of social phenomena including what one more recently refers to as collective intentional phenomena. Of Schütz's view, Gurwitsch argues, the "subjective interpretation of meaning" [*subjecktiver* or *gemeinter Sinn*] is not peculiar to analysis, but "proves to be a common practice of social life in the world of everyday experience."[41] All social interaction is based on expectations guided by typifications functioning anonymously. That is to say, that one has expectations that roles will be fulfilled more or less as they should be by those associated with those roles. The social world can only have sense to it if it has a sufficiently stable structure of anticipations. "Unless I had such an idea, it would be impossible for me to come to terms with [the other], to interlock my course of action with what I may expect his to be; there would be nothing to orient and guide me in the negotiations on which I am about to enter."[42] Schütz argues that this sort of reciprocity is a requirement for all social interactions.

For Schütz that one's inherited expectations and type-forms are intelligible only in relation to one's biographical situation supports subjective individualism. This is why cultural variances can lead to frustrations in social interaction, as the categorization of types and their corresponding expectation structures can vary.

> My fellowmen see the same things I see, though they see them differently, from different perspectives. ...Furthermore, our goals and systems of relevancy cannot be the same, since the "biographically determined situations" in which they originate must by necessity differ for different persons.[43]

Further, it is not only others who bear roles that are shaped through typification, one regularly assumes such roles oneself.[44] The very sense "other" or "stranger" that is part of one's experience is framed within the context of a lived situation.

Schütz's instrumental emphasis regarding social relations need not be agreed to in full. However, there is a sense in which it bears true and which is important to note in regard to the question of evidence. "All cultural objects—tools, symbols, language systems, works of art, social institutions, etc.–point back by their very origin and meaning to the activities of human subjects."[45] At the same time, "The overwhelming majority of the rules and recipes are complied with as a matter of course, and are hardly ever explicitly formulated, still less reflected upon."[46] That is to say, most persons don't stop and reflect about what they experience in the social world, i.e., don't seek evidentiary fulfillment for their intentional acts within their everyday lives. Rather, they continue operating under their largely inherited anticipatory schemes (horizons) unless some sufficiently transparent incongruity presents itself. Since social phenomena are evidenced in relation to harmonious continuities of appresentational contents, it should not surprise one if incongruities between what is taken as experience and evidence must generally be of a relatively obvious nature to provoke reflection. So long as one's intention and what transpires, in both individually and collectively contexted cases, is close enough for one's purposes to continue or to require adjustments that are not contrary to one's interests, the play of passive synthesis continues uninterrupted and without express awareness. It should be noted that typification poses a problem for the charge that subjective individualism is normativity free. Each type, insofar as it has a specific horizon or expectation structure to it, grounds and informs normative expectations. Each type has a normality appropriate to it that is identified in experience, such that the experience of something abnormal in association with a type expectation is incongruous and puzzling to one in a basic experiential sense.

It is clear that in addition to asserting that consciousness is always and only found in individuals, one sees that intentionality, intrinsic intentionality to be more specific, is always and only found in relation to consciousness. There is a rigid dependence relation between each instance of intrinsic intentionality and the subject whose act of consciousness that involves, as well as rigid dependence in relation to the act itself. If this is the case, then intrinsic intentionality is only ever manifest in consciousness of individual subjects. Since groups do not possess consciousness, they cannot be said to possess intentionality in an intrinsic manner. Nor do groups execute intentional acts in an intrinsic sense. As such, whatever intentionality groups do express must be derived intentionality.

Where Schmid claims "If we conceive of collective intentionality in a non-atomistic way, I think it becomes clear that the question about the relation between collective intentionality and the group is futile since *collective intentionality* is *the group*,"[47] the status of said intentionality can only be of a derived intentional nature. This is also in conflict with Searle's claim that: "collective intentionality gives rise to the collective and not the other way around."[48]

It could be said that Searle claims that collective intentionality is a form or mode of intrinsic intentionality. However, Searle's use of "collective intentionality" is ambiguous. Collective intentionality refers on the one hand to the intrinsic intentional states wherein an individual's consciousness takes on a plural as opposed to a singular form. On the other hand, collective intentionality is also used by Searle to refer to the derived intentional attributions of status on objects that can be accepted by groups or communities of individuals. Schmid would appear to be denying collective intentionality in the intrinsic sense and embracing it in the derived sense. It is unclear, however, how the latter can exist independent of the former. Note also Schmid's express reference to atomism as that helps motivate the concern, addressed below, that there may be a conflation between atomism and individualism in Schmid's arguments.

Of collective intentionality in the intrinsic sense, i.e., intentional states of consciousness that are in a we-mode, one can say that they are rigidly dependent on the subject of and acts of consciousness just as intentions in the singular-mode.[49] Of collective intentionality in the derived sense, i.e., attributions of intentional characteristics that supervene on some object, event, or state of affairs, one can say that they are generically dependent on the existence of conscious beings. They have ontologically subjective natures, as opposed to ontologically objective natures. Without beings with consciousness, ontologically subjective beings could not exist. However, derived collective intentional achievements are also historically dependent on acts of intrinsic intentionality. Were this not the case, there could be ontologically subjective phenomena that have no origin in the acts of subjective beings. If the dependence of derived collective intentional states on intrinsic intentionality is correct, then Schmid's position faces further difficulties and the denial of subjective individualism appears yet further from a tenable thesis.

The matter gets more complicated where one introduces questions of evidence and horizon intentionality in association with the variant types of intentionality. The basic nature of phenomenological evidence has already been introduced. However, it is important to introduce the basic idea of horizon intentionality and discuss more nuanced considerations about the nature of evidence before returning again to direct consideration of Schmid's criticisms.[50]

One related note about evidence worthy of mention before turning to horizons per se is Husserl's non-trivial observation that one rarely concerns herself with evidence in everyday life. Rather, one tends to accept the sedimentations of cultural and individual achievements as given, folding these into our experiences without critical attention to their evidentiary merits. Such sedimentations are merely part of, and thought to be supported in the uncritical state of mind by, one's experiential horizons. For instance, few work out for themselves proof for things like the Pythagorean Theorem, relying instead on the testimony that it has been done. One generally accepts such achievements on the ground of a utility within a practice, wherein the achievement's–like the Pythagorean Theorem's– instrumental value is taken as sufficient evidence for it. Observe further that there are historical shifts in connotations that also are taken up into one's consciousness mostly unwittingly and one finds potential barriers to proper analysis that are manifest inheritances of socially constituted experiences. This helps motivate Husserl's interest in grounding predicative judgments and their evidentiary requirements in prior pre-predicative foundations.[51] If a given predicative claim does not have some prepredicative foundation in experience, it is likely groundless. Unfortunately, such claims regularly permeate culture and rely on collective intentional achievements for their formation and persistence.

The uncritically adopted meanings and practices one accepts in virtue of one's surroundings and cultural contexts are features of the background of our experience insofar as they delineate potentialities that are present to the horizon structure of one's experience. In many cases one finds potentialities of linguistic reference associated with linguistic communities. Horizons represent for Husserl a "...*fundamental trait of intentionality*."[52] He states:

> Every subjective process has a process "horizon," which changes with the alteration of the nexus of consciousness to which the process belongs and with the alteration of the process itself form phase to phase of its flow–an intentional

horizon of reference to potentialities of consciousness that belong to the process itself.[53]

Further,

> Thus, as consciousness of somethin*ç*, every consciousness has the essential
> property, not just of being somehow *able to change into continually new modes
> of consciousness of the same object* (which, throughout the unity of synthesis,
> is inherent in them as an identical objective sense), but of being able to do so
> according to–indeed, *only according to those horizon intentionalities.*[54]

Only by uncovering these implicit and predelineated possibilities in consciousness can the phenomenologist make understandable how "anything like *fixed
and abiding objective unities* can become intended and, in particular, how this
marvelous work of 'constituting' identical objects is done *in the case of each
category of objects....*"[55]

Husserl distinguishes between internal and external horizons, amongst other
horizon structures. David Vessey characterizes the distinction well. "Internal
horizons are horizons that arise from the nature of the object either as an object,
such as taking up space, or as the kind of object that it is. When we see someone
from the back, we perceive him or her as having a face. It belongs to the internal
horizon of a head to have a face."[56] An internal horizon arises from one's identification of something as being of a certain type. The internal horizon of a person
is distinct from that of a statue. A statue is not expected to be able to move or
think or have a fleshy organic composition. Hence the surprise when the street
performer posing as a statue grabs one's shoulder, as the precedent horizon is
"shattered."[57]

> External horizons are horizons established by the relation between the object
> and its surroundings. If there is a telegraph pole partially obstructing our view
> of a house, we recognize the parts of the house on both sides of the pole as still
> belonging to the same house as being located behind the pole. ...All relations
> get their character from the external horizon, including the relation of belong-
> ing to one spatio-temporal whole with everything else.[58]

Where each object of experience has its own internal horizon, when they are
placed in relation to one another, there emerges yet another horizon in experience, that consisting of relations. Horizons bear reference to potential and actual
relations, as well as inform type associations in categorially rich experience,
affording some ground for normativity. Relationality and normativity are both
things Schmid has claimed the subjective individualist cannot address, both of
which are present in the works of subjective individualist phenomenologists.
Barring arguments against Husserl, Schütz, and Gurwitsch, Schmid's assertions
regarding the supposed shortcomings of subjective individualism faces robust
counter-examples to both claims.

Intrinsic intentional states have horizon structures. Horizon structures are rigidly dependent on the individual subject and historically dependent on the subject's biographical narrative. Derived intentional states do not and cannot have horizon structures. If they did, stop signs and sentences and the like would have potentialities that are available to the stop signs and sentences *themselves*, as distinct from the potentialities available *for some subject*. Further, derived collective intentional states are dependent on subjects establishing them and the systems of indication whereby they become accessible as intentional. Subjects not party to the systems of indication cannot access the derived collective intentional contents. Such systems of indication are part of the horizon structure of consciousness. As such, they are generically dependent on the existence of beings with consciousness, i.e., subjects, as well as founded upon the intrinsic intentional acts of subjects. This is to say, while the meanings associated with derived intentional phenomena within socially constituted horizons are often accepted or inherited as part of one's social context rather than explicitly generated by the individual herself, such phenomena have origins in human praxis and are thus founded on some intrinsic intentional basis; at least where the foundation relation is open to being evidenced and not founded on empty intentions, which is, of course, possible.

Where intrinsic intentional states have fulfillment conditions that are specifiable in relation of the act-content correlations inherent in such states themselves, derived intentional states appear to consist only in contents without an obvious act correlation. This is lent credence in virtue of how derived intentional states only manifest intentional characteristics in relation to subjects' actualizing those potentialities through acts of consciousness. Given that the act-type of an intentional state is essential to establish a fulfillment condition, it is most probably the case that derived intentional states do not properly speaking have fulfillment conditions specific to themselves in isolation from acts of subjectivity.

If one attempted to argue that derived intentional states did have fulfillment conditions associated with the acts of subjects, then it seems one accepts that derived intentional states are dependent on individuals for their fulfillment conditions. If that is the case, one is committed either to the view that (i) derived intentional states themselves have no fulfillment conditions proper to themselves, or that (ii) derived intentional states have fulfillment conditions that are rigidly dependent on or that are reducible to fulfillment conditions specifiable only in terms of intrinsic intentional states. If the later is the case, then whatever fulfillment conditions there are for derived intentional states are dependent on a specifiable horizon structure according to which the intentionality exhibited is intelligible to some consciousness.

The impact of this on Schmid's arguments against subjective individualism is the following. Earlier it was shown that Schmid's sense of collective intentionality should be understood as intentionality in a derived, not intrinsic sense. That in itself is not problematic. However, in that derived intentional states are themselves dependent on subjects and their acts, being founded on intrinsic intentional acts, being ontologically subjective in Searle's terminology, the denial of subjective individualism poses a serious quandary. If intentions are not something anyone "has," then how can there be intentional states or achievements at all? Further, there are good reasons to believe that there are no horizon and probably no evidentiary structures associated with derived intentional states. Yet horizon intentionality, an essential feature of intrinsic intentionality, is necessary for derived intentional states to be intelligible. And if there are evidentiary structures associated with derived intentional states, they too have dependence relations that require the acts of subjects in order to manifest.

An example will illustrate better what I take the differences to amount to. I will use Searle's example of people in the park escaping from the rain.[59] Consider two variants of this case that are identical in all details but one. There are many people in the park. As it begins to rain, they all move to get out of the rain. In the first case, 1) the people in the park have no intentions to act together; in the second case, 2) the people in the park have intentions to act together. All characteristics otherwise in both cases are identical. As I understand the matter, when Schmid denies subjective individualism he's unable to differentiate these cases because all other relations are identical. However, the subjective individualist can point to a clear difference. The first case involves relations between individuals, but not of the important kind in that it lacks collectivity in virtue of the fact that the intentionality of the subjects is lacking. The individuals involved do not *have* the appropriate intentional states. Any apparent collectivity is accidental. The second case involves collectivity as the important kind of relation bears true. The introduction of the intentional states of the individuals changes the relations in a non-trivial way.

More pointedly, take the example of two individuals engaged in sexual intercourse. The activity itself can be assumed to play out identically in both cases. Again, if the intentionality of the subjects is removed the relation between the individuals changes dramatically. Cases where one individual's intention to engage in intercourse with the other is lacking clearly differentiates rape from consensual intercourse. Denying subjective individualism prevents one from having the ability to differentiate these cases. The case where neither individual has the appropriate intentional state might be called zombie action. In essence, this is what one who denies subjective individualism takes on: zombies can act collectively, since intentionality of the subjects is not important.[60]

In Schmid's defense, I believe he might argue that I've misinterpreted his position. For instance, he could argue that it is the intentional structure of the phenomenon itself that varies. The cases of consensual intercourse and rape differ precisely because the phenomena, collective actions, themselves differ. Similarly, the difference between Searle's two cases of people intending to get out of the rain is not so much the individuals' acceptance, but a question of the different intentionality manifest in the phenomena themselves. While in cases of small groups, pairs and other small groupings, the position may be hard to appreciate, it's clearer in cases of collective actions of larger scale. When we behave as a collective, there's no necessity to any individual's accepting the activity of the collective itself. As such, one might claim that the individuals don't intend the action, and such actions have independent intentional structures.

I respond to such an argument by asserting that while it is true that individuals' intentions never summatively produce a collective action, it does not follow from this that the action itself has a complete intentional independence from the individuals themselves. One can admit that collective actions have derived intentionality, but doing so requires a dependence relation to intrinsic intentionality. There is no derived intentionality free of some intrinsic intentional agents' acting collectively. While collective acceptance might not be the best model, something like collective adherence may work. Acceptance seems to fail as one can argue that it is possible for no individuals in a collective to accept action or position of the collective. Adherence on the other hand is neutral regarding individual commitments to the specific collective action. At the same time, there is nothing inconsistent with asserting that collective adherence to a common action is dependent, ontologically, on the intrinsic intentional states of the individuals involved. In some sense the agents adhere to the activity of the collective. As such, what's missing in the case of the park example is adherence to a collective plan. Similarly, in the case of rape there is no adherence to any common goal.

Conclusion

Given the problems latent in the denial of subjective individualism, it seems clear that, at the very least, subjective individualism is a thesis that is less problematic in comparison with its denial. Denying subjective individualism makes collectivity something bereft of a kind of relation to individuals–thereby eliminating a feature that appears to be essential to collectivity. A theory of collective intentionality should embrace the ontological subjectivity of the social world and seek to clarify the dependence relations to consciousness and individual subjects, not deny that foundation.

It may be that Schmid is meaning to criticize atomism and not individualism. Granted, there are historical associations of the two positions. Also, Schmid's critiques appear to emphasize the inadequacies of the philosophical theories of the Modern era, which often have an implicit atomistic bias. If the problem is atomism, then the positions must be carefully disambiguated. Doing so will reveal the lack of an essential relation between atomism and individualism.

Consider, for instance, Philip Pettit's manner of differentiating the two theses. Pettit identifies his position as one that is both individualist and holistic, i.e., individualistic and opposed to atomism.[61] On Pettit's view, individualism and collectivism are positions as to the vertical relations between individuals and the social wholes to which they stand in relation. Collectivism is a view that "we would realize that the intentional image of ourselves as more or less autonomous subjects–as autarchical agents–is a conceit that lacks foundation in reality."[62] Individualism is the position opposed to this thesis, held by those "who deny that social forces or regularities are inimical in this way to intentional autonomy or autarchy."[63] More plainly, individualism is the claim that individual autonomy and self-directedness is not contrary to there being non-trivial social forces and regularities of influence that bear on individuals through relations they have to society. Atomism and holism, on the other hand, are positions as to the horizontal relations between individual subjects within such social wholes. "Atomists occupy an extreme position, according to which it is possible for a human being to develop all the capacities characteristic of our kind in total isolation from her fellows, if indeed she has any fellows."[64] Holism denies the claim of atomism, "arguing that one or another distinctive capacity–usually the capacity for thought–depends in a non-causal or constitutive way on the enjoyment of social relationships."[65] Holistic individualism, then, appears to be the position that Husserlian phenomenology embodies as well–even if denying elements of Pettit's naturalism.[66]

If Schmid's claim is that subjective individualists are committed to atomism, it appears to be presented with a clear counter-example in Pettit's case, to which one can add Husserl, Gurwitsch, and Schütz at the very least. Phenomenological philosophers tend to whole-heartedly agree with Pettit's assertion that: "There is no prospect of the solitary thinker, no prospect of the sort of possibility that the atomist has to countenance."[67]

Given that it has been demonstrated that subjective individualism is not unable to accommodate normativity or relationality, there may be further reason to take atomism as the intended target of the critique. It wouldn't be unreasonable to argue that atomists have problems with relationality, in that atomists deny relations to others are necessary for personal flourishing. What's more, atomism may very well have problems with normativity having intersubjective extension, as wholly self-sufficient beings who are not dependent on social relations whatsoever might be thought to be construed as isolated subjects who are bound by norms only by virtue of their own private commitments to those norms.

A further potential problem for Schmid is where Gurwitsch roundly criticizes those who conflate the subjective individualism with atomism, being very critical of Max Scheler, for instance, in Scheler's pressing a "Robinson Crusoe" like conception of the individual as being like an island unto themselves.[68] The atomistic conception of the subject is fiction, Gurwitsch asserts; its model of self-sufficient *"pure individuals"* in community with one another is an abstraction that "need not be universalized."[69] Additionally,

> The originary encounter with fellow human beings does not signify a coming together and a being together of isolated individuals who, in their mutual encounter, have severed their collective relations to the surrounding world and, so to speak, find themselves together but detached and "horizonless," as *mere individuals* such that this sort of encounter would be a *mere being together*. Instead, we continuously encounter fellow human beings in a determined horizon, namely in that of the relevant concrete sector of our "natural living."[70]

And,

No encounters of fellow human beings are ever given that would be *absolutely* without a horizon such that two "monads" unrelated to the surrounding world would simply confront each other, i.e., "monads" whose being together would not be embedded in a sector of the lived world.[71]

It should be clear that the subjective individualist–not to be conflated with an atomist–is not damaged by Schmid's arguments.

In sum, then, subjective individualism, being the view that only subjects have intentionality in an intrinsic sense, is not equivalent with atomism. Nor does subjective individualism presuppose or entail atomism. Subjective individualism is consistent with the claims that individual subjects need to exist in relations to others in order to develop their capacities; atomism is not. However, the dependence relations one's material capacities depend on are largely epistemological and historical.

Notes

1. Schmid 2003a, 2003b, & 2006
2. "Every experience points to further experiences that would fulfill and verify the appresented horizons, which include, in the form of non-intuitive anticipations, potentially verifiable syntheses of harmonious further experience" (Husserl 1999:114/144).
3. Schmid 2003b: 205
4. Schmid 2006: 19
5. Bratman 1999
6. Schmid 2006: 18
7. Schmid 2003b: 205
8. Husserl 1999: 105/135
9. Bratman 1999: 94ff.
10. ibid: 111; Margaret Gilbert discusses the thesis as to whether or not groups can be said to have beliefs under the headings "psychologism about beliefs" and "anti-psychologism about groups." Her use, despite being well intended, of 'psychologism' is unfortunate as it differs from what concerned Frege and Husserl in their discussions of psychologism (Gilbert 1992: 238).
11. Bratman is careful to distinguish his account of shared intentions, which is individualistic and expressly reductive in spirit, from Searle's collective intentions, Raimo Tuomela's we-intentions (Bratman may be incorrect on this point, see Tuomela 2000), and Gilbert's plural subjects (Bratman 1999: §5-8). Bratman insists that his shared intentions are of a narrower focus than either Searle or Tuomela's objects of concern, which do not involve distinguishing between an individual's intention for a group's activity and an individual's intention for shared activity (ibid: 116n17, 145n6). I have no objection to Bratman's distinction. However, I would suggest that his shared intentions be viewed as a species of collective intentions. The success conditions are more stringent, but what

goes more generally for collective- or we-intentions follows with respect for shared intentions. I understand such a distinction in the following manner. The object of a shared intention is shared cooperative activity. The object of a collective intention is collective activity. I view shared cooperative activity as a species of collective activity.

12. Leo Zaibert has argued that Searle is committed to formal individualism in virtue of his taking both a non-summative approach to collective intentionality and his subjective individualism (Zaibert 2003). I don't see why that would have to be the case, but cannot here respond to Zaibert's argument in full.

13. Schmid 2003b: 212; Schmid 2006: 18, 19, 21

14. Carr 1986: 525

15. ibid.

16. ibid: 526

17. Schmid 2006: 18

18. Schmid 2003b: 212; Schmid 2006: 18, 19, 21

19. Schmid 2006: 21

20. ibid: 19-20

21. Schmid 2003b: 212-213

22. ibid: 209

23. ibid: 210

24. ibid: 211

25. See also Meijers 2003

26. D.W. Smith 1989: §3.3

27. Schmid 2006: 20

28. Schmid 2003b: 213

29. In a paper published online, Leo Zaibert and Barry Smith insightfully argue that it is common in contemporary philosophy to speak of normativity as a homogenous whole and that this is clearly inadequate. (http://ontology.buffalo.edu/smith/articles/ Normativity.pdf) Zaibert and Smith find at least three kinds of normativity (labels mine): 1) Rule normativity–normativity derived from constitutive rules; 2) Grounding normativity–normativity which is necessary as a pretext to the possibility for social action; 3) Phenomenological normativity–normativity dependent on the essential structures of mental phenomena (Zaibert and Smith, 17). In particular, I find the third category interesting, as the later Husserl began to give explicit treatment to such "proto-normativity" constitutive in the structure of experience (Husserl 1970, 1973).

30. Searle 1964

31. ibid: §III

32. ibid: 54

33. ibid.

34. Schmid 2003b: 214

35. Thomasson 1997: 126

36. Drummond 2003: 83

37. ibid.

38. For instance, in phenomenology, the sense of one's agency is dependently related to one's experiential awareness of one's agency. Animals and small children are not agents in that they are unaware of the self-directed nature of their activities, i.e. they don't experience themselves as directors of those activities: "In its proper sense, we understand agency to depend on the agent's consciousness of agency. That is, if someone intentionally causes something to happen, that person is not an agent of (even if they are a cause) if they do not know that they have intentionally caused it to happen. ...The kind of conscious knowledge involved in agency does not have to be of a very high order; it could be simply a matter of a very thin, pre-reflective awareness, and in most cases it is just that. Sometimes, however, there may be an explicit consciousness of acting for reasons. ...The *sense of agency* (or self-agency) for my actions, then, may involve a thin, pre-reflective awareness of what I am doing as I am doing it, or it may involve a more explicit consciousness filled with well-developed reasons" (Gallagher & Zahavi 2008: 158).

39. Schmid 2003b: 203
40. ibid: 214
41. Gurwitsch 1962: 68
42. ibid: 67
43. ibid: 62
44. ibid: 66
45. Schütz 1962: 10
46. Gurwitsch 1962: 56
47. Schmid 2003a: 93
48. Searle 1997: 449

49. I am sympathetic to the objections of phenomenologically informed philosophers against Searle's use of "mode." Kevin Mulligan, for instance, forcefully registered at the Collective Intentionality VII conference in Basel the view that modes do not represent. Agreeing with that, one can argue that there is a difference between the mode of an intentional state and the representation of a mode in an intentional state. Searle could evade objections of Mulligan's kind were he to endorse the latter. More to the point, one can understand Searle's phrase "we-mode" intention as signifying a multi-rayed intentional content. That is, what differentiates the I-mode and We-mode intentions is not, strictly speaking the mode of intentionality, but that the intentional contents refer either singularly or plurally. I-mode intentions, on Searle's language, refer only to one subject's intentionality in regard to their fulfillment conditions. We-mode intentions, on Searle's language, refer to multiple subjects' intentionality in regard to their fulfillment conditions.

50. The question of evidence and the modes of evidence in Husserlian phenomenology is a rich discussion. Husserl distinguishes between apodicitic and assertoric evidence (Husserl 1998: §137). Apodicitic evidence is evidence of something's necessity, and may be pure or impure in nature. Assertoric evidence is evidence to the effect that something is such-and-so, and can either be adequate (complete) and inadequate (capable of being increased) (Husserl 1998:

§138). Evidence can also be immediate or mediate (Husserl 1998: §141; Husserl 1973:§5, b & c). Husserl also notes that evidence relations have their own dependence relations, such that the evidence for a complex intentional act–like most intentional acts in everyday experience–can only be as strong in character as the weakest part (Husserl 1973: §5-10). As noted earlier in the paper, the kind of evidence associated with a given type of phenomena is dependent on the nature of that phenomenon. However, he further establishes that there are essential differences between kinds of phenomena (Husserl 1998: §138). In Husserl's system, since the entire social world is founded on the basic intersubjective encounter of one subject's experience of another as other, all specifically social phenomena will have the same basic evidentiary form (Husserl 1999: §55ff.). For Husserl, this will be evidence associated with a harmonious synthesis of appresentational profiles, and can only be thus insofar as the states of consciousness of others are implicated in such phenomena (Husserl 1999: 105-106/135-136, 109/139, 114/144, 149/175). As such, the horizons of the social world and the phenomena therein are always indexed to potential others of greater or lesser specific biographical makeup. This I take to be the basis for Gurwitsch's claims to the co-presence of others, whether physically present to one's experience or not, in the horizons related to social phenomena (Gurwitsch 1979). This is also why Schütz emphasizes the importance of the subjective interpretation of meaning and all meaning's dependence on one's biographical situation (Schütz 1962, Gurwitsch 1962). If someone has no context of reference for something's specific socially designated significance, i.e., they lack the appropriate horizon, that object will not bear the socially designated significance it would for those whose horizons do so include those possibilities.

51. For Husserl, this seems to express a truism: the predicative is founded on the prepredicative.

"But the return to objective, prepredicative self-evidence obtains its proper emphasis and full significance only with the stipulation that this *relation of founding concerns not only judgments grounded in experience but every self-evident predicative judgment in general, and therewith also the judgments of the logician himself,* with their apodictic self-evidence, which, after all, make the claim of being valid 'in themselves,' i.e., regardless of their possible application to a determinate range of substrates" (Husserl 1973: 20).

Further: "For all generality and plurality, even the most primitive, already refers back to an act of taking several individuals together and, therewith, to a more or less primitive logical activity, in which what is taken together already receives a categorial formation, a forming of generality. *Original substrates are therefore individuals, individual objects,* and every thinkable judgment *ultimately* refers to individual objects, no matter how mediated in a variety of ways" (ibid: 26).

52. Husserl 1999: 44/82

53. ibid; "*Every experience has its own horizon*; every experience has its core of actual and determinate cognition, its own content of immediate determi-

nation which give themselves; but beyond this core determinate quiddity, of the truly given as 'itself-there,' it has its own horizon" (Husserl 1973: 32).

54. Husserl 1999: 45/83
55. ibid: 48/85-86
56. Vessey 2009: 534
57. Schütz (1962) and Gurwitsch (1962) each rely heavily on the sense of types or theory of typifications, which is closely bound up with the explication of horizon intentionality, in Husserl's *Experience and Judgment* (Husserl 1973). Zaibert & Smith, in a paper published online also reference Husserl's work (Zaibert & Smith: 17). In all cases, there is recognized to be a normative or proto-normative structure functioning in experience itself where typification is manifest, typifications are dynamic sense structures that are associated with one's horizon intentionality. I am indebted to Sara Heinämaa for the term "proto-normative," which captures nicely Husserl's sense of this being something prepredicative and prior to judgment proper.

58. Vessey 2009: 534-535
59. Searle 2002: 92
60. I realize that zombies are usually understood as lacking qualia. But to have an intent to act collectively with others is something it is like to have a certain sort of experience. The point is that collectivity becomes a vacuous notion that automatons could engage in if intentionality is not tied to subjects but merely manifest in relations independent of consciousness.

61. Pettit 1993: 112
62. ibid: 111
63. ibid.
64. ibid: 111-112
65. ibid: 112
66. Pettit & Schweikard 2006 outlines a third distinction, that between what they call singularism and pluralism. Singularism is the view that denies singular subjects are capable of forming "plural centers of intentional life" (Pettit & Schweikard 2006: 36).

67. Pettit 1993: 114
68. Gurwitsch 1979: 100-102
69. ibid: 36, 37
70. ibid: 35-36
71. ibid: 36

Chapter 5
The Phenomenology of the Social World and Gilbert's Plural Subject Theory

This chapter develops the analysis of plural subjects from the preceding chapters. This is done in two main ways. First, Aron Gurwitsch's social phenomenology is examined. This continues the development of the subjective individualist account of plural subjects, buttressing the Husserlian approach further against Hans Bernhard Schmid's challenges. Additionally, Gurwitsch focuses his analyses around horizon intentionality's role in the social world. Attending to it here allows a more positive development of the place of horizon intentionality in the social phenomena than the preceding chapter's response to Schmid allowed. Gurwitsch offers an account of three primary types of community with others, which he calls: partnership, membership, and fusion. Each constitutes a distinctive type of horizon of involvement one can have with another. This helps emphasize the heterogeneous nature of social phenomena.

Second, the phenomenological approach to understanding plural subjects and collective intentions is drawn into contrast with Margaret Gilbert's plural subject theory. There is a great deal in common between Gilbert's approach and a phenomenological one and I believe that both phenomenological and the Gilbertian approaches can benefit from dialogue with one another. They each share a denial of formal individualism, each rejects atomistic conceptions of the subject, and each aims to account for plural subjects in non-reductive fashion. Importantly, both accounts outline a middle position between the extremes of atomistic individualism and collectivism. This is not to say that there are not significant differences between the approaches. Where my phenomenologically motivated account aims to defend a non-atomistic individualism, steering clear of the excesses of collectivism or holism, Gilbert's view appears to tend more towards collectivism or holism in order to avoid the excesses of precedent individualist approaches.

More importantly, however, confronting Gilbert's view reveals a problem latent in some of the analytic literature on collective intentionality, namely, a faulty or incomplete understanding of intentionality. These differences in theories of intentionality have non-trivial consequences for one's theory of collective

intentionality. Arguments are offered showing how starting from the action oriented, voluntaristic sense of intentionality [*Absicht*] runs afoul of the more basic
phenomenological sense of intentionality [*Intentionalität*]. An account of the
former, because of its being founded on the latter, must be consistent with accounts of the latter. More simply, since agency depends on consciousness or
mind, the intentionality of consciousness or mind grounds the intentionality of
agents in action.

Gurwitsch's Social Phenomenology

Aron Gurwitsch takes one of the more wholly systematic approaches to examining the possibilities of being with others in plurality. Gurwitsch's account is
one also rigorously subjectively individualist, consistent with Husserlian phenomenology broadly construed.[1] Gurwitsch speaks first to the importance of the
transcendence of intentionality, as well as the horizonal structure of intentional
experience.

> No situation is "autarchic" and made self-sufficient such that it does not of it-
> self refer to something lying outside it, and it is precisely in this reference to the
> "co-included" horizon that the situation reveals itself as "intramundane," i.e.,
> precisely as a situation of the *surrounding world.*[2]

That reference to the surrounding world is not unimportant as others are present
in that world.

> *Thus in the horizons which are "co-included," something like a world of fellow
> human beings is found. Insofar as every situation refers beyond what is inher-
> ent in it, it also continuously refers, therefore, to "other people."*[3]

Others are not extra to or accidental to one's experience, nor are others products
of inference; others are latent in our experiences often affecting the shape of our
experiences. As to what Gurwitsch understands as "co-included" horizons he
expressly identifies the protentive temporal horizon, the broader contextual
community, one's fellows, and so on.[4]

The "co-included" horizon, Gurwitsch argues, is as much a conviction as it
is knowledge. It is knowledge in the lived sense, implicit or tacitly functional
part of the background of our consciousness. It's not intentional in nature, i.e.
not directed at an object. It is more like a mood state or akin to Searle's notion
of the background.[5] Because of this one cannot speak of the intersubjective nature of consciousness or experience just in epistemological terms. In that the co-
included horizon is not intentional in nature it is not readily expressible in propositional form, or at least expressions of it in propositional form will inherently
be incomplete or entail a lacuna.

Gurwitsch identifies three different types of being with: partnership, membership, and fusion. Under the heading of partnership Gurwitsch considers first

being together in a common situation. He stresses that a *common* situation (situation in common with others) does not mean an *identical* situation. Gurwitsch uses an example of two workers cobbling a street together; one laying stones the other knocking them into place.[6] In that the other worker in a situation of this sort is part of what makes this situation what it is, part of its constitution as their cobbling the street together, "the other also belongs to the situation in which I stand; his presence also contributes to the constituting of the situation and to making it what it is *in concreto*."[7] Our cobbling the street together gives meaning to and informs what we are doing, as well as giving meaning to each individual's role in virtue of the situational context.

This same form of being-together also functions where we work contrary to one another under a singular aim, as in a game of chess or in a multiplayer game environment on the Internet. Gurwitsch identifies the particular sense of one's comportment in taking one's own measure and anticipating the other's reactions to be *only* present in cases of *partnership*.[8] In partnership, how we comport ourselves is determined by our having partners, i.e., in virtue of the co-constituted situation. Our relation to one another in partnerships is *founded* in that relation and involves prescriptions of *roles* to be filled by individuals in relation to the "prescriptive" situational context.[9] Partnerships are also temporally limited, having definite beginnings and endings. This is the case even if they are repetitive, as in the relation of one's co-workers being a partnership whose roles are determined in relation to a workday.[10] While some partnerships have implicit or explicit contracts, contracts are *not* essential to all partnerships, even though this form of being-together "continuously needs an explicit or implicit agreement."[11] Partnership is not a spontaneous coincidence of a plurality of individuals, but involves having some purpose(s) in common that informs and contributes to the constitution of the plurality and through which individual roles can be determined.

Affirming subjective individualism, Gurwitsch argues that in partnerships "the individuals precede consociation [*Verbande*]: the association [*Verbindung*] is only subsequent."[12] He elaborates:

> The primacy of the individual over social wholes and the "essential separateness" of individuals even in the associations in question does not mean that these consociations are mere accumulations of people socially related exclusively to one another and who otherwise do not stand in any material and meaningful relation to one another. We must rather understand by this the pure, materially motivated being-together which alone is grounded in the situational encounter.[13]

Thus, subjective individualism is necessary insofar as there is a requirement for a situational context's authority as something definitive of *our* experience that individuals accept or determine that situations' meaningfulness. One cannot say that we are playing chess together if I don't know what chess is or don't accept the rules of chess as constitutive of the game. In such cases I refuse to accept the role the situation, in this case a game of chess, dictates in order for our entering into partnership to be meaningfully determined. That is, the situation determined in common or had in common plays a constitutional function in establishing a purpose that in turn is definitive toward the roles each determine in reference to that end in common.

Beyond partnership, Gurwitsch discusses membership. Underlying this notion is a distinction Gurwitsch makes between two different senses pertaining to a grouping of subjects together: society and community. For Gurwitsch, being in society with others refers to cool, distanced, loose forms of being-together. By community Gurwitsch understands a societal relation with a supervening positive sentiment [*Walther*]. Being in community with others involves more warmth and closeness, founded on some shared positive sentiment, and requires a sense of "inner unity" or "inner inseparability" not necessary for being in society with others.[14] Why a positive sentiment directing the unity and not a negative one? Quite simply, negative sentiments can bind variant groupings of individuals together who wouldn't otherwise share this positive sense of unity. In other words, alliances against a common goal don't always represent memberships with, as they tend to be more like partnerships between member-communities. Alliances might represent a kind of unity with without having community with. Communities are grounded in a life-context, they are not merely economic or material alignments of interests. One is a member of a community and communities are merely aligned against others, but also consist of a vision for what the community and its members stand for. Membership is not nearly as loose or free as partnership.

Consider how one is born into a community, yet one freely enters into and dissolves partnerships. "One already finds himself as a member of the community. One is born into a community, grows up and in it."[15] This has further significance to it: "*In advance, a human being is not solus ipse; insofar as he is communalized and historicalized, he always already belongs to other human beings....*"[16] That is to say that, as social animals, human beings always find themselves in an intersubjectively constituted world of meanings. In a sense, the whole, the community, has a certain priority over its parts. This leads Gurwitsch to say that being in community with others is not a mere "*being together of individuals as individuals*" as with partnerships.[17] Members of communities are together in a manner that involves the mediation through the community and its inheritance. Thus co-members of a community do not need to be aware of other *individuals* specifically to whom they stand in this relation with as those in partnerships do–at least in the abstract sense of an appreciation of other roles to be played in the partnership relations.

This isn't to say that all aspects of one's life are under the control of a community, as Gurwitsch's language might seem to suggest. Rather, communities have limited boundaries.

> ...there remains to the member of the community a private sphere, i.e., a realm of life and action with respect to which the member does not grow older with others and for which, as a consequence, no regulations based on the life of the

community even exist. If he lives *in this relation,* then the members of the community (as well as the community in question) are determined as the members they are in their given case, namely as "present."[18]

As such, it is not a problem that there can be variant factions within a community. Rather, by community one only understands that *common ground* or *common basis* in reference to which one's life takes shape. Unlike functioning in society with others, which is determinative of roles one might play, being in community with others is determinative of a basic way of comportment. Partnerships dictate *what* we do relative to a situation, memberships dictate *how* we orient ourselves to our surroundings. Where partnerships are purpose oriented, memberships are context-determinative or context structuring.

There is a potential problem here for Mathiesen's plurality condition and Carr's requirement for a sense of unity in relation to the phenomenological account of plurality subjects presented in earlier chapters in the present work. A problem arises in relation to the potential for unity across a plurality in a nonbinding way, as is the cases with alliances against something in common. This only represents a *prima facie* problem, however, as there is an ambiguity in how "unity" is understood between the two instances. The face-value unity of the alliance is not as strict as the deeper sense of unity invoked in relation to memberships. Also, the sense of unity operative in the everyday sense of a we-intention, wherein a plural subject is intended, only need be of the former, weaker form. An accompanying sentiment is accidental to the basic act of a we-intention. For clarification, the sense of unity is not accident, but its strength or any accompaniment of sentimental affect is accidental to plural subjects as such–even if there are restrictions on these in relation to specific kinds of plural subjects.

A final form of intersubjective being Gurwitsch discusses is fusion. Gurwitsch uses the term group to specifically distinguish fusion from partnership (society) and membership (community). Fusion involves a state in which emotional bonds or feelings bear a constitutive meaning, "...*feeling as 'one'* and *identification.*"[19] "Feelings of being united as 'one' have a meaning for the constitution of groups as well as for the actual being together of the members of the group."[20] "The feeling united as 'one' with the 'spirit' is constitutive for being together in the group by which one is united as 'one' with another."[21] When fusion occurs, individual differences are "cancelled out."[22] Gurwitsch gives the example that churches function as communities, whereas cults–like the one in the Jonestown massacre–operate as groups in the specialized sense he gives that term here. Fusion is not just meaning-giving as community relations are, but is "world-making," transformative, and revolutionary.[23]

Fusion is not necessarily a pejorative category, as I would argue cults exploit the possibility of this type of relation and are not representative of the essence of fusion *per se,* only representative of one of its possible manifestations. Rather, this category appears to be what romantics think a marriage should be and this appears to be where one ought to place Aristotle's genuine friendships.

For instance, on marriage, and with an eye to the same sorts of cautionary worries Gurwitsch also expresses, Gilbert states: "The term 'fusion' may be an apt label for certain problematic forms of marital relationships. At the same time, many people have obviously thought that something aptly referred to as 'fusion' has the capacity to strongly enhance a marriage."[24] In both the case of the romantic notion of marriages and Aristotelian friendships one finds unities of individuals that involve rich identifications. Both involve notions of mutually reciprocated good will that unifies the individuals together through a strong bond, enhancing each individual's life without effacing their individuality.[25]

As a point of summation, partnerships are where one has a situation in common with another and in virtue of that situation one bears a role determined in virtue of how that situation is shaped, principally by the purpose(s) operative within it. Memberships are where one's background contexts and ways of orienting oneself and ascribing value is shared with others, as directed in relation to some shared positive sentiment in unification; the community(s) of one's birth on some level(s) are instances of memberships. Fusion is where individuals come together "as one" with others, where a deep sense of identification permeates the relation. These are not just common situations or common sentiments acting as unifiers between subjects, but where one's very sense of self and world-understanding "fuses" with another's.

In Gilbert's treatment of fusion she emphasizes that "every instance of fusion provides a basis for a *sense of unity*, even a sense of *intimacy* or *closeness* within the single 'we' that is involved"[26]; in addition to emphasizing the intensity, continuity of intensity, and stability as characteristic of such cases.[27] "Stable untrammeled fusion is likely to be reflected in a fully justified, strong sense of mutual trust."[28] Where in a membership the community's orientation and values are more or less constitutive of one's world-view or at least a partial view of some region of the world, a fusion with another is where one's own identity is constituted in reference to that relation. In memberships one can still identify herself as an autonomous individual and may reassess their membership with the community.[29] In fusion, one may retain actual autonomy, but their individuality becomes intrinsically tied to the other(s). While this should give some the creeps, I stress again that this need not be construed as wholly pejorative. There are positive social relations through which we consider our identities intrinsically wrapped up with others that aren't necessarily threats to our wellbeing as individuals.[30] Gilbert stresses a continuum of how totalizing a fusion can be from "the totally 'unfused' ego, the 'unjoined person'" to total homogenization of subjects.[31] While Gurwitsch would deny fusion in the cases of the person at the one extreme, I believe he would acknowledge some continuum along the lines of Gilbert's proposal. Though, Gilbert doesn't stress the identity formation component in her essay, she does note that one might call "*deep* fusion" those cases where fused subjects accept the joint value or whatever predicates their identification as a pairing of individuals can manifest itself as "*positively correlative fusion*."[32] This does not mean that Gilbert would think Gurwitsch's worries are illegitimate; she adds: "fusion as an ideal must, clearly be viewed with caution."[33] Yet, as Gilbert rightly points out, fusion *"does not require the obliteration of the egos in question."*[34]

Gurwitsch stresses that these are conceptual distinctions and that the three categories of partnership, membership and fusion do *not* designate *determinate* relations. "Instead, they involve the manner in which people *sociate* [*soziiert*] with one another in concrete social associations."[35] These are *modal categories*, not stages or a hierarchy of social relation. "The three 'modal categories' are fundamental regional-ontological categories precisely of the object-region, any *'societas'* whatever. ...*They constitute the Being-structure just of this and no other realm of objects.*"[36] This is important in that in everyday life the same people could stand in different modes of relations to one another simultaneously. For example, Venus and Serena Williams are sisters and also embody relations related to each of their professional tennis careers: as doubles-partners–which in a match involves fluid role changes depending on which of the pair is serving for instance–or as competitors in singles competition. They are both members of professional tennis associations and likely share other membership relations as well.

Construing these as modes of relations has the further benefit that doing so does not require us to reassess the nature of an individual's relation to others in essential terms. One does not need to afford a special metaphysical status to collectives or to assume subjective collectivism. Collectivities or groups are variable dynamic expressions of systems of intersubjective relations.[37] It is in lieu of this that they are able to bear predicates that their individual participants do not; the predicate is borne by the system of relations, attaching itself to that set of relations as its grammatical subject.

Gilbert might point out that one thing common to all three of Gurwitsch's identified modes of being with others is that they all have action-directed consequences. That is, one might argue Gurwitsch's view might support the primacy in her account of *Absicht* over *Intentionalität*, or a more co-dependent understanding of their relation that exonerates her account from the sorts of criticisms I raise in more detail further into this chapter. The problem with this response is that it collapses the *Absicht-Intentionalität* distinction with the theory-praxis distinction. It is right to stress that theory is naught without praxis, even that theory originates in and through praxis, just as it is also correct to emphasize that theory affects praxis.[38] As such it might seem reasonable to consider the same dynamic in relation to the two senses of intentionality. However, the analogy does not hold. *Intentionalität* is not a purely theoretical activity, just as *Absicht* is not strictly a form of praxis. Rather, both theory and praxis involve *Intentionalität*. Whether or not both involve *Absicht* will here be left an open question. That Gurwitsch's modes of being with others have action-directive consequences is a product of its being theory, especially within the phenomenological tradition with its habit of drawing connections to praxis; it is not owed to the presence of intentionality in the theoretical framework of Gurwitsch's analyses themselves.

One might ask whether Gilbert's view can be nicely fitted with a view like Gurwitsch's. It is natural to wonder if Gilbert's theory should be understood in relation to one or several of Gurwitsch's particular modes of relatedness with others. My suspicion is that Gilbert's analyses rather handily supplement and expand on Gurwitsch's first two senses of being with: partnership and membership. Though, perhaps Gurwitsch's account could offer greater clarity and distinction to how Gilbert addresses these different types of phenomena. In the case of fusion, it has already been shown that Gilbert has a discussion of the phenomena that tracks with Gurwitch's discussion nicely. Though, for Gilbert all plural subjects express fusion, just to variant degrees.[39] To this end, I believe both views can suggest improvements for one another. Gurwitsch's view could be improved by Gilbert's discussions of the variant ways in which fusion can manifest, as she better details how fusion need not be problematic even if it does contain a danger for effacing individuality. Gilbert's view could be improved by restricting the sense of fusion to a specific type of plural subject experience as opposed to any and all. At the very least cause is given to introduce a qualitative distinction into Gilbert's view for clarity's sake; as strangers conversing on a bus don't obviously share the same kind of bond that the genuine Aristotelian friendship expresses. Further, the grounding in a broader theoretical context of intentionality as such, and not just action-oriented intent, should further ground and strengthen the basic intuitions Gilbert has, even if requiring some restructuring and revision at the same time. A phenomenological account should be largely commensurable with Gilbert's basic intuitions, especially when understanding those as involving principal interest in addressing the domain of action-oriented intent in the collective mode. The integration and grounding of the social ontology in relation to the ontology of consciousness is important and necessary, given that the social world is both described in terms of and is grounded on acts of consciousness.

Many of our experiences of the world involve co-intentional references of or to others, in varied capacities and levels of determinateness. When one intends socially constituted objects or states of affairs (e.g. money, economies), artifacts (e.g. tools, televisions, works of art), or institutions (e.g. the Federal Reserve, universities), one's experience involves tacit references to others. All social objects are dependent on intersubjective belief and collective acceptance or adherence–not to be taken in all cases as an expression of endorsement or preference.[40] Social objects or meanings are not things that are possible without an intersubjective or social context. Given the necessity of that context and its essentially social nature, others are tacitly referenced by one's intentions of objects, events or states of affairs dependent on them. For example, experiencing a work of art as a work of art involves a determinate or indeterminate reference to someone as its creator. In addition it indirectly implicates others involved in one's linguistic community whose conceptual categorization schemes one applies in the expression of one's articulate experience of the work of art as work of art. One's experience, if in the context of a museum or gallery, might also co-reference those institutions and their members. The experience might be constituted as viewing with others if public or as involving systems of exchange if at auction. These references to others are an abstract *part*–a moment in Husserlian terminology–of the intersubjective character of the content of one's experience. Not only a part of its *content*, it is a requisite part of that content's sense-formation and sense-articulation, as one experiences always articulate wholes of certain kinds; one never first experiences bare qualia, such as redness or blueness. Others are not parts of the individual's *act* of intending social objects, but the acts of intentionality of others, constitutive of social objects, are tacitly or indirectly referenced in through that content, being that they are necessary conditions to *intersubjectively* constituted contents and their iterated levels of meanings. None of this entails a notion of collective consciousness, or collective intentionality whose act-structure transcends individual consciousness' standing in relation to one another as *individual*. Strong instances of "we" experiences, involving we-intentions, include and reference others as being privy to the contents of their own subjective experiences. The priority of the shared experience over shared action emphasized by Carr is apt. It is that common ground which is part of what is implicit in one's inclusion of others in their "we," with variant grades of determinateness. Determinate cases are where one has in mind particular persons or a particular grouping of persons. Indeterminate cases leave unspecified the particular subjects of co-reference, though it is not clear that requires indeterminacy of the socially constituted content itself in respect of one's intentional experience.

Husserl accepts a basis of shared experiences. Husserl's transcendental interests also lead him to appeal, in more substantive ways to shared conditions for experience. The transcendental preconditions for human experience factor into the shared commonalities that base the collective intentional formations. This can be seen through the use of the Leibnizian metaphor of the monad used in some of Husserl's writings. In more basic language, Husserl was keen on underscoring the formal continuities that figure into establishing the range of material possibilities. There is a formal structure to an experience as an experience. Some conditions for experience are: someone for whom there is *experience*, consciousness, intentionality, etc. As such any subjectivity, any conscious experiencing being, has some basic formal similarities with all others in virtue of that capacity. Human being happens to be one specific instance of this general form. Being a human being itself brings further formal constraints to the material nature of experience–as I doubt any would argue that dog consciousness is identical to human consciousness, though both are instances of consciousness. The metaphor of the monad is intended only to allow some means of speaking about the general formal characteristics which underlie intersubjectivity as such, of which interpersonal human interactions represent more specific materially informed instances.

Husserl speaks also of higher order pluralities, I understand these to refer to intersubjectively constituted hierarchies of meaning, what contemporary philosophy has rediscovered in the collective intentionality literature. Higher order pluralities function not as entities endowed with consciousness in their own right, but as a sort of short-hand in reference: in terms of subjects who are participants to these groupings, subjects co-intended as operating in and contributing to these particular domains of reference (individuated worlds), and contents available in meaning.

Gilbert on Plural Subjects

I turn now to an examination of one of the more established view of plural subjects in the contemporary literature, that of Margaret Gilbert. I begin by laying out Gilbert's position on plural subjects, then subject her account to critique. I argue that Gilbert's view, while powerful in many respects, is inadequate. Her normative emphasis is not adequately founded on a pre-normative foundation; more pointedly her view is not wholly consistent with a broader ontology within which it should be situated. This inadequacy stems from its failure to be sufficiently based in an adequate phenomenology. The strength of Gilbert's position rests in its astute moral analysis.

If moral values depend on non-moral properties and relations to have sense, then the account one gives pertaining to the key non-moral or pre-moral properties and relations should bear significantly important implications for how one understands the former. On this view, the analysis of what constitutes the grounding phenomena for moral values and other forms of value will carry specific sorts of constraints for the value-oriented analyses.[41] For instance, the theory of intentionality one adheres to will impact the theory of collective intentionality and anything that follows from that in regard to moral analysis of social wholes dependently related to collective intentionality. This is likely why some in collective intentionality circles appear interested in establishing reference to some theory of mind as a background to their views.[42]

Even if there is no dependence relation for moral values on non-moral properties, there remains a question as to whether or not Gilbert's account, which is heavily dependent on subjective psychological states, is based on a sufficiently basic understanding of the phenomenology of or ontology of consciousness. Were a view of the social world inconsistent with the nature of consciousness, and consciousness is accepted as standing in a foundational relation to the social world, that would pose a serious problem. My view is that Gilbert's position has difficulties avoidable where a more comprehensive understanding of the phenomenology of consciousness is presented. Specifically, I believe that Gilbert's view has difficulties brought on by the dependence her view of plural subjects has to individual psychology, to consciousness; difficulties that could be avoided by a more systematic phenomenological analysis. By contrasting Gilbert's view on plural subjects with David Carr's one can see problems latent in Gilbert's view more clearly, as well as to see what a more complete phenomenology might entail. The problems stem from an insufficiently basic notion of plural-subjecthood in distinction from what a phenomenologically rigorous account would offer.[43] In this chapter, then, I aim to show the shortcomings of Gilbert's view in relation to phenomenology and propose revisions.

Gilbert defines "plural subject" thus: "A plural subject in my sense is founded on what I call a *joint commitment*. Two or more people constitute the plural subject of a goal, for instance, if they are jointly committed to accepting that goal together, or, as I have preferred to put it, *as a body*."[44] In another instance, she states: "People form a plural subject, in my sense, when they are jointly committed to doing something as a body, in a broad sense of 'do.'"[45] Gilbert also refers to a "plural subject perspective,"[46] and offers a more formal definition:

> For persons A and B and psychological attribute X, A and B form a *plural subject* of X-ing if and only if A and B are jointly committed to X-ing as a body, or, if you like, as a single person.[47]

Accidental coincidences of psychological states or shared experiences, a loose sense of "we," are once again treated as insufficient to form a plural subject. Rather, what is necessary is a stronger sense of "we," one dependent on some firmer basis. What is troubling however is the notion of *joint commitment,* as it presupposes a much less basic starting point than the bare sort of experience that one might otherwise utilize. Gilbert's model is dialogical; the phenomenologist seeks something more primitive, something that underlies the possibility for the dialogical model. A dialogical model operates on the level of language. Yet, Gilbert relies heavily on appeals to psychological states, states of consciousness in the grounding for plural subjects. The role of psychological states operating in her view of plural subjects makes her view liable to critique in relation to an ontology of consciousness. Phenomenology provides an ontology of consciousness (a model of first-personal experience).[48] As such, if Gilbert's view is in tension with the underlying phenomenology or ontology, then proposals for revision should be made and the charge of being in conflict with what's basic to the phenomenology or ontology of consciousness is substantiated, as I hope to demonstrate.[49] One should stress that Gilbert's view is not wholly inconsistent with phenomenology, and I do not intend to be offering a critique of the whole of her view, only to critique its assumptions and to propose adjustments accordingly.

Gilbert also focuses on worldly conditions as bearing on plural-subjecthood–that A and B each are in the right frame of mind *and* both committed to collective belief, action, etc. For Gilbert, if A daydreams about doing something with B, that does not involve a plural subject. Phenomenologically, however, it would appear that A's daydreaming of "our" action, essentially inclusive with B, would involve a plural subject. This underscores part of the difference between the two views, as the experience of a plural subject is had in daydreaming, and that doesn't necessitate a state of affairs in the world involving B as such. This is because the *act* of consciousness was *daydreaming*. As such, the conditions for fulfillment of what is daydreamt reference the daydream

itself, not anything else. If it is true that A's daydream was of their action together with B, then A's daydream is evidenced. Deny this and one can't make
sense of how A's daydream was of something *together* with B, in that one would
deny that the daydreamt action was experienced as plural in nature. Phenomenology is interested in offering description of what sort of act of consciousness
is operative in cases where one experiences something *as shared, as together,*
with others in experience itself, less so than dictating on the basis of theoretical
constraints what must be the case. Changes in act-type alter the conditions for
satisfaction or fulfillment, even if the contents of the experience are the same in
both cases, just as changes in content-type also alter the conditions for fulfillment, regardless of act-type identity.[50]

A further consequence of a phenomenological position on plural subjects is
that it will allow us to diagnose why collectivist leaning authors overreach, and
impart consciousness to a plural subject (implicitly reifying the plural subject
into an object that is able to have consciousness predicated of it) by appending
speculative argumentation to phenomenology. Insofar as the plural subject or
collective intentionality can be understood as a ground for all higher-order intersubjective constitutional achievements, plural subjects and collective intentionality represents an integral part of a complete account of intersubjectivity. Plural
subjects or collective intentionality are essential parts of such things as common
meanings like those found in language, cultural objects, social objects, institutions, etc.

Gilbert's Plural Subject Theory

Gilbert calls the intentions of a plural subject, intentions of the form "we intend to do A," shared intentions. One may thereby count shared intentions as
species of collective intentions. Gilbert identifies three criteria for an account of
shared intention: 1) obligation, 2) permission, and 3) compatibility with the lack
of the corresponding personal intentions.[51] In addition, she stipulates that having
a shared intention minimally means "both parties know they share the intention
in question and both know this is so."[52] For present purposes, collective intentions are understood as any intention the expression of which requires a we-form.
Plural subjects are the subject implicated or referenced in a collective intention,
the *who* of the *we*. All plural subjects thus entail collective intentions. As such,
one can say that plural subjects are coextensive with collective intentions.[53]
Shared intentions are, for present purposes, counted as specialized instances of
collective intentions, "we x" where the plural subject is related or directed toward action, as per Gilbert's view. As such, Gilbert's could be thought to be
more specialized, representing a narrower set of phenomena than the broader
phenomenological account. In the broader account, recall that collective intentions are not necessarily action oriented, e.g. "we heard Beethoven's *Pathetique*."
It is argued that the broader collective intentional account is not wholly consistent with Gilbert's specialized view.

Regarding obligation, Gilbert uses an example of two persons walking together. When one stops, the other rebukes her for violating their agreement to walk together. From her example, she believes three conceptual features regarding the criteria for obligation relative to plural subjects may be discerned. These are:

"First, each participant has an obligation not to act contrary to the shared intention."

"Second, corresponding to these obligations are rights or entitlements of the other parties to the appropriate performances."

"Third, if one participant does something contrary to the shared intention, the others have a special entitlement to rebuke that person." [54]

If two individuals share an understanding that they are to do something together an obligation arises on the basis of that shared understanding. That obligation corresponds to a right of expectation relative to the fulfillment of the understood course of action. A failure by one party to the shared intention to fulfill their obligation entitles others involved to chastise the person for their failure. For instance, if on a football field a player misinterprets the call in the huddle and does not execute the play called in the huddle, their teammates have a right to chastise the failure to execute the play as called.

In respect to the second criteria, permission, Gilbert states: "Participants in a shared intention understand that they are not in a position to remove its constraints unilaterally by a simple change of mind, announced or unannounced. The concurrence of the other participants must first be obtained." [55] When we do something together with others the fact that it is *together* with others, and not coincident with others individually, means that to retain the togetherness of the action *one* cannot act alone to redirect *our* actions. For instance, if a football player decides on his own that an alternative play would be preferable they can't by stroke of their individual action affect a new plan of action for the group.

One might argue that this is precisely what happens when an audible is called prior to the snap: where there is a change of play by the quarterback, or a coverage or blocking scheme change by a position leader. In such cases, while it is an individual whose announced action does effect a change for the team or positional scheme on the field, it is not without the implicit permission of the other parties involved. Part of the game involves the other players' acknowledgement beforehand that the quarterback has the authority to revise their play scheme prior to the snap. Those individuals maintain a tacit permission to make alterations in a way that does not constitute an adequate counter-example. This is similar to where a singular executive mandates or institutes change governing an institutional policy. The authority of their declarative act is dependent on an underlying acceptance of such authority being held by that office or individual in the context of the institution. [56] This is to say that apparent cases of counter-examples to Gilbert's point regarding the collective acceptance underlying changes of plural subject aims actually conform to her account on analysis.

By the third criteria for shared intentions that contribute to plural subjects, compatibility with the lack of the corresponding personal intentions, Gilbert says "...(at a minimum) each of us must personally intend to behave appropriately to our doing A,"[57] where A is the action of the shared intention. A shared intention has directive influence in relation to the action of the individual participants in a plural subject. My intention that "we *x*" affects how I act in some significant fashion that is not reducible merely to the individually referential intentions of participating parties, i.e. not reducible to a set of intentions expressible in the form "I intend *x*" and "you intend *x*." A further reason for this criterion is that Gilbert notes how individuals involved in group activity don't always agree with the action chosen by the group. Individuals who are part of a plural subject might not engage in the action of the plural subject were they to act individually. As part of a group or plural action, however, one does act in such a manner, whether or not they agree or would engage in the action individually. This underscores the non-reducible nature of shared intentions. "My central claim is that *it is apparently possible in principle that the corresponding personal intentions are lacking when a shared intention is present.*"[58] Consider, for example, the case of a whistleblower. While whistleblowers are often complicit in questionable actions taken on the part of their corporation or group, they also often object to the actions themselves, sometimes prior to or simultaneous with the action's performance.[59] Another example would be of a politician who publicly tows the party line while privately disagreeing with their party's position on the issues in question. The basic point being that with a shared intention, or intention in the we-form, it is possible that the we-intention be compatible with the lack of an I-intention directed at the same end. This is because there is no equivalence between individuals and communities.[60] A community, as individuated, is not equivalent to the mere sum of its individual subject members or parts.

Gilbert puts all of this together in what she calls Schema S. The key elements of Schema S are: "For the relevant psychological predicate '*X*' and persons *P1* and *P2*, *P1* or *P2* may truly say 'We *X*' with respect to *P1* and *P2* if and only if *P1* and *P2* are *jointly committed* to *X*-ing *as a body*."[61] When *P1* and *P2* are jointly committed to *X*-ing as a body, "they constitute what I call a *plural subject*."[62] Gilbert acknowledges that one might object to the phrase "as a body," as was done in relation to Carr's account earlier. Gilbert considers "as a body" to be substitutable with "as a unit" and one adds, for further clarity, "as one."[63] The ground for that singularity of action or intention, what unifies this set of individuals, is a joint commitment.

It is important to note in relation to present purposes that Gilbert expressly appeals to psychological states. I assume that by 'psychological state' Gilbert refers to a state of consciousness. If so, the nature of those psychological states must be consistent with a broader understanding of consciousness and intentionality. If this assumption is not accurate, I am uncertain what is meant by reference to psychology.

A joint commitment is precisely a commitment to and for those parties involved. An example is offered for emphasis: "Ruth and Lil's joint commitment is, precisely, the commitment *of Ruth and Lil*."[64] Joint commitments are based on common knowledge and they are "not an aggregate of personal [individual] commitments."[65] Gilbert understands this to mean that "...a joint commitment does not properly speaking have *parts*."[66] Gilbert understands we-intentions to be basic in the sense that they aren't founded on I-intentions, plural subject intentions are not founded on singular subject intentions. The claim that they have *no* parts whatsoever is mistaken. This is not to quarrel by claiming that we-intentions decompose into more basic intentional states. Rather, it is to disambiguate, pointing out that all intentional states have parts: we-intentions have parts just in the same manner that singular-intentions do: act-characters, act-matters, contents, etc.[67]

In sum, there are three discernable elements that Gilbert understands as operating in conjunction with one another: joint commitment, shared intention, and plural subject. She states "Persons *P1* and *P2* have a shared intention to do *A* if and only if they are jointly committed to intending as a body to do *A*."[68] And, "Persons *P1* and *P2* have a shared intention to do *A* if and only if they constitute the plural subject of an intention to do *A*."[69] In other words, a set of individuals are not said to act or operate as one, as a plural subject, unless they are jointly committed to something. And that joint commitment to common action if it involves uniformity of action, gives rise to a shared intention. Not only is a joint commitment necessary for a plural subject, but it is necessary for there to be some prior understanding of what a joint commitment is as well. Gilbert claims, "One cannot be subject to a joint commitment without having the concept of a joint commitment and having exercised it."[70]

Critique of Gilbert's View

Now that Gilbert's account of plural subjects has been presented, let us examine where it has potential problems; again with specific interest as to a contrast with the phenomenological account of plural subjects. A first place where Gilbert's view runs into conflict with the phenomenology is in everyday cases where individuals experience a 'we,' with its full sense of togetherness; for instance, an individual's experience with their pet or a child's imaginings. Both types of cases fail on Gilbert's account in virtue of the failure of possible joint commitment on the part of the other(s) intended. Further, children, even of very young ages, play together in rather sophisticated ways without any sense of what a joint commitment is or pressing concerns over even loosely defined obligations.[71] Michael Tomasello's research into preverbal children, for instance, demonstrates the possibility of cooperation prior to conceptualization.[72] Also, those with mental disabilities or deficiencies regularly have experiences describable as together with others, yet it's unclear how they can always be said to have a concept of joint commitment. Granted, Gilbert might respond by arguing that

that is ground for not holding such individuals responsible. But this only underscores the differences between her theory of plural subjects of action–with an emphasis on moral evaluation–and a phenomenological theory of plural subjects–with an emphasis on describing the most basic sense of being together with another. Even many animal species behave in social forms that aren't easily accounted for in terms of aggregate individually directed intentionality. Where in all of this is there an operating sense of "joint commitment" or obligation that governs these interactions? I take this as a critical weakness in Gilbert's view, in virtue of her choice of a theoretical starting point which foists abstract constraints contrary to the evidence instead of beginning from the body of evidence and working from there. The baseline for an account of plural subjects, even if it is a paradigmatic sort of case, should not begin and end with the interactions between fully articulated rational adults–regardless of whether or not this is the type of experience philosophers are most familiar with in relation to their work.

Before I turn to the specific examples, I want to deflect the charge that my criticisms are being unfair to Gilbert. In *On Social Facts*, Gilbert characterizes her approach as an *intentionalist* approach.[73] On her view, "if we are to give an adequate account of our everyday concept of a social group, we will have to appeal to the intentional or meaningful acts of human beings."[74] One gets the sense here that 'intentional' refers to purposefulness or intent, and not the aboutness or directedness of the experience. In the chapter in which she defends the view, one position she defends is that of "the logical independence of intentions from society."[75] And it is her view that the "concept of a human social group can indeed be explicated in terms of human thoughts and intentions."[76] All of these statements demonstrate that Gilbert's view is that she is articulating a view predicated on the intentionality latent in thought as being foundational to social wholes. Gilbert is open to criticisms from the phenomenologist regarding how she orders the intentional achievements in question and how well her analysis captures the intentionality of lived experiences.

In fairness to Gilbert, her view has shifted some since *On Social Facts*. She speaks less about psychological states now. Consider, for instance, where she argues:

> [J]oint commitments are not necessarily brought into being with any clear conscious intent to do so. ...[P]eople may relatively unconsciously take up one another's relatively unconscious hints to the point that they become confident that there is a joint commitment, without being able to point to the time it came into being.[77]

There are a couple problems with this claim, if taken too broadly. Gilbert is only denying that all joint commitments are formed expressly or with full cognizance of the participating subject(s). This does not entail that the structure of a joint commitment is not intentional. Even if one can claim the joint commitment arose without explicit or premeditated intent [*Absicht*], as a joint commitment it is still a commitment about what we are to do together and therefore intentional

[*Intentionalität*]. The basic problem remains, as joint commitments are about something or directed towards our doing something together. Even if one can't say exactly what the commitment's express nature is, one must have some less determinate sense about it in order for it to direct one's actions or beliefs. Joint commitments require intentionality.

Phenomenological Instances of Plural Subjects that Fail to Meet Gilbert's Criteria

I argue that an individual can have the experience of a joint commitment irrespective of whether or not the party(s) they experience having a joint commitment with themselves reciprocate. The apparent cases in individual experience and genuine cases, with respect to the state of affairs at large, should be the same in all respects, except for the lack of the possibility of intentional fulfillment in the case of the former. Nonetheless, the experience, as experience for a subject, is real. This is precisely where Gilbert's view of plural subjects and the phenomenological position diverge. The phenomenologist argues that Gilbert puts the success conditions prior to that which the success is predicated upon, i.e. she is inverting the order of intention and evidence. More specifically, Gilbert is dictating that a *de facto* joint commitment be prior to the experiences had by the individual subjects of that joint commitment. Individuals must experience joint commitment, implicitly or expressly experience of oneself as being part of a group, in order for there to be a joint commitment. Those experiences themselves are not dependent on the consequent factual state of affairs of the resultant *de facto* plural subject. The individual plural subject experiences carry the same meaning-content in intention that the *de facto* state of affairs does. As such, the *de facto* state of affairs is not necessary in order for an individual to have a plural subject experience. Further, one can experience being part of a "we," with all the connotative elements, obligations, etc., that are brought with said experience without there being a state of affairs in the world to satisfy the experience's intention in evidence. As such, the examples in this section focus on what an *individual* can experience as to the *experience* of a joint commitment, or the set of conditions Gilbert provides for such. Phenomenologically, the experiences of obligation, commitment, guilt, etc., are important and real to one's experience. Even if instances of "Jewish guilt" or "Catholic guilt" are not warranted, to the subjects experiencing them they are very real. Granted, one might ask as to whether or not that which one experiences is rational or not. But this does not discount what is experienced as unimportant and one can't discount what individuals experience as unimportant where one accepts their psychology or intentionality to be constitutive of the phenomena.

Take as a first case going for a walk with one's dog or playing Frisbee with one's dog. For argument's sake, consider that the dog is a German Shepherd. In this respect one can also allow into the range of phenomena to consider those acts of canine companions who are specifically trained to be able to assist human beings. Many people have experienced having a pet, or even a working animal companion in the case of the disabled, epileptic, or elderly. What can Gilbert's view say in relation to simple things like a family taking their dog for a walk or a child playing with their dog?

Leave aside for a moment the question as to whether or not one's dog can be said to be in the "right frame of mind" on Gilbert's view. It seems we might be able to grant that obligation and permission both factor into the experience of taking one's dog for a walk. When one walks their dog they have expectations as to the dog's behavior on their walk. Owners who are more familiar with training their animal are better at defining and projecting their animal's "obligations" or expectations for their walk.[78] A well-trained dog, for instance, should sit when their handler stops, heel while walking at a pace with their handler and follow their handler's signals as to changes in direction, even if the handler is a toddler.[79] The better trained the animal, the better understanding between both handler and animal as to the system of rebukes for failures of cooperation. Indeed, one might argue that the dog projects some of their own expectations as to their handler's leading them. The animal expects not to be scolded if it follows directions and the handler expects the animal's cooperation as well. In some sense the animal knows who is in charge of setting the pace or which direction they are to proceed. Less able handlers often cede the alpha (directive) role to the animal, where more apt parties project the alpha status in relation to their pet, that is they fail to project a superior "rank" in the pack order to the animal and animal behaviors are very predictable in virtue of the understanding of "rank" order.[80]

As per the question of the lack of a compatible personal intention, this is where Gilbert might object to the example. It seems clear, however, that "I intend to take the dog for a walk" need not be a necessary condition for our, the dog's and my going for a walk together. A conscientious animal owner will appreciate that even if they, the human being, doesn't want to go for a walk or entertain their animal's request for play, that they ought to despite a lack of personal interest. Even if this is a contentious example, it is consistent with Gilbert's requirement for a lack of personal intention. The action in question is undertaken because of what the plural relation requires of the individual, and could not be accounted for solely with reference to the individual's motivations taken singularly. In addition, if Gilbert's view is that the animal cannot possibly have the psychological state necessary for participation in a plural subject then the animal can't possibly fail this criterion any more than a rock or tomato plant could. The inability to have the compatible personal intention as psychological state whatsoever is consistent with her criterion for consistency with the lack of that compatible personal intention.

It seems unambiguously clear that animals have consciousness, and having consciousness, i.e. having experiences, requires intentionality–as experiences are about things.[81] This is true even if animal consciousnesses are not as sophisticated in terms of a set of capabilities as the consciousness manifest in human beings.[82] Animals clearly experience objects–they can distinguish between food and non-food, danger and safety, etc. That a dog can chase a Frisbee requires that a dog be able to have an experience of said object. Granted, dogs don't have the linguistic category or abilities to generalize away from particulars to the best of our knowledge. Accepting that some form of consciousness is present in animal species, and given that many animal species tend to have some form of social organization, it seems clear that animals are capable on some level of group behavior. Granted, one should admit of a gradation of sophistication, perhaps denying non-human animals the capacity to iterate their social intentions or organize them into systems dissociable from immediate interests. If Gilbert's view would ignore both the human interaction with animals and animals' own interactions with one another, it seems clear that it cannot be a complete account of how *experiences* together with other beings can be constituted. An account that can't deal with very primitive or simplistic experiences–no matter its merits at the higher levels of sophistication–is necessarily incomplete and is in wont of revision. The point is that where human interactions with animals are experienced *as* social in nature, Gilbert has potential problems.

Gilbert would respond by pointing out that one is appealing to complicated cases, and that one ought to begin their analysis by *"using the least ambiguous data."*[83] In *On Social Facts,* she considers the case of infants and their relation to the social world.[84] She acknowledges that such questions are complicated, and rely more on assumptions about the intentionality infants are capable of than evidence. For instance, she notes that we project onto infants more than is probably actually happening in their minds.[85] Granted, this is accurate and one might be doing this with non-human animals to some extent as well. However, none of this negates that infants and non-human animals are conscious, and if conscious there is intentionality of some form operative in their experiences by necessity. The problem, I argue, stems from how Gilbert understands intentionality. More of the differences between the classical theory of intentionality and contemporary uses of the term are noted in earlier parts of the work and are again revisited below. While I have no objection that her view might begin from simpler cases and work to extend itself to more complex ones, what I'm arguing in this section is that her view as it is presented actually fails to adequately handle those more primitive cases and that further work is therefore required.

Take as a second case where the phenomenology would be present, but which won't pass on Gilbert's view: the projections of children, considering especially very young children (not infants in this case). Søren says to his mother, "We are going to have a party," but Søren is speaking of him and his stuffed animals. Or take a child's utterance of "we" as inclusive of their pet rock or their tomato plant. Where the previous case of animals pairs our experiences with other animate organisms, other conscious beings, these cases exhibit how a "we" can range in experience to include inanimate objects. That is, "we" is not restricted as to its application in relation to only other human beings. If a child is at play with their stuffed animals, and their experiences are of something as *together* with their stuffed animal, I see no good reason not to count that as another intentional act ranging over a plural subject, "we" being inclusive of the child and their stuffed animal. In other words, the projection of a we-intention does not in itself always demand reciprocity from those inclusive to the intentions. Reciprocation is too strict a criteria if we are describing experience as such and not only offering an account of success conditions, the dependence on which moral evaluations are predicated. More "grown up" examples include where members of a corporation count the software or computer systems they use to be a part of the group's constitution; or, a cyberneticist's intending that "we are going for a walk about campus" where "we" refers to their team and their robot. Whether or not these are anthropomorphizing intentional gestures without evidentiary merit, we regularly express such thoughts and experience the world this way.[86] What such experiences are inclusive of is arguably a meaningful part of how one understands a plural subject's unity as distinct from the mere collection of members. Children don't experience a lack of unity with their stuffed animals in play–they even rebuke them for their imagined transgressions!

Gilbert's view is oriented such that plural subjects can only be experienced in relation to sentient beings with a sufficient rational capacity. My critique amounts to pointing out that other sentient beings, non-human animals, and even non-sentient beings can be included in an individual's plural subject intention (experiences one has *as–or about*–something as together with another). Where I believe Gilbert goes wrong is in failing to respect the distinction between conditions for satisfaction and conditions for intention or experience in the first place. This stems from a failure to first appreciate the range of possible act-types that can be at play in experience.

Our experiences of a singular content aren't bound by a singular act-type. It isn't as if there is just "I thinks" or "I intends," there are an array of species of intentional acts. Different act-types, or modes of experiencing a content if one prefers, bear distinctly different conditions for fulfillment. "I saw a unicorn" and "I imagined a unicorn" refer to two very different types of act, the latter can be fulfilled with evidence; the former–barring some unknown instance in the universe of an actual unicorn–is essentially an empty intention, i.e. an intention incapable of fulfillment through evidence or adequation in experience. Pet owners, children with active imaginations, the psychologically disturbed, and most normal everyday people have experiences or have intentions that don't bear out in respect to the evidence or fail to achieve fulfillment. Gilbert may be assuming that "we" is restricted to one act-type or one species of act-types, or at the very least assumes that plural subjects are only meaningfully understood in relation to satisfied or fulfilled intentions. This wouldn't be a problem for her if her view were restricted only to a very specific range of phenomena.

In addition to the self-avowed intentionalist approach, when Gilbert discusses the influence of David Lewis on her view, she offers no objection to referring to all actions, beliefs, preferences, etc. as "actions."[87] This is very important if one recalls that Gilbert stresses in her initial characterizations of plural subject that they involve joint commitments to doing things as a uniform body "in a broad sense of 'do.'" She understands herself as giving an account of plural subjects as such–presumably including having perceptual experiences together with others. If the types of experiences I point to are experience in which *we do* X, then they are types of experiences her view purports to cover by her own admission. The imaginative projections of children aren't non-sensical; they are real experiences, experiences directed at or about doing things with others, whether real or fictional.[88] Certainly they are a different type of experience from the narrowly construed action-oriented view of Gilbert. Then again, walking with one's dog is meaningful as an experience and it represents an instance of Gilbert's action-directed type of intentional act that her view appears to be unable to account for.

Another problem for Gilbert's view is with simple cases of shared perceptual experience, the sorts that Carr and Gurwitsch count as relatively basic to experience. These also don't appear to have any ready consistency with Gilbert's view. For Gilbert our experience of taking in the sight of Denali in Alaska is not sufficient in itself to constitute a plural subject, nor seeing the Dalai Lama speak, nor listening to an orchestral performance of a Beethoven symphony, etc. All of these are experiences had together with others, experiences about what we do together and which bear as basic to those experiences the sense of togetherness. They are not aggregated experiences, but experiences had in a we-mode. Each is an experience of something as *together* with another or others. "We are looking across Glacier National Park at Denali" is something that is meaningful. Neither party needs the other's permission to experience it. That it is experienced as together is not accidental to the individuals taking in North America's highest peak. Nor are there any obligations at work in experiencing Denali together in this way. There may have been obligations at play in our trek together to our viewing point, but not in relation to perceiving Denali itself. Whether or not that is experienced as intended in common seems less important than that there is another subject essentially co-intended in relation to one's experience, in whatever mode that experience manifests. This follows if one accepts that we-intentions are not reducible to I-intentions and accepts that we-intentions are possible in relation to the perceptual experience of something as being perceived in common with others. "We" and "I" are each formally indicative with respect to how act-content correlation manifests in experience.

Gilbertian Plural Subjects that Fail to Qualify on the Phenomenological Model

There are also cases where a Gilbertian plural subject might be satisfied, but the phenomenological plural subject is suspect. For instance, splitting a cab with someone or two persons "hooking up" for a casual sexual experience. While both experiences might pass on Gilbert's notion of a plural subject, both are unclear in relation to the phenomenology at various levels, especially in relation to those complex action-oriented dimensions around which Gilbert's view is built. In splitting a cab with a stranger it is possible that both parties are merely acting as individuals seeking to arrive at proximate but distinct destinations or even the same destination. For anyone who's traveled alone and has ridden in an airport shuttle to a conference, this is sort of the experience I have in mind. However, where an airport shuttle might not count as a plural subject on Gilbert's view,[89] as each individual pays their individual fare, splitting a cab would—as there is *one* fare to be split by the parties involved. There is a tacit appreciation in splitting a cab that the fare is split—in many cases in half. If one party bolts from the cab without paying a share, the other is rightly allowed to count that as a betrayal and to express their right for the other's share. And the intent to split a cab is consistent with the lack of a personal intention to take a cab—one might rather take the train or a shuttle, but the opportunity to save a bit in splitting a cab and expedite one's travel presents itself as an appealing alternative. Similarly, the party who bolted without paying their share might never have intended to split the fare even if they intended to take advantage of the cab's services.

The other example, that of a causal sexual encounter, also requires multiple parties to participate and presumably counts as a plural subject on Gilbert's view given the shared action in common, the sexual activity. However, here again one can see—I presume—how the individual parties might not have any interest or experience of this in a plural mode beyond the most basic perceptual levels. Or even just in so far as there be another to make the act possible, where *who* is entirely fungible. One imagines that a transaction with a prostitute might also function this way—as one party is primarily engaged in a financial transaction, where the other is seeking to be engaged in sexual activity. Both understand their commerce with the other differently yet appear to "act as a body" to a third-personal observer. Such an arrangement appears to have an obligation structure, permissions likely related to an economic scale, and the compatibility with lack of personal intention given that an act requiring multiple parties is not something that individuals can intend in isolation (cases of failure to have a plural structure extended across both parties' intentionality are, of course, generally identified as rape).

It should strike one as odd that a plural subject could be constituted without a permeating sense of togetherness in relation to the experience at hand. Some normally plurally-conditioned activities appear to be instances of individuals co-functioning as opposed to operating together. In more general terms, third-personal objective descriptions are not always consistent with first-personal phenomenological descriptions. If psychological states are important to Gilbert's view, as it seems they should be, then some further accounting for how subjective experiences aren't pre-figured by third-personal observational categories is in order. Carr underscored this with his *qualitative* distinctions.

It should concern one if a Gilbertian plural subject would fail to also constitute a plural subject in the more basic phenomenological sense outlined in the previous chapters. This would be cause for concern in that it should not be possible to lack the essential sense of togetherness constitutive of the plural subject in the phenomenological sense in relation to the plural subject's unity on Gilbert's view. This should strike one as counter-intuitive, if not impossible. However, there should be little, if any, concern regarding cases of phenomenological plural subjects that don't meet the criteria of Gilbert's account. If one accepts that not all plural subject experiences are essentially normative, while allowing that the specific action-oriented cases of Gilbert's direct concern are essentially normatively conditioned, one avoids problems. One avoids potential problems this way in that one can account for that normativity either with the prior non-normative or proto-normative[90] phenomenological ground in shared experience or in virtue of some species-specific properties of the sort Gilbert bases her view on. For instance, one recognizes there are expectational structures to experience, and that these are not necessarily accompanied by the sense of force associated with a traditional norm.

Gilbert would likely respond that what I count as a plural subject in the phenomenological sense is not a plural subject on her view, as it lacks a joint commitment. This response is inadequate, however, as what the phenomenology points to is what constitutes the grounding phenomena for joint commitments and Gilbert's more restricted sense of plural subject. As argued in first establishing the phenomenological account, shared experience is the ground for shared action. Here one expands on that point and asserts that joint commitments are not possible without shared experiential foundations. Even if joint commitments might be said to be simultaneous with a Gilbertian plural subject, something must motivate one to form a Gilbertian plural subject in the first place. Without some prior sense of togetherness or plurality, it's not clear how a Gilbertian plural subject ever could be formed or sustained.

Gilbert's Criticisms of Searle's Subjective Individualism and Response

Gilbert responds to the sort of subjective individualist position at work here where she criticizes Searle's position. She identifies two senses of holism, her term for what she opposes to individualism, which others have termed collectivism. Gilbert understands internal holism to be where "…according to one's account of shared intention the *participants* in such an intention irreducibly ascribe to an action to something they together constitute."[91] External holism is where "…if one's account of shared intention itself irreducibly ascribes an action to the participants in a shared intention."[92] Her view is that Searle's position is one that embraces internal holism and rejects external holism.[93] She counts her own view by contrast as holistic in both senses.[94] In terms of labeling both accounts by these standards, I find no fault.[95]

Of Searle's view Gilbert claims:

> It is not clear how, on [Searle's] account, one is to explain the obligations and entitlements I have argued to be inevitably associated with shared intention and action. Nor is it clear how to explain that, as I have also argued, those who take

themselves to be acting together in the relevant sense inevitably understand themselves to have these obligations and entitlements.[96]

In other words, she argues that it is not clear as to how obligations or entitlements function on Searle's view.[97] The complaint, in that she favors being doubly holistic, is that Searle's internal holism, subjective individualism as it has been previously termed, fails to prescribe actions for individuals in relation to group action. To Gilbert, Searle's counting we-intentions as irreducible, his formal collectivism, allows one to associate oneself with a plural subject, and constitute that plural subject on the basis of some common ground. However, it is claimed that Searle's subjective individualism makes it unclear how one sees a prescription for one's *own* action issuing from or in reference to the *collective* action or shared intention of the plural subject. Searle doesn't find Gilbert's puzzle to be an insoluble mystery.

Searle addresses this issue as an instance of what he calls the paradox of obligations. The paradox, Searle argues, traditionally arises in relation to promises and is often raised against his position in relation to constitutive rules or institutional facts. In relation to promises the paradox arises thus: "How can the obligation of promises come into existence without a prior promise to abide by promises?"[98] In its most basic form, the potential paradox can be stated in this way: normative propositions seem to assume other normative propositions in order to be possible or to have force. Gilbert's solution is to make normativity essential to any collective or shared intention. We are immersed in naturally occurent, interrelated normative frameworks that are functional independent of individuals. Searle avoids making that claim, being uncomfortable with the notion that normativity is somehow not robustly linked in an ontologically dependent fashion to the achievement of individual intentional acts, and thus is forced to offer an alternative answer.

Searle begins by noting that human beings have the capacity to impose status functions.[99] For example, all members of a primitive community regard one individual as their "chief" or "leader." In virtue of individuals collectively intending that status in reference to this individual, who does not by virtue of their physical being possess that status or its powers, the status is imposed on her.

To Searle, the imposition of status functions, when regularized or formalized, issues in a constitutive rule.[100] However, not all cases of our utilizing our ability to impose status functions require a constitutive rule; for instance, if one uses a three-hole punch as a paperweight. There's no rule to the effect that three-hole punches are paperweights in certain contexts, rather one simply imposes that function on it when they use it as such.

For Searle, status functions "are always matters of positive or negative powers."[101] These powers are not at all like brute physical powers. There is something peculiar, for instance, in calling both the power of one's car's engine and the power of an individual acting as the President of the United States "powers" without respecting that there is some ambiguity. The powers prescribed by status impositions or by institutions "are always matters of rights, duties, obligations, commitments, authorizations, requirements, permissions, and privileges."[102] Searle calls these *deontic powers.*

An interesting observation that appeals to socially embedded theorists is that language appears to be constitutive of socially constituted facts in a way that it is not in the case of physical facts.[103] And yet a new potential paradox arises in that language itself is a social institution.[104] Admittedly, Searle does have a potential circularity problem involving language, if language is necessary for social constitutions and language itself is socially constituted. However, if one accepts his claims elsewhere to the effect that language's intentionality is derived, and only the intentionality of consciousness is original, then one can evade vicious circularity.[105] It is originally through acts of cognition, where subjects intend something to be the case, that social institutions like language are made possible, the symbolic expression of which is secondary. The regularity of reference pertaining to a language is dependent on a prior cognitive foundation in which intentionality first manifests and in relation to which a basis in experience serves as a necessary foundation.[106]

In response to Gilbert, then, Searle's position should be that normativity is present when it's supposed to be (when we impose it or have a predicate for it), but is not automatic as Gilbert believes. If one accepts that deontic powers don't arise in relation to *every* instance of a we-intention or plural subject, but only certain types of we-intentions one can see both why Gilbert is puzzled by Searle's view (a lack of clarity on Searle's part) and why Gilbert's concern is ultimately only a superficial one (as a ready answer is latent in a broader account of intentionality). Gilbert's narrower focus for her theory is intended only to account for those cases of collective intentionality wherein deontic powers are operative. However, what the phenomenology of plural subjects suggests, and finds agreement with Searle's philosophy, is that there are instances of collective intentionality or plural subjects where deontic powers are not operative in or constitutive to one's experience. The apparent mystery is only that Searle has been insufficiently clear in exposing the more basic phenomenological modes of plural subjects by failing to connect various parts of his view together adequately and not that Searle's view can't answer Gilbert's concerns.

Couple Gilbert's complaint regarding normativity with the stringent epistemic requirements above–i.e. knowledge of shared intention and knowledge of its being shared *and* that having a concept of a joint commitment are necessary for a we-intention–and one can begin to diagnose an underlying problem with Gilbert's view. Though, Gilbert has since appeared to loosen her epistemic requirements.[107] Nonetheless, it may be that Gilbert is implicitly operating with a Cartesian subject in mind. The paradigm of subjectivity she's operating with is that of a rationality endowed epistemologically responsible party. It is because of this that her account runs into issues with children, the disabled, and animals– as they are all "less rational" or at least less capable epistemically speaking. Plainly small children and animals don't meet Gilbert's requirements, but they nonetheless appear to formulate we-intentions and experience themselves as parties to plural subjects, experiences as in the mode of being *together* with others. What else appears to contribute to Gilbert's arriving at this sort of position?

Gilbert admits to being heavily influenced by David Lewis's work on conventions,[108] which she identifies as being individualistic. She states of Lewis' view, "It appeals only to the personal actions, beliefs, preferences, and so on– 'actions' for short–of particular human individuals. ...There is no essential appeal at any level to the action of anything composed of two or more human individuals."[109] That is, Lewis's view does not address plural subjects, and is therefore inadequate. Lewis, by only addressing individuals in an atomistic fashion, neglects to account for our group functions, which are essential to understanding how conventions operate. Something that appears to have rubbed off on Gilbert is a feature of the way Lewis's view operates–with an eye to epistemic judgments: subject-predicate relations expressed in the forms of propositions. Gilbert does not seem to shirk this aspect of Lewis's analysis, as her view seems to operate on the same model. However, judgments aren't the whole of our experiences, only a subset. As such, not everything can be reduced to subject-predicate relations and a view that operates with that background assumption and directs its inquiry to such things, while valuable as a kind of analysis, is not going to be able to capture the fuller range of experiences found in everyday life.

In distinction from this propositional framework one should stress that plural subjects aren't merely the *objects* of judgments but something experienced involving relations between subjects. Useful is Thomas Owen's introductory statements on the emergence of intersubjectivity in contemporary philosophy through its reaction to the Modern philosophical paradigm. Quoting Owens:

> Both the topic (intersubjectivity) and the method (phenomenology) are relative newcomers to philosophy and in a sense they arrived together. Ever since Descartes, philosophers have labored to explain how a subject knows an *object*. But not until the twentieth century did they begin to ask the much more fundamental and vastly more mysterious question–how does one subject encounter another subject precisely *as another subject*?[110]

The difference is not a trivial one. The reason so many attempts to solve the problem of other minds or variants of the problem of solipsism inevitably fail is that they treat one individual's relation to another on the model of the perception of any other *object*, especially as it can be expressed in a proposition or by a judgment.[111] One neither experiences objects in the world nor other subjects primarily as variables pertaining to subject-predicate places in epistemic relations. Our epistemological concerns arise out of and in relation to that prior experiential framework. One experiences others precisely as *other*, with all the uncertainty that brings with it. This doesn't make one's experiences of other subjects an anomaly or unwarranted inference or lacking justification. The model of the subject as inference generator or proposition computer is not adequate to experience. Phenomenology's break from that model is to respect the *subjec-*

tive elements of cognition that are irreducibly associated with their objective correlates.

A further important point to make in regard to Gilbert's discussion of Lewis is that Gilbert sees no objection to calling actions, beliefs, preferences, etc. all "actions," that plural subjects involve joint commitments to doing things as a uniform body "in a broad sense of 'do.'" Thus, it's not unfair to count her as having understood herself as giving an account of plural subjects as such–which would then include having perceptual experiences together with others. Certainly she counts herself to be discussing beliefs, as she expressly addresses that subject in her writings when discussing what it means for the scientific community to change its view on some matter and the relation the view of the scientific community as such endorses to the views of individual scientists functioning as part of that community.[112] Again, one can raise the question, what do her three criteria for plural subjects mean in relation to very basic kinds of plural subject experiences? My answer has been that Gilbert's criteria don't apply in many cases, and that is because she's describing a subset of we-intentions. Specifically, Gilbert's account only addresses *intent* and not *intentionality*. She addresses that subset of plural subjects in which deontic powers are operative, not plural subjects as such. Gilbert mistakes a part for the whole, or a species for the genus. Her account counts as the whole of the phenomena in question those instances of plural subjects related to *intentionality [Absicht]* without an adequate appreciation as to how that sense of intentionality is dependent on the more fundamental cognitive sense of the term, *Intentionalität*.[113] In short, Gilbert's view is not sufficiently buttressed by an adequate philosophy of mind and appears to have insurmountable inconsistencies with viable theories of mind. At the very least Gilbert may stand to benefit from supplementing her view with phenomenology.

Conclusion

By starting with intentionality *[Absicht]* and not offering an account of how that is dependent upon or integrated with intentionality *[Intentionalität]* Gilbert inherits unnecessary theoretical problems. Gilbert's *theoretical* edifice is insufficiently *phenomenologically* grounded. The theoretically motivated account ends up ignoring or effacing a range of the sorts of phenomena she claims to address in virtue of her staring point. As a result the account runs into trouble and results in strained accounts of everyday phenomena in virtue of a commitment to the theoretical foundation that forces one to construct a fix for phenomena that a more basic starting point would encompass. By starting an account at a level of greater complexity, and accepting that as basic to one's view, one necessarily inherits as problematic being able to account for what is more basic. A parallel to this arises in the history of aesthetics, for instance, where traditional views assumed a notion of art with reference principally to static or plastic art objects as being definitive of the basic category "art." By doing so, however, those views ran into terrible difficulty, if not the impossibility of accounting adequately for dynamic art forms.[114] In like capacity, Gilbert appears to have started from what is best classified as a species category and tries to account for its genus in terms of the species; rather like trying to construct an ontology of candy by assuming all candy contains chocolate. If, on the other hand, Gilbert actually starts from intentionality [*Intentionalität*] then it is clear that the account she offers is at best partial and at worst lacking in regard to the nature of intentionality itself.

Notes

1. Arguably, Aristotle did some of this same work himself in his ethical and political writings. A comparative analysis of Gurwitsch and Aristotle should yield fruitful results.

Another subjective individualist in the broad vein of Husserlian phenomenology is Alfred Schütz. When I use the phrase 'Husserlian phenomenology' broadly I mean it primarily as a point of contrast, specifically in distinction from Heideggerian phenomenology or French phenomenology, namely the later "phenomenological" traditions that reacted against Husserl. The early writings of Sartre and a good amount of Merleau-Ponty's phenomenological writings might be classified as Husserlian. While Schütz along with the early Sartre and Gurwitsch are critical of Husserl, Schütz's approach to phenomenological philosophy is more in line with Husserl than Heidegger, the French tradition or any later developments.

2. Gurwitsch 1979: 96
3. ibid. Husserl and Schütz both distinguish in places between Nature, the horizon of the natural world, and Society, the other-inclusive horizons of our cultural and social heritage and history.
4. Gurtwitsch 1979: 96
5. ibid: 99. On the Background in Searle see Searle 1983: Chapter 5 and Searle 1992: Chapter 8.
6. Gurwitsch 1979: 104
7. ibid: 104
8. ibid: 105
9. ibid: 109
10. ibid: 116-117
11. ibid: 118-119
12. ibid: 118
13. ibid.
14. ibid: 120
15. ibid: 124
16. ibid: 127
17. ibid: 130
18. ibid: 131. Hannah Arendt distinguishes between private, social, and public spheres. Communities presumably have primary determinative *constitutive* roles in relation to *social* spheres, and through that exercising an influence

on individuals' private lives. It seems right to understand the public sphere as "exterior" to communities, i.e. as a contextual horizon "in" which communities can arise and operate but which is itself not bound by specific community "governance." See Arendt 1998 for discussion.

19. Gurwitsch 1979: 139

20. ibid: 141

21. ibid: 142

22. ibid.

23. ibid: 150

24. Gilbert 1996: 216

25. See Aristotle, *Nicomachean Ethics,* VIII-IX. Yu 2007 also places strong emphasis on the mirroring of virtue in Aristotle's friendships.

26. Gilbert 1996: 221

27. ibid: 222

28. ibid: 223

29. Fusion *"...does not require the obliteration of the egos in question."* (Gilbert 1996: 220)

30. Gilbert (1996) distinguishes between positively and negatively correlated fusion on p. 224-225.

31. Gilbert 1996: 223-224

32. ibid: 224

33. ibid: 225

34. ibid: 220

35. Gurwitsch 1979: 151

36. ibid: 152

37. Any number of philosophers (Plato, Aristotle, Kant, Nietzsche, Kierkegaard, Heidegger, etc.) have examined the potentially negative impact of too great a reliance of an individual on social groups. These analyses lose their edge and are potentially marginalized if one adopts collectivism. Certainly some philosophers have gone too far in pitting the individual *in opposition to* communities (e.g. Hobbes, Locke, Mill, etc.), but most seem concerned with the extent to which one uncritically adopts communal influence–that is in critically examining the best way for individual to *relate with* or *comport in respect of* their community, often by adopting a critical eye for evidence or epistemic justification–as opposed to eschewing communities and their practices altogether. However, adopting collectivism as true would seem to require that most of these sorts of analyses be construed as reactionary and misguided. This would be so where the view holds that social wholes are properly understood as objects with an independent status in relation to their parts, as opposed to dependent expression of parts in systems of relations.

38. Husserl 1979

39. Gilbert 1996: 215-225. "I take the phenomenon I shall refer to as 'fusion' in this essay to be central to human social relationships in general" (ibid: 216). "One possible model for *fusion* is that of *plural subject formation,* or *'we'-*

formation in the correlative sense" (ibid.). She claims that a conversation between strangers on a bus can constitute fusion on p. 221.

40. Husserl referred to co-intentional reference as implicit in experience of something as objective, i.e. in relation to any object of experience. The sense of the world and of Nature in particular, as Objective Nature [object of physical or *natural* sciences] includes "thereness-for-everyone. This is always co-intended wherever we speak of Objective actuality" (Husserl 1999: 92/124). "These Objects, in respect of their origin and sense, refer us to subjects, usually other subjects, and their actively constituting intentionality" (ibid.).

I take Gurwitsch to be speaking of more specific cases than are Husserl's concern. Gurwitsch's view, being more oriented to explicitly social dimensions of experience is focused on co-intentional references founded through the social *constitution* of the objects themselves. Whereas, Husserl's concern with objectivity as such focused on the co-intentional references founded in the quality or modality of the experience itself.

41. Recall the passage quoted earlier in text from *Logical Investigations* (Husserl 2001a: 38).

42. Pettit 1993, Searle 1995, Bratman 1999, Gilbert 1996

43. A natural objection to this from the phenomenological tradition might be to argue following Levinas that morality precedes ontology (Levinas 1969). While representing a reasonable challenge, my suspicion is that Levinas' meaning of "priority" is not the same as the Husserlian notion, being more an existential or psychological sense of the term rather than an ontological or logical one. However, the complexity of Levinas is prohibitive to and orthogonal to present purposes.

44. Gilbert 1996: 2

45. Gilbert 2000: 2

46. Gilbert 1996: 3

47. ibid: 348

48. Strictly speaking, to call "experience" first-personal should be considered redundant.

49. The phrase "phenomenology or ontology," to a Husserlian would be redundant. To Husserl, the aim of all rigorous philosophy, which phenomenology establishes the methodology for, is to produce ontological results. (See Husserl's "Philosophy as a Rigorous Science" in McCormick & Elliston 1981.)

50. *Prima facie* this may appear to disadvantage the phenomenologist. However, that would be to forget that there is a distinction between experience, and the intentionality manifest in experience, and conditions for satisfaction or fulfillment of the intention. As discussed earlier, one does not fail to have a plural form experience just because worldly conditions are not consistent with one's experience. Rather, one's experience involves empty intentions and isn't evidentially verifiable.

51. Gilbert 2000: 14

52. ibid: 16

53. Phenomenologically, the coextensive relation would likely be owed to a plural subject's being a proper part of a collective intention. I am uncertain that Gilbert would agree to this accounting for the coextensive relation, and note it as a potential point for future development.

54. Gilbert 2000: 17

55. ibid.

56. It is worth noting the parallels with Searle's description of why specific instances of inked cloth-paper are money and why others aren't. Searle 1995: 48

57. Gilbert 2000: 17-18

58. ibid: 18

59. See, for example, Michael Davis' complicity theory of whistleblowing (Davis 1996).

60. Gilbert 2000: 37-38

61. ibid: 19

62. ibid.

63. ibid.

64. ibid: 21

65. ibid.

66. ibid.

67. For a fuller account on intentionality's part-whole structure, see Husserl's *Fifth Logical Investigation,* "On Intentional Experiences and Their 'Contents'" (Husserl 2001b: V). See also Sokolowski 1974.

68. Gilbert 2000: 22

69. ibid.

70. ibid: 40

71. Where Gilbert might respond that either these children are actually behaving as jointly committed or as-if jointly committed, I maintain my criticism. If she concedes that they are jointly committed and behavior is sufficient to demonstrate such, I respond that she appears to be equating her criteria with the basic sense of togetherness manifest in experience. If that's the case, her criteria are weaker than her presentation suggestions. If she claims that they are merely acting as-if jointly committed, we have a disagreement over how to interpret the phenomena of a very difficult nature. I prefer to interpret these cases as representative of plural subjects in a basic sense, counting what Gilbert's doing as referring to either sub-species or more complex kinds of these types of phenomena. Gilbert's view is that basic forms of cooperative behaviors are insufficient to form plural subjects. I take my view to be preferential on the grounds that it is more flexible and more inclusive; Gilbert would respond that the broadness of my view is indicative of too liberal a view of plural subjects. Part of the disagreement is a quandary over why to stress the differences as being so significant, unless the concern is that if small children can be said to form plural subjects that this would imply moral agency and moral responsibility in a robust form. If that's the concern, I disagree that such an implication would follow and point to this as an example of where the primacy of her moral orientation has led to a problem in analyzing the basic phenomena prior to axiological concerns.

72. Tomasello 2008 and Tomasello 2009
73. Gilbert 1989: Ch. III
74. ibid: 58; the claim is repeated on p. 128
75. ibid: 131, see also p. 58 & p. 128
76. ibid.
77. Gilbert 2000: 6
78. I use scare quotes around obligation here because 1) I don't know what German Shepherd consciousness is like, and 2) to dissuade one from thinking I'm granting moral agency to the animal. Some animals, dogs like German Shepherds certainly, appear to recognize something like obligation in experience, that's all that's being affirmed. Animals also have expectations in relation to experience, that much is also clear.
79. Here I speak from experience, as while a toddler my parents' German Shepherd, a 90 lb animal well beyond my ability to control physically, would respond to my cues—even though I knew nothing at the time of how said cues operated. Similar interactions occur between my German Shepherd and my son, who at the time this was first written was himself a toddler.
80. I am told that "the Dog Whisperer," Cesar Millan, effectively states the same in respect to how responsible owners are to interact with their animals for the animals' benefit. Rank does not mean some all-encompassing claim to superiority over one's pet with carte blanche to do to them whatever one will.
81. If Gilbert charges me with presenting a red herring here, asserting that animals have different kinds of consciousness, my response is that this is a difficult question. Phenomenologists tend to believe, on the basis of argument, that there is a basic structure of consciousness that any and all instances of consciousness would have to have in common. If true, the question as to whether or not this is a red herring is entirely dependent on the extent to which there is overlap between given cases of animal and human consciousness. However, this does not affect the point about the individual human's experience as a potential counter-example to Gilbert's view.
82. Searle makes a very strong claim as to the relation of biology to consciousness and consciousness to rationality. His view is basically that from the complexities of these naturally arising systems certain further dependent systems or system-level properties emerge which are not reducible to nor equivalent with the individuated physical properties. If one accepts that Husserl's use of the term organisms in relation to his discussions of consciousness is not metaphorical but is intended to be taken rather literally, as is the view of Hans-Georg Gadamer with specific reference to Husserl's writings (*Husserliana* VI or Husserl 1970), then Husserl's view potentially shares even more with Searle's than most admit (Gadamer 1989: 249). This raises an interesting question as to how to interpret Husserl's anti-naturalism on the one hand as well as Searle's naturalism, especially as to whether or not their terminologies diverge in relation to 'naturalism.' A terrific set of discussions regarding the contemporary status of Husserl's critique of naturalism is in Petitot et al. 1999, especially in the introduction.

Husserl's language in *Crisis* also opens the door for a possible reconciliation between the early and late Husserl over the question of "realism." Though, the realism-idealism dispute in relation to Husserl, as with Kant, is largely premised on a category mistake on the part of commentators that neither Husserl nor Kant fell sway to. Realism and idealism are not opposed categories for these thinkers. As such, while I count myself as a realist follower of Husserl, I don't understand that commitment to entail an outright rejection of Husserl's transcendental idealism.

For positive comparisons of Searle and Husserl see Fitzpatrick 2003: 53, Zahavi 2000: 20, Carr 1989: 303-304, 308n7, Johansson 2003: 235 for example.

For Searle's reaction to such comparisons see Searle 1999 and Searle 2005. In both cases it is clear that Searle's ignorance of Husserl is owed to his accepting Hubert Dreyfus' understanding of Husserl as an accurate representation of Husserl's views, as he acknowledges not really bothering to read Husserl with any seriousness. Searle's resistance to the comparison is thus motivated by Dreyfus' Heideggerian reactionary posture to Husserlian phenomenology. I take Dreyfus to have grossly misunderstood Husserl, and Searle's attempt to count Dreyfus as *the* authority on all things Husserl to be irresponsible from a scholarly standpoint. Better for Searle to claim ignorance, as would be accurate, and to resist Dreyfus's mischaracterizations of Searle's view without lashing out with an uninformed resistance to what is intended, in most cases, as a flattering comparison.

83. Gilbert 1989: 132

84. ibid: 131-132

85. ibid: 132

86. To be clear, even if the intentionality attributed to the robot or stuffed animal is not intrinsic, perhaps only as-if intentionality, this doesn't affect the intentionality manifest in the experience of the individual person nor its formal requirements. The experiences of the cyberneticist and child are in plural form and not inconsequentially so. One cannot overlook the plural form of their experiences even if the plurality operative in experience is not reciprocated. The revisited *Battlestar Gallactica* series (2004-2009) played with similar types of concerns having to do with human-Cylon relations, asking whether Cylons are conscious or merely mechanisms, as well as if that even matters to the experiences of human subjects. In particular, take the example of Chief Tyrol and Lt. Agathon's respective relationships with the Cylon Sharon Valerii.

87. Gilbert 2000: 155

88. While I'm not equivocating between imagination, perceptual experience or action-oriented experiences, the point is twofold. 1) Plural subject experiences can manifest in relation to a more varied set of act-types in consciousness than Gilbert's view is readily able to address. 2) Some projections in experience are not qualified as imaginative projections by the individual engaging in said behavior. Children are great examples, but adults do these things too. And one can't discount these projections out of hand. To do so, again, represents in many

cases conflating the intentionality of the experience itself with the conditions for satisfaction in relation to what is experienced.

89. The act of riding in the same shuttle doesn't meet Gilbert's criteria itself. However, in her essay on "fusion" and marriage, Gilbert asserts that a conversation by strangers on a bus would qualify on her view as a plural subject (Gilbert 1996: 221). Gilbert takes "fusion" to consist in the symmetrical awareness of participants in an actual state of affairs, that is "central to human relationships in general" (ibid: 216). Later, she attributes fusion to cases of plural subjects: "I now suggest that one possible model for *fusion* is that of *plural subject formation*, or *'we'-formation* in the correlative sense. I propose that two egos may be said to have fused just in case the people in question for a plural subject of some kind" (ibid: 220). Further, "every instance of fusion provides a basis for a *sense of unity*, even a sense of *intimacy* or *closeness* within the single 'we' that is involved" (ibid: 221). All of this complicates Gilbert's view making it more applicable to everyday experiences. I take this as further evidence that Gilbert's intent is to provide a basic account of plural subjects. Again, my criticism is that her view doesn't adequately address such basic cases, as her criteria are too restrictive. To say this another way, her view operates on a different level of analysis, one which requires founded intentional achievements. That's not to say in respect of the analysis given that her view is inadequate, only that it doesn't adequately account for the basic phenomena which serve as founding intentional achievements.

90. I have in mind the type of "normativity" associated with typification in the later writings of Husserl. Granting that there's a *prima facie* concern with the statements regarding normativity at the beginning of the chapter, I will only say that resolving that concern neatly is too difficult for the present work to engage in. Sara Heinämaa's work in feminist phenomenology includes material that has immense promise for how the potential problem can be resolved.

91. Gilbert 2000: 157

92. ibid.

93. ibid.

94. ibid: 158

95. I would like to note that Philip Pettit's alternative categorical distinctions afford an alternative way to recast the dispute between Gilbert and Searle. Pettit would likely argue that there is a terminological confusion at root in their dispute as Pettit identifies his position as one that is both individualist and holistic (Pettit 1993: 112). Individualism and collectivism are positions as to the vertical relations between individuals and the social wholes to which they stand in relation. Collectivism is a view that claims "we would realize that the intentional image of ourselves as more or less autonomous subjects–as autarchical agents–is a conceit that lacks foundation in reality" (ibid: 111). Individualism is the position opposed to this thesis, held by those "who deny that social forces or regularities are inimical in this way to intentional autonomy or autarchy" (ibid.). Atomism and holism are positions as to the horizontal relations between individual subjects within such social wholes. "Atomists occupy an extreme position, ac-

cording to which it is possible for a human being to develop all the capacities characteristic of our kind in total isolation from her fellows, if indeed she has any fellows" (ibid: 111-112). Holism denies the claim of atomism, "arguing that one or another distinctive capacity–usually the capacity for thought–depends in a non-causal or constitutive way on the enjoyment of social relationships" (ibid: 112). Holistic individualism, then, appears to be the position that, at least by definition, Husserlian phenomenology embodies as well–while denying elements of Pettit's naturalism.

On Pettit's view, one could view the dispute between Gilbert and Searle in the following manner. Gilbert is accusing Searle of atomism, an atomism that appears to be latent in Searle's individualism. Hans Bernhard Schmid expressly calls out Searle's supposed atomism in Schmid 2003a: pg. 93. What's more, my criticisms of Gilbert could be seen as mainly directed at her collectivism and not her holism. As Pettit notes, the influence of Durkheim has motivated collectivist views (ibid: 112-113). And Durkheim is influential to Gilbert's views. While this is an interesting and even potentially illuminating recasting, to avoid confusion in what follows, I respond to Gilbert's criticisms of Searle on the terms already in use throughout.

96. Gilbert 2000: 157

97. This is not at all an uncommon critique of Searle. See Meijers 2003, Tuomela 2003, Schmid 2003a and Schmid 2003b as examples

98. Searle 2004: 90

99. ibid.

100. ibid: 91-92

101. ibid: 92

102. ibid: 93

103. ibid. See previous discussions and Searle's discussions of the distinction between brute facts and institutional facts in Searle 1995: 2, 27, 31-57; as well as Searle 1998: 121, 123.

104. ibid: 94

105. I have since argued that Searle's revisions to his view, found in *Making the Social World* (2010), result in the circularity becoming unavoidable. I also argue that phenomenology can escape the circle in a way that Searle is unable to. The paper was presented to the Cave Hill Philosophy Symposium in 2011.

106. Gilbert 1989: III responds to Kripke's Wittgenstein's arguments about private languages in a manner that suggests, or could be taken to suggest, that Gilbert accepts the intentionality of thought to be distinct from the intentionality of language.

107. Gilbert 2000

108. Lewis 1969. Gilbert's criticisms of Lewis' view are given in Gilbert 1989: VI.

109. Gilbert 2000: 155

110. Owens 1970: 1

111. It is worth noting that attentive readers of Husserl accept that he is not concerned with solipsism. See for example: Hutcheson 1981, 1982a, 1982b, Allen 1978b, Carr 1973, Donohoe 2004, Staehler 2008, Zahavi 2001a, 2001b.

112. Gilbert 2000: 37-38

113. Action in any morally laden sense of the term is dependent on a view of autonomy and volition. Those in turn depend on consciousness, which itself depends on intentionality. As such, *intent*–the expression of one's autonomy or of one's volition from out of or in response to one's experience (consciousness)– depends on the more basic notion of intentionality (as an expression of intent requires that one's experiences can be *about* or *directed at* or *of* something in a meaningful capacity).

114. One of the lesser-appreciated critiques to this effect in aesthetics, but which is getting more notice of late, is that expressed in the works of Susanne Langer. The most notable of Langer's works are Langer 1996 & Langer 1953.

Chapter 6
Responses to Two Criticisms Motivated by Realist Concerns

In this chapter, I respond to two related challenges to Husserl's views on inter-subjectivity motivated by realist concerns. The first is a challenge to Husserl presented by Barry Smith. Smith objects to the Husserlian approach to intersubjectivity with specific regard for the phenomenological notion of a world. His worry is one of an implicit relativism. One should recall from the earlier discussions of David Carr, that Carr's view is that each community or plural subject has a world. As such, Smith's objection and the methodological issues raised therein are not unimportant. I argue that only a misunderstanding of Husserlian phenomenology would regard it as involving the specter of relativism and rely on other early phenomenologists, who were realists, to support my case.

Predicated on similar concerns, Han Georg Gadamer has also objected to the Husserlian approach to intersubjectivity and the experience of others. Gadamer's objection to Husserl hinges not around the phenomenological notion of world but on the notion of a phenomenological horizon. Gadamer's mistake, I argue, is to downplay the asymmetry inherent in intersubjective experience. This is not to say that Gadamer, or Smith for that matter, don't present meaningful criticisms. Rather, I argue that both objections amount more to calls for further clarification than anything devastating to the Husserlian project.

Barry Smith's Criticisms of Husserl on Intersubjectivity

Barry Smith argues that there is a problem in Husserl's philosophy involving the plurality of worlds.[1] Smith identifies the problem of intersubjectivity as one "of accounting for the existence of harmony among the different worlds which arise when 'world' is relativized to your and my subjective appearances and of accounting for the possibility of a single universal science which would govern the modes and manners of such appearing."[2] By 'single universal science' Smith means phenomenology, though he may intend more specific reference to only constitutive phenomenology. Smith is correct in emphasizing that, especially for Husserl, success in addressing the problem of intersubjectivity was central to the very possibility of phenomenology. One can understand more about what is meant by relativized worlds where Smith states:

> There are the ideal worlds of mathematics or legal objects, of financial instruments, folk tales, chess, and so on. Each such realm of objects is an interpersonal, cultural accomplishment, presupposing a certain association of human beings. The world of common-sense, too, is an accomplishment of a community of persons recognizing each other (or better: taking each other for granted) as normal, as similar as in agreement.[3]

Smith is characterizing the phenomenological sense of world–a totality of reference–and he is noting that such an understanding of "world" does not preclude there being multiple "worlds" relativized to specific contextualized environments. One can speak of what is normal to people in Buffalo, the "world" of the Buffalonian, what is normal to people in Hong Kong and so on. There is also a sense in which each individual has an idiosyncratic "world." It is the reconciliation of these systems of meaning, their unification or demonstration as to their possible continuity, which Smith sees as one of the main issues to be addressed by a satisfactory account of intersubjectivity. Alternatively, one might object to the need for any reconciliation between worlds, noting that this is only a problem that arises if one glosses over the intersubjectively rich way in which we experience the world together, as entertaining a false problem.

The problem of intersubjective interaction between or across worlds presents itself most fundamentally on the level of individuals. One individual's world–in the phenomenological sense of a unified totality of meanings, a system if one prefers–may not be wholly consistent with the world of another. At the level of groups–cultures, corporations, governments, etc.–this refers to the interactions between and overlaps of specialized domains of meaning, the worlds or systems of meaning such collectives represent and maintain. As may be clear by now, the solution to Smith's concern lies precisely in the shared experiential basis Carr touts and the brute facts on which Searle's view depends. Different worlds, representing specific or specialized meanings and meaning-formations, are only problematic where there is nothing to mitigate or reconcile differences, or where there could be no possible way to adjudicate disagreements. Additionally, there must be some regularity in the form of those subjectivities themselves. The shared humanity of humans is not just a point of moral emphasis. Rather, it picks out the form of subjective experiences that the given type of subjectivity has. It delimits the range of possible act-content correlations in the field of experience. Bat or dolphin experiences, by comparison, are not structured the same as human experiences, humans, for instance have no sonar, wings, fins, etc. Within a type of subjectivity there is also a vast range of variance across subjects. These are owed to genetic differences in constitutional development of individual consciousnesses, i.e. they represent material differences played out in systemic fashion against the backdrop of a common formal delimitation of possibilities. The commonalities don't consist merely in terms of their contents–specific experiences themselves. The commonalities in question also include the form of experiences (including act-species), represented as a limiting horizon of the range of the types of experiences possible for these subjects. These bases of shared experiential forms–the formal attributes of a type of subjectivity's phenomenology–form the basis Smith finds wanting. It is, however, a legitimate question as to whether Husserl would include or accept such an account.

Smith is correct to claim that each such realm, domain or world, presupposes a community, or association of subjects, in this case specifically human subjects. This is not a claim that I believe one should reasonably challenge. It is also a claim I believe Husserl embraces. This view is captured in the very notion of the lifeworld [*Lebenswelt*]. In part, Smith is pointing out that, per Husserl, the kinds of worlds he acknowledges above are each dependent on higher-order communities, themselves dependent on more basic elements, ultimately with respect to subjectivity. It is exposing such basic constitutive sense-elements that Husserl aimed for with his analyses of intersubjectivity. A complete phenomenological description of community-accomplished worlds would be dependent on description of the variant levels of phenomenological communalization present in said phenomenon.

There are at least three components needed to answer Smith's challenge:

1) A common experiential basis
2) A framework within which new intentional formations can be established by subjects acting in concert with one another
3) A description of what is present in the identification of other subjects as subjects to ground (2), and relate it to (1)

Briefly, these three elements amount to the following. A common experiential basis represents some common ground between subjects, and by reference to which they are able to mitigate differences between their personal and founded worlds. This basis, on a realist interpretation, would involve, though not necessarily be exhausted by, the "external world." However, phenomenology's methodological neutrality precludes any easy endorsement of such a position, or similarly structured alternatives. The common experiential basis may also invoke a common or shared structure for a given type of subjectivity. Again, bat subjectivity, if there is such a thing, is different from human subjectivity. Though, this point may be taken too far if one neglects that all animal life on Earth operates within the same set of physical constraints, as well as participating in evolutionary biological developments in common. Second, the framework for new, higher-order, intentional formations is best understood, in my view, by contemporary discussions of collective intentionality. Collective intentional achievements constitute essential moments of intersubjective wholes (higher order pluralities): local or cultural worlds, institutions, etc. This helps address Smith's challenge by excavating the workings of subjects operating in plural. Finally, there is the description of the intentionality involved in the experience of another subject as a subject. This represents a necessary intentional basis for any shared or collective intentional formation, and is the standard subject matter of those writing on intersubjectivity in Husserl. Take for example, Husserl's rather amusing example of seeing a wax-woman across a hall, as first described in *Logical Investigations*, an example he was known to use in the classroom as well.

> Wandering about in the Panopticum Waxworks we meet on the stairs a charming lady whom we do not know and who seems to know us, and who is in fact the well-known joke of the place: we have for a moment been tricked by a waxwork figure. As long as we *are* tricked, we experience a perfectly good percept: we see a lady and not a waxwork figure. When the illusion vanishes, we see exactly the opposite, a waxwork figure that only *represents* a lady. Such talk of 'representing' does not of course mean that the waxwork figure is modeled on a lady as in the same waxworks there are figure-models *of* Napoleon, *of* Bismarck etc. The percept of the wax-figure as a thing does not therefore underlie our awareness of the same figure as representing the lady. The lady, rather, makes her appearance together with the wax-figure and in union with it. Two perceptual interpretations, or two appearances of a thing, interpenetrate, coinciding as it were in part in their perceptual content. And they interpenetrate in conflicting fashion, so that our observation wanders from one to another of the apparent objects each barring the other from existence.[4]

The figure of the wax-woman is not met first as waxen, but first taken as person, as a living embodied whole with its own consciousness and all that entails, including all the anticipations associated with such. When one's expectations are dissolved, and only a wax-figure remains, one no longer attributes to the figure the sense of living embodied whole with its own consciousness. It is what is left behind in sense constitution when the trick of the waxen-figure is made clear to us that needs description—what is it that one attributes and how is that sense structured when one identifies something as a living being, a conscious being, or more specifically a human being. As a necessary basis upon which collective intentions are founded, the basic intersubjective experience, experiencing another subject *as* subject, itself constitutes an instance of a common experience. In pointing back to individual subjectivity and its experiences as well as operating through individual subjective achievements, collective intentionality implicitly draws on these experiences and their form in relation to whatever social or intersubjectively rich dimensions of experience there are. In essence, these three elements represent three parts of a description of subjectivity itself: the form of its structure and experiences, its specific (material) experiences of other subjects, and its extension into society with other subjectivities.

While it is correct that the problem of a plurality of worlds is part of the problem of intersubjectivity, or one of the associated problems under that heading, it does not itself constitute the whole. Husserl acknowledges there being a host of problems, not a singular monolithic problem. Carr notes the rather remarkable admission by Husserl that in the first thirty years of phenomenology he "had published no systematic or extensive treatment of the problems falling under the heading of intersubjectivity, e.g., the problem of our experience of another consciousness and of the concept of a plurality of subjects."[5] More recently, Dan Zahavi has introduced the further categorical distinction between the constitution of intersubjectivity and the constituting intersubjectivity.[6] The problem of one's experience of another consciousness, and like issues, is part of the subset of problems under the heading of the constitution of intersubjectivity. As Carr notes with reference to *Cartesian Meditations*, the issue is "not Husserl's [or anyone else's] ability to prove that others exist, which is not in question, but his ability to make 'phenomenological sense' of other egos."[7] As any phenomenologist of Husserlian persuasion should note, the existential question must be off the table owed to the method of *epoché*. However, this does not exclude the question of how existential sense figures into one's experience, how something is experienced *as* existent. The problem of a plurality of subjects, as experienced from first personal conscious experience, is a part of the subset of problems under the heading of the constituting intersubjectivity. This includes matters relating to how intersubjectivity affects individual conscious experience, e.g. being enculturated into a specific worldview. Smith's problem represents only a part of the totality of intersubjective problematics.

However, there is also an ambiguity to Smith's critique in that the problem of relativized worlds could be seen either as an intrasubjective problem relating to the constitution of intersubjectivity or as an intersubjective problem relating to constituting intersubjectivity. By intrasubjective here I refer to what Husserl references by the phrase "sphere of ownness," what is essentially part of the individual subject's experience independent of any reference to others (as such, essentially non-linguistic in character); from this position how does one come to recognize as genuine the possibility of there being others independent of oneself?

Husserl confirms a ground for intersubjective experience in a shared basis of experience as being grounded in relation to the natural world where he claims that the cultural world is given "...on the underlying basis of the Nature common to all and on the basis of the spatiotemporal form that gives access to Nature and must function also in making the multiplicity of cultural formations and cultures accessible."[8] Carrying on, he states:

> Everyone, as a matter of a priori necessity, lives in the same Nature, a Nature moreover that, with the necessary communalization of his life and the lives of others, he has fashioned into a *cultural world* in his individual and communalized living and doing—a world having human significances, even if it belongs to an extremely low cultural level.[9]

This shared foundation does not preclude the possibility of differences, however.

> But this, after all, does not exclude, either a priori or de facto, the truth that men belonging to one and the same world live in a loose cultural community—or even none at all—and accordingly constitute different surrounding worlds of cul-

ture, as concrete life-worlds in which the relatively or absolutely separate communities live in their passive and active lives.[10]

One should note that the appeal to common foundation, a uniform Nature, is not to be conflated with appeals to a naïve realism. One could, for instance, see Husserl's appeal to a common Nature as a similar sort of grounding move that Searle makes in appeal to brute facts in order to ground institutional (socially constituted) facts.[11] Searle's appeal is to an existent reality. Husserl's appeal, on the other hand, must be understood in relation to the larger project of phenomenology. Husserl cannot directly appeal to an existent objective world entirely independent of all experience, Instead, Husserl can only reference an external world as it is a possible object of experience.[12] The sense "objective" essentially involves reference to others.[13] He could however, refer to the common essence or common nature of all individual consciousness—as phenomenology is focused on exposing essences and universal themes, not individually unique psychologies. Husserl's appeals must refer to meanings or sense in some fashion. The appeal to a common essential form to consciousness for all (human) subjectivity as a basis must be understood as such an appeal. It is in virtue of the common basis in meaning-constitutions that we are able to have community with one another and build up higher order systems of meanings.

This is not inconsistent with Searle's and other realist's views. One could even draw the two types of approaches closer were one to offer an argument parallel to Husserl's argument for why one can say they experience others *as* existing, i.e. indirect evidence born of harmonious appresentative contents passively synthesize with the contentful whole as experienced. "…[E]very sense that any existent whatever has or can have for me—in respect of its 'what' and its 'it exists and actually is'—is a sense *in* and *arising from* my intentional life, becoming clarified and uncovered for me in consequence of my constitutive syntheses, in systems of harmonious verification."[14] Or, "Every experience points to further experiences that would fulfill and verify the appresented horizons, which include, in the form of non-intuitive anticipations, potentially verifiable syntheses of harmonious further experience."[15] Or even, "The Objective world has [the sense of] existence by virtue of a harmonious confirmation of the apperceptive constitution…"[16] The point being that one recognize a common ground for experience and this common ground, which conditions one's own experience, imparts sense to the experience of others. The point is not that one analogizes the particularities of one's experience, though that happens as well, but that one analogizes the form of experience in reference to the other.

A similar moment arises in Kant's *Critique of Judgment*. Kant seeks to ground aesthetic judgments in a common sense, i.e. in our subjectivity in common. By common sense Kant does not refer to a common or vulgar understanding, i.e. not *content* in common but powers in common. Quoting:

…we must [here] take *sensus communis* to mean the idea of a sense *shared* [by all of us], i.e., a power to judge that in reflecting takes account (a priori), in our thought, of everyone else's way of presenting [something], in order *as it were* to compare our own judgment with human reason in general and thus escape the illusion that arises from the ease of mistaking subjective and private conditions for objective ones, an illusion that would have a prejudicial influence on the judgment. Now we do this as follows: we compare our judgment not so much with the actual as rather with the merely possible judgments of others, and [thus] put ourselves in the position of everyone else, merely by abstracting from the limitations that [may] happen to attach to our own judging; and this in turn we accomplish by leaving out as much as possible whatever is matter, i.e., sensation, in the presentational state, and by paying attention solely to the formal features of our presentation or our presentational state. Now perhaps this operation of reflection will seem rather too artful to be attributed to the ability we call *common* sense. But in fact it only looks this way when expressed in abstract formulas. Intrinsically nothing is more natural than abstracting from charm and emotion when we seek a judgment that is to serve as a universal rule.[17]

The parallels to Husserl's analyses of intersubjectivity in *Cartesian Meditations* and *Formal and Transcendental Logic* are palpable. In both cases there is an admission that it is in relation to the material composition of individuated experience that one recognizes and elevates differences. However, one can get past the materially idiosyncratic experience and recognize their formal identity, be it in relation to content-types or act-types in cognition or the form of subjectivity itself. Further, Kant argues that this is an entirely natural feature of experience that only appears foreign or strange in virtue of its being given abstract expression in philosophical discourse. Also important is that Kant is expressly discussing experiences he accepts as non-inferential and non-cognitive, i.e. it is not a conceptual process carried on through argumentation; it is a reflective aesthetic judgment wherein the result of judgment is non-conceptual, i.e. non-inferential in nature. Husserl's view, taken at its word, also appeals to this non-inferential quality of experience whereby the phenomena are experienced as rich and saturated in a manner not describable from the standpoint of a strict empiricism. While Smith, I believe, accepts this dimension of Husserl's view, he appears unnerved by Husserl's endorsement of transcendental idealism and is thereby wont for some coherent account of the ground for the view of intersubjectivity. As with Kant, however, there is not intended to be a tension between realism and idealism. Naïve forms of realism, particularly those endorsed by empiricism (e.g. Locke or Hume), are discounted and treated as inadequate on the ground of their eliminativist consequences, i.e. denying the reality of one's experiences or any mental phenomena in favor of only brute physical facts. However, the epistemologically motivated turn to a transcendental idealism does not imply idealism as the totality for one's ontology.[18]

Smith's criticism may be reduced to a conditional. If Husserl's idealism is pervasive and entails a denial of ontological realism, then there is no possibility for a sufficient common basis of experience by which to adequately account for the plurality of worlds. However, one is not forced to interpret Husserl that way.

Smith's argument offers strong reasons why not to adopt such an interpretation: the problem is not one integral to phenomenology as such. Those who deny realism in a simplistic manner end up having to accept an unsustainable form of relativism. In response, first, Husserl's idealism is not ontological in nature as Berkeley's is often thought to be, an idealism he criticized and expressly dissociated himself from.[19] "If anyone reading our statements objects that they mean changing all the world into a subjective illusion and committing oneself to a 'Berkeleyan idealism,' we can only answer that he has not seized upon the *sense* of those statements."[20] Nor is Husserl's idealism absolute in the manner of Hegel, someone Husserl had no interest in emulating.[21] If one assumes that the Neo-Kantians or Hegelians have the proper sense of transcendental idealism, one will surely be mistaken in relation to Husserl and likely for Kant as well. What exactly Husserl's idealism means beyond including examination into the conditions for the possibility of idealities (*eidos*) is not as clear as Smith's arguments appear to suggest.[22] Further, Husserl's *Crisis* fills out for one the genealogical history of sedimented meanings, with specific emphasis on the latent possibility for one to resuscitate the experiential praxis underlying the theoretical edifice and to re-enliven their correlation to lived experience. At the same time Husserl acknowledges that the formal constraints of human subjectivity don't entail univocity with respect to how one systematizes or orders the meanings of experience.[23]

In the *Crisis* Husserl was expressly concerned as to whether or not his conception of humanity, European humanity, had come to embody more than "an empirical anthropological type," accepting that the philosophers of the Eighteenth Century had employed a naïve rationalization of the state of humanity in Europe as being related to the rest of humanity in a superior position.[24] Granted, Husserl did believe that a theoretical attitude, specifically as definitive of a community of scholars was unique to the West, originating in Greek philosophy. From the Greeks one finds:

> ...as a communal form in which this interest [a world-encompassing interest directed to the discernment of universals] works itself out for internal reasons, being the corresponding, essentially new [community] of philosophers, of scientists (mathematicians, astronomers, etc.). These are the men who, not in isolation but with one another and for one another, i.e., in interpersonally bound communal work, strive for and bring about *theoria* and nothing but *theoria*, whose growth and constant perfection, with the broadening of the circle of coworkers and the succession of the generations of inquirers, is finally taken up into the will with the sense of an infinite and common task.[25]

That this is founded from out of and refers back to the practical attitude is no accident. Yet what is truly important is that the material constituents of life are in a state of flux, without any clear implication in respect of the form *humanity*. "The concrete contents of culture change and according to a relatively closed historical process. Humanity (or a closed community such as a nation, tribe, etc.), in its historical situation, always lives under some attitude or other. Its life always has its norm-style and, in reference to this, a constant historicity or development."[26] This is the natural attitude, the attitude of our everyday lives. However, one can transcend the natural attitude, which is intrinsically practical in its orientation by donning the *theoretical attitude*.[27] It is only from the position of a theoretical attitude that one is able to take in the contrasting forms of life and culture and from that distinguish between world-representation and actual world, from which a notion of truths transcendent of locality or convention emerges.[28] It is these universal forms at which, through a process of abstracting away material differences, philosophy aims. Instructive are passages from Adolf Reinach:

> For the essential point is this, that phenomenology is not a system of philosophical propositions and truths...but rather it is a method of philosophizing which is required by the problems of philosophy, which is very different from the manner of viewing and verifying in life, and which is even more difference from the way in which one does and must work in most sciences.[29]

And,

> But here also we must succeed in grasping the phenomena purely, in working out its essence without preconceptions and prejudgments: - the essence of color, extension and matter, light and dark, tones, and so on. We must also investigate the constitution of the phenomenal thing, purely in itself and according to its essential structure. In that structure, color, for example, certainly plays another role than does extension or matter. Everywhere it is essence laws that are in question. Existence is never posited.
>
> In all of this we are not working against science. Rather we are creating the basis upon which its structure can be *understood for the first time*.[30]

Given Husserl's aim, the aim of all philosophy, his position on intersubjectivity could not reduce to a simplistic relativism of meanings without falling into gross incoherence. Naïve realism or naïve relativism is a false choice, just as is naïve realism or ontological idealism. Recall what is, in effect, Smith's conditional: If Husserl's idealism is pervasive and entails a denial of ontological realism, then there is no possibility for a sufficient common basis of experience by which to adequately account for the plurality of worlds. Husserl's methodology is ontologically neutral, hence does not necessarily entail a denial of realism. Husserl's idealism is limited in nature and not ontological, as he asserts repeatedly. As such, the possibility for a sufficient common ground in experience by which to account for the plurality of worlds is still, in principle, available.

Gadamerian Criticisms of Husserl's Approach to Intersubjectivity

Gadamer treats Husserl's problem of intersubjectivity in basically similar fashion to how Smith does.[31] It is worth noting at the outset that Gadamer is aware of the mereological dimensions to Husserl's analysis, in that there is a part-whole dynamic at play with our interactions of others in an abstract manner that is similar to the concrete part-whole experiences related to everyday perceptual experience.[32] Gadamer accepts that there is a fusion of horizons across or between subjects, such that plural subjects could be said to be constituted through horizonal fusion. What is a horizon? "Horizons might function as a limit at a particular time, but they are also gateways to something beyond."[33] Horizons are not insurmountable limits, they are the limit of what is present and in relation to which the undetermined is anticipated in relation to the experience of an object as a whole.

> This horizon, however, is the correlate of the components of undeterminateness essentially attached to experiences of physical things themselves; and those components–again, essentially–leave open the possibilities of fulfillment, which are by no means completely undetermined, but are, on the contrary, motivated possibilities *predelineated with respect to their essential type.*[34]

In the case of another, the other's consciousness is essentially part of the horizon of one's experience, just as is any physical dimension not given at a particular moment, i.e. part of the projected totality of the whole. The recognition of the other as a living conscious being carries a distinct kind of horizonal intentionality from the intentional horizons associated with the experience of an inanimate being. Hence, a change in significance and projected possibilities are manifest in experience when one's seeing a waxen-woman as a person is found erroneous and one sees the waxen-woman *as* waxen-figure.

Merleau-Ponty identified three themes in relation to horizons: objects never appear without a horizon; horizons establish the set of expectations associated with the perception of an object; object's horizons are structured in connection with our finite-perspectives.[35] As David Vessey points out, horizons "demarcate what can be directly sensed from what can't be directly sensed, but they don't limit the perception of the object to what can be directly sensed."[36] Also, "The horizons are what make it possible to perceive more than what is directly sensed. Horizons open up possibilities of future perceptions of the object and in doing so provide it with its character."[37] The consciousness of other subjects is always found in the horizon of one's experience, and not ever entirely absent. That horizon undergoes modifications in experience.

As Roberto Walton has demonstrated, horizons are not entirely indeterminate, as the above passages from *Ideas I* might suggest, but they vary in degree of determinacy.[38] With respect to intersubjective experience, then, one can recognize two elements: 1) the other's consciousness, being unavailable in immediate evidence to me, is undetermined in my experience–my expectations of another's thoughts, etc., is a projection regarding what is unavailable to me; and 2) the other's consciousness or character need not be seen as entirely opaque. If that were the case, then there would be no difference in how well one knew one subject from another, but that isn't the case. One does know some subjects other than oneself better than others. It's not because one has gotten evidence in the original sense, one doesn't have the other's consciousness given to them directly. Rather, it's owed to the modifications horizons in relation to that person has undergone. Given the absence of any possible direct evidence with regard to our determinations in respect to the other, their "inner" life will always retain some indeterminacy, no matter how well one comes to "know" the other.

Vessey identifies three basic kinds of horizons in Husserl: "internal," "external," and "temporal."[39] "Internal horizons are horizons that arise from the nature of the object either as an object, such as taking up space, or as the kind of object that it is. When we see someone from the back, we perceive him or her as having a face. It belongs to the internal horizon of a head to have a face."[40] An internal horizon, then, results from one's identification of something as being of a certain type. The internal horizon of a person is distinct from that of a statue for example, as a statue is not expected to be able to move or think. Hence the surprise when the street performer posing as a statue grabs one's shoulder, as the precedent horizon is "shattered."

> External horizons are horizons established by the relation between the object and its surroundings. If there is a telegraph pole partially obstructing our view of a house, we recognize the parts of the house on both sides of the pole as still belonging to the same house as being located behind the pole. ...All relations get their character from the external horizon, including the relation of belonging to one spatio-temporal whole with everything else.[41]

Where each object of experience has its own internal horizon, when they are placed in relation to one another, there emerges yet another horizon in experience, that consisting of relations. And yet, objects are not merely spatially extended, but temporally extended as well. "For Husserl, the temporal horizon is the most important as all objects appear to us as temporal objects, as extended in time just as they are in space."[42]

Consider, as an example for all three senses of horizon the experience of seeing a bunch of bananas on a kitchen counter. As an experience with the sense "banana" and not plastic replica of a banana, one expects that they could peel the fruit and access the meat of the fruit. This is an expression of the internal horizon—what is undetermined in experience but expected in virtue of its being a banana. Yet, there is not merely a single banana, but a bunch. One expects that the tips protruding from the bottom of the bunch and the stems meeting at the top match in regular fashion, even if one can't see the second layer of bananas behind those at the top of the bunch. This is an expression of the external horizon, the bananas that one has obstructed partial views of are bananas, and not banana fragments. Finally, one expects the bunch at first to change from a greenish-yellow coloration to a yellowish hue, signifying ripening. Left to sit on the countertop longer, the yellowish coloration will begin to take on brown spotting, and eventually turn to a brown-black coloring. This is an example of the temporal horizon, in particular as it relates to the object's internal horizons.

The fusion of horizons in Gadamer is not to be conflated with Gurwitsch's notion of fusion discussed in the previous chapter.[43] Gurwitsch's notion of fusion is a narrower sense of fusion than what Gadamer means. Gadamer uses fusion more as a metaphor for the interaction, especially through successful communication or shared understandings, of subjects in common. Vessey argues clearly that for Gadamer:

> Horizons fuse when an individual realizes how the context of the subject matter can be weighed differently to lead to a different interpretation from the one initially arrived at. Either new information or a new sense of the relative significance of available information leads, at the very least, to an understanding of the subject matter, and ideally to a new agreement between the two parties about the subject matter. In any case, the original understanding is surpassed and integrated into a broader, more informed understanding. Our horizons are broadened; we have a new perspective on our old views, and maybe new views as well. This is the meaning of 'the fusion of horizons.'[44]

With Gadamer's sense of the fusion of subjects' horizons in and through intersubjective experiences one could argue that this is operative where plural subjects are verified evidentially, i.e. intentionally fulfilled. At the very least, fusion occurs when some coming together of divergent sets of understandings, thereby sets of expectations, meet in productive fashion–representing a shared experiential basis in the acknowledgement of and effect had through *our* exchange, even if totalizing or univocal agreement is not found. This can also function as the sort of basis from which an action-oriented view like Margaret Gilbert's can work. That is, a fusion of horizons operates in the constitution of plural subjects of *Intentionalität*, enabling the possibility of the plural subject per *Absicht*. Gurwitsch, on the other hand, isolated a specific type of fusion of horizons, namely wholesale fusion, fusion of a totalizing nature that effaces individuality. With Gadamer, and presumably Gilbert as well, the fusion or scope of shared intention need not be totalizing and individuality can be maintained. For example, that John and Jane do something in the "we" mode does not entail that they are in all respects as one, only that they are as one in reference to the specific objects of their intentionality or intent at play.

Gadamer's discussion takes place in a section of Gadamer's work titled "Overcoming the Epistemological Problem." The problem of intersubjectivity is tied to the issue of constitution, the aim being to penetrate to a universal achievement, the ground of the intersubjective world as such.[45] This relates also to the perennial issue of the one over the many.[46] According to Gadamer:

> [Husserl] is trying to penetrate behind the actuality of the sense-giving consciousness, and even behind the potentiality of shared meaning, to the universality of an achievement that is alone able to measure the universality of what is achieved–i.e., constituted in its validity. The all-embracing world horizon is constituted by fundamentally *anonymous* intentionality–i.e., not achieved by anyone by name. ...This world horizon is a presupposition of all science as well and is, therefore, more fundamental. As a horizon phenomenon "world" is

essentially related to subjectivity, and this relation means also that it "exists in transiency." The life-world exists in a constant movement of relative validity.[47]

The "outer" horizon of experience as such, not the "nearer" horizons of our scientific achievements or even our potential shared meanings, is an open intersubjective horizon within which all possible and actual meanings are situated. An open horizon is one that is in a state of dynamic activity, with the possibility for new subjects and its revision always open. Closed horizons, on the other hand, would be those that are settled and unopen to revision. Arguably, hate groups tend to have closed horizons, that is, they foreclose possibilities of relation with certain persons or groups of persons.[48] It should not surprise one that those domains of meaning more common to our everyday experience are found within the open intersubjective horizon of the life-world, if we point out that specialized bodies of knowledge, such as the natural sciences, represent descriptions of domains "nested" within the objective limits of possible experience as such.

Basically, a potential problem arises in virtue of the varied set of worlds or systems of meanings that one encounters in experience, from cultural variances to idiosyncratic individuals differences. To avoid wholesale relativism one must offer some constant as a ground for the relativities, in phenomenology this is a status subjectivity itself takes on.[49] Subjectivity in bare essence functions as the ground, not in actual potency with world-reference. To say this another way, subjectivity in a particular instantiation cannot serve as ground, in that, doing so one affirms relativism in a manner that results in incoherence. Instead, the form of subjectivity generally speaking is the ground that unifies and establishes the range in which the particulars may manifest distinctly.[50]

For Gadamer and many others after Husserl, the appeal to subjectivity–especially where taken as one's starting point for analysis–is exactly the locus of the problem.[51] To Gadamer, Husserl's view involves a "two-step empathy" that is "a very artificial construction."[52] Gadamer believes that, for Husserl, one first encounters the other as object and only secondarily "ensouls" the perceptual object. "In starting with transcendental subjectivity, Husserl insists that the Other must first of all be intended as something perceived… Only then, in a second, 'stepped-up' act, is ensoulment bestowed upon the perceived thing."[53] To one taking Husserl's analyses in their context, even reviewing the case of the waxenwoman, it's clear that Husserl would insist that one *first* sees the living person, and that the stepwise elements are only found in the constitutive analysis within the reflective analyses seeking what is essential in or "underneath" the everyday experiences of unreflective life.[54]

The apparent threat of subjective relativism one might take from Husserl is not really a reaction to relativism properly speaking. One is not speaking of relativism as much as one is speaking of a kind of particularism, a classic Aristotelian position embodied paradigmatically in Aristotle's theory of virtue.[55] This view is an outgrowth of respecting the particular nature of phenomena while also recognizing phenomena have formal natures that play an essential role in determining the phenomena themselves while also contributing to identity across particulars. This form of particularism accepts variations with regard to how particulars function or manifest without accepting that those differences imply a lack of a universal or essence in common across particulars, in contrast with relativism which denies the common essence. That is, even if there are general or universal principles that play constitutive roles in relation to phenomena, those principles underdetermine particulars. If they completely determined particulars, it is hard to see how there could be differences between particulars at all. The study of the unity of a kind is insufficient for the particularist, as the study of difference is of coequal importance. For Aristotle this wasn't just a hallmark of moral theory, but of metaphysics or ontology itself.[56] Particularism allows that within a system the same types of things will appear or behave differently in virtue of the variables local to them, and asserts that this is only to be expected. Material differences do not imply formal differences just as formal analyses don't prescribe every material facet of a particular, only what is essential to its being a particular of a given kind.

A reason for understanding the lifeworld or "outer" most horizon as being open is that as our bodies of knowledge expand and our technological capabilities expand we alter the domain of potential knowledge and experience for actual subjectivities of our particular form. What Husserl has identified is that subjectivity itself, in its raw essential form establishes the "outermost" limits of any possible *experience* whatsoever. As such, Gadamer is correct when he states that: "Transcendental subjectivity is the Ur-Ich ('the primal I') and not 'an I.' For it the basis of the pregiven world is superseded. It is the absolute irrelative to which all relativity, including that of the inquiring 'I,' is related."[57] The very possibility of intersecting horizons with others is owed to the shared essence of subjectivity as such, and more specifically to the shared species forms of that essence: human being. Within the genus of subjectivity as such, the human being is not alone, or not necessarily alone. Thus an opening is available for the possibility of our coming together in experience with other forms of subjectivity–for instance, dogs or bonobos–even if the richness of that togetherness can never be as strong as interpersonal relations between human beings. Indeed, one might also understand cultural differences as further "narrowing" of the basic forms in actuality, explaining why cross-cultural interactions sometimes aren't as "smooth" as intra-cultural interactions, especially where the "cultural-world-horizons" of cultures is potentially of greatly distinct *specific* forms; though, their *generic* forms are uniform in kind. The theme that relativities or particular variances of particulars of a shared form require some fixed anchor to be possible is one that is not unique to Husserl, but certainly a position of nuance that too few philosophers appreciate, or which too few are willing to accept the challenge to defend.[58]

Gadamer presents concerns about the possibility that Husserlian phenomenology could adequately address experiences of, hence with, others. Indeed, he seems of the mind that Husserl's framework makes the accounting impossible. Specifically, being motivated by realist concerns, Gadamer finds the move to transcendental idealism to be a predominant problem.[59] Yet, if one considers the issue from the phenomenological position, as opposed to the objectivist position of what is true or likely true from a global perspective, dissociated from individuated phenomenologies, one sees that realism is also inadequate to surmount the fundamental issue. There is a fundamental asymmetry to experience. As Husserl puts it clearly:

> Properly speaking, neither the other Ego [*Ich*] himself, nor his subjective processes or his appearance to his own essence, becomes given in our experience originally. If it were, if what belongs to the other's own essence were directly accessible, it would be merely a moment of my own essence, and ultimately he himself and I myself would be the same.
>
> ...An appresentation occurs even in external experience, since the strictly seen front of a physical thing always and necessarily appresents a rear aspect and prescribes for it a more or less determinate content. On the other hand, experiencing someone else cannot be a matter of just this kind of appresentation, which already plays a role in the constitution of primordial Nature: Appresentation of this sort involves the possibility of verification by a corresponding fulfilling presentation (the back becomes the front); whereas in the case of that appresentation which would lead over into the other original sphere, such verification must be excluded a priori.[60]

One's experience is always and only *their own*. One can never experience the other's experience. It is that de facto asymmetry between my experience, my consciousness and the other's which leads to the variance in our respective horizons or "worlds" in the first place. Since it is implausible to deny the asymmetry to conscious experience, one must aim for descriptions of how we operate that work with that fact of experience, as opposed to simply seeking to work around it.

There are two potential worries that a Gadamerian might respond to this with. First, one might object that Gadamer is not motivated by realism but with an effort to preserve facticity. Second, one might object that Gadamer's approach better represents lived experience, that Husserl's approach is overly artificial.[61]

The first objection argues that realism is not Gadamer's concern, only facticity—capturing the factical nature of our lived experience. This objection argues that we find ourselves thrown into the world at the outset, immersed amongst others already, and enmeshed within historical and cultural formations. In response to this objection, I acknowledge that Gadamer is not a naïve realist, but wonder how the motivation for facticity isn't the same in kind as the motivation for realism. Gadamer's hermeneutics focuses on how the same fact or object under interpretation may be interpreted as bearing distinctly different meanings to different subjects. That is, facts alone do not determine meaning, though they certainly constrain them. A concern for facticity amounts to a concern for identifying that which is to be interpreted, that which is the basis for interpretation, or that which an evidentially sound interpretation of the phenomenon in question must accept as part of its interpretation. The three listed possibilities are not identical with one another, but each reflects the same sort of concern had by the realist, capturing as accurately as possible the non-subjective elements of a state of affairs and for transcending one's idiosyncratic interpretation of beings. Husserl never denies those factical elements, only brackets them in order to unearth evidentially supported descriptions of them in order to ground meaningful statements about intersubjective states of affairs.

The second objection argues that Gadamer's concern with facticity and aim to preserve lived experience first is preferable to the Husserlian approach. The argument is that Husserl's emphasis on the subject tends to reifying the subject and thereby dispose his account to an artificially intellectualist approach to dealing with others. Instead of focusing on lived form of communal life, Husserl focuses on the very experience of the other, as if that is alien to one in everyday experience. In response to this objection, I argue that Husserl never denies the presence of others in everyday experience. Phenomenology treats the world as we experience it as its point of origin, and radically so–denying theoretical pre-commitments, no matter how entrenched, as being an adequate starting point. The Gadamerian confuses the founded nature of everyday acts of communal experiences. Husserl's claim is that those experiences contain as part of their constitution the more basic formal dimensions his analyses focus on. Further, he would reemphasize again that the other is always "exterior" to one, and that fact is inescapable. To attempt to bypass the asymmetry essential to the experience of another fails to capture the factical nature of experience.

Do we experience others in our everyday lives without much trouble: certainly. Is there an asymmetry to our respective experiences: certainly. Phenomenology respects both, as both are true to experience. While Gadamer and Smith direct our attention in fruitful critical directions, neither presents a devastating critique. Rather, each points to places where more work needs to be done and clearer descriptive analyses can be presented.

Notes

1. B. Smith 1995. This appears to be, for all functional purposes, the same criticism levied against Searle in Smith and Searle 2003. Smith's criticisms of both Husserl and Searle demand a more precise accounting of how pluralities of meanings or references function. Basically, if one cedes to some form of realism and stresses the importance of evidence in relation to the intersubjective task of testing the fulfillment of intentions, the subject-world relation mediated by others while maintaining a capacity for variety and plurality is not an open or capricious plurality–as it is bound by reference to the world.

2. B. Smith 1995: 429

3. ibid: 424

4. Husserl 2001b: V, §27, 137-138

5. Carr 1974: 82

6. Zahavi 2001a, see also Donohoe 2004, Zahavi 2001b, 2003, 2005

7. Carr 1974: 88

8. Husserl 1999: 134/162

9. Husserl 1999: 133/160; I believe the sense of *a priori* here is consistent with other developments of that term in the early phenomenological movement. For example, those of Adolf Reinach (2002) and Mikel Dufrenne (1966). What this means is that Husserl's appeal to the a priori status of a common Nature in which we all live, is that he's acknowledging a necessity to this fact as a constitutive part of the world–which conditions our experience from the outset.

10. Husserl 1999: 133/160

11. Searle 1995: 27-29

12. At least, this is how Husserl is commonly understood. I'm tempted to say either the interpretation of Husserl is wrongheaded or that the Münich realists, who are able to assert such consistently with phenomenology, had a position that is better. However, even they acknowledge that there are key epistemological differences between their methods and those of empiricists, paradigmatically the case of Hume.

13. Husserl 1999: V, Husserl 1978: VI

14. Husserl 1999: 91/123

15. ibid: 114/144

16. ibid: 125/154, see also 105/135, 107/137, 114-115/144-145, 125-126/154, 148/175

17. Kant 1987: 160/293-294

18. This is a rather huge problem, that of realism and idealism. I must here shelve the issue and move on. I would refer one initially to Husserl 1983: §§21-22 as key to filling out the nuances of Husserl's view.

19. Husserl identifies Berkeley's nominalism, which underlies his idealism, as a mistake in the same place he counts Platonic realism as a mistake (Husserl 2001a: II, §7: 248-249). See also Husserl 2001a: II, §§15, 18, 20, 28-31

20. Husserl 1983: §55: 129/106-107

21. Husserl called Hegel's dialectic a fiction (Husserl 2001a: Prolegomena, §55: 130). Later Husserl offers a scathing statement on the value of Hegel: "Of the ambiguous profundity of that systematic philosophy, which rather aimed at thinking out world-conceptions and a world-wisdom, and which hindered the progress of scientific philosophy so badly by its unholy blend of discordant intentions, Bolzano–the contemporary of Hegel–shows no trace" (ibid: Prolegomena, Chapter 10, Appendix: 142-143).

22. Consider also Reinach's statement about the difficulties of getting the phenomena themselves, as opposed to conceptualizations of them: "right at the beginning of this task we have wholly to do with ideal objects (*Ideelles*)" (Reinach 2002: 181).

23. It is also incoherent to claim that *all* attempts at systemization are of equal worth. Reinach 2002: 185

24. Husserl 1970: §6, 16

25. Husserl 1970: Appendix I, *The Vienna Lecture*, 280

26. ibid.

27. ibid: 282

28. ibid: 286

29. Reinach 2002: 180

30. ibid: 194-195

31. Gadamer's full set of criticisms of Husserl's views on intersubjectivity is too massive a project to tackle here. As such, I focus just on the arguments centered around the notion of horizons. Key components are Gadamer 1989: Part II, 3, A and Gadamer 2000. Insightful critical appraisals of Gadamer's reading of Husserl can be found in Vessey 2005, 2007, 2009.

32. Gadamer 1989: 245

33. Vessey 2009: 533

34. Husserl 1998: §27 & §44

35. Vessey 2009: 535; Merleau-Ponty 1958: 78-79

36. Vessey 2009: 535

37. ibid: 535-536; Elsewhere Vessey points out that Gadamer saw Husserl's innovation of horizonal intentionality as both a means of avoiding psychologism as well as idealism and the pitfalls of Neo-Kantianism (Vessey 2007: 10).

38. Walton 2003

39. This list is clearly incomplete, but sufficient for present purposes. If one consults, for example, the masterful research of Roberto Walton, one sees a much richer account—one that contrasts Gurwitsch's use of horizon with Husserl's (Walton 2003). See also Kwan 1990.

40. Vessey 2009: 534

41. ibid: 534-535

42. ibid: 535

43. Gadamer is good to refer to Husserl's acknowledgment of William James' influence on the notion of "horizon," specifically through James' notion of "fringes" (Gadamer 1989: 245-246 n. 148, reference is to Husserl 1999: 264).

44. Vessey 2009: 540

45. Gadamer 1989: 246

46. ibid: 248

47. ibid: 246-247

48. Arguably the present state of our political culture in the United States consists of two mostly closed horizons, resulting in the volatile and intolerant talk across party-lines. The open sectors of these horizons consist of those few places where consensus is had, and at the level of individuals who don't operate under a closed horizonal schema in their political lives. One could make a case that open political horizons are better than closed ones, acknowledging that these horizons will naturally be at odds with one another. Closed horizons foreclose the possibility of fusion through either consensus or reasoned compromise, often being detrimental to national interests.

49. Gadamer 1989: 248. The idea of grounding localized relativities in some objective basis is discussed in some depth in Boghossian 2006.

50. Consult, for instance, Husserl's insightful discussions of the genetic developments of material differences as they contribute to the individuation of formally identical monadic wholes: Husserl 2001: Supplementary Texts, Section

4, B-C. According to David Vessey, Gadamer sat in on some of these lectures in 1921 (Vessey 2007: 4)

51. Gadamer 2000: 282-283; for discussion see Vessey 2007: 17ff.

52. ibid: 283

53. ibid: 282

54. Remember that the transcendental attitude is "the attitude according to which everything previously existing for us in straightforward consciousness is taken exclusively as 'phenomenon,' as a sense meant and undergoing verification, purely in the manner in which, as correlate of uncoverable constitutive systems, it has gained and is gaining existential sense" (Husserl 1999: 95/126).

Vessey has carefully indentified at least three problems latent in Gadamer's own alternative position in Vessey 2005.

55. See Nussbaum 1993; I believe Nussbaum rightly points out that Aristotle's virtue ethics is not relativistic. The same lesson is fruitfully applied to Husserl's phenomenology. It's that the sophisticated nuance of the formal analyses and sensitivity to particulars in material analyses gives off the impression of relativism to the critic whose understanding or respect for differences in analytical aims from place to place is less than acute or whose tolerance for subtlety is low.

56. Aristotle, *Metaphysics*, IV.2, 1004a15-b1

57. Gadamer 1989: 248

58. For instance, Paul Boghossian concludes that any relativism can only be coherent within some non-relative framework. That is, relativism can be true over a domain if and only if there is some non-relative foundation for it (Boghossian 2006).

Another example is that of Nussbaum's argument, noted earlier, to the effect that Aristotle's particularism does not entail relativism. That is, that variable moral practices are not inconsistent with a denial of relativism in virtue of their foundational reference to humanity as such (Nussbaum 1993).

59. "For Gadamer the difficulty Husserl had with issue of intersubjectivity, the body, and practical life were signs Husserl erred when he turned away from the realism of the *Logical Investigations* toward the idealism of the *Ideas...*" (Vessey 2007: 8). Full discussion is insightful (Vessey 2007: 8-9).

60. Husserl 1999: 109/139

61. My gratitude to Theodor George for registering these objections at the 2011 Central Division meeting of the American Philosophical Association in Minneapolis, MN.

Chapter 7
Responding to Sokolowski's Criticisms of Husserlian Individualism

Robert Sokolowski has recently given very clear voice to a common criticism of Husserlian individualism. Sokolowski begins:

> I believe that his [Husserl's] analysis of how logic emerges from experience is a major advancement in philosophical thinking, but I also think that his description does not take intersubjectivity sufficiently into account. He describes categorial articulation as though it were done by a solitary mind, which first perceives an object in a manifold of appearances and then moves upward into categorial form as it articulates and recognizes parts and wholes in things.[1]

Sokolowski's alternative recommendation is that:

> Instead of describing categorial intuition as something my own mind accomplishes, we should describe it as something a speaker does for a listener. The formal structures of logic arise between two (or more) persons, not primarily in the mind of a single person by himself.[2]

That is, Sokolowski counts the categorial articulations of our conscious experiences as primarily oriented on an intersubjective plane, instead of a personal one. Our articulations, he suggests, are done with an eye towards others, not for our own sake. As such, syntactic articulations arise "because two people can be so related to a given object that one of them can focus their attention on that object as a whole and then focus their attention on an aspect of that object."[3]

In response to the challenge that the operations of mind could be done individually to each person, Sokolowski replies: "If the transition from perception to thought happened in privacy and immanence, then communication would be impossible."[4] He is referring specifically to how perceptual acts, or precategorial acts, form the basis for our categorial articulations with part-whole structures—more simply, meanings–as manifest to consciousness. For Sokolowski, meanings arise in the intersubjectively saturated relations between persons, others and the world. "It is that interaction or coupling of focus, which is an almost legal achievement and documentation, that installs a syntactic form."[5] This statement rather nicely articulates the basic intuitions of theories of collective intentionality, but makes meaningful experience dependent on intersubjectivity. One need not disagree that intersubjective experiences and intersubjectively oriented experiences (collective experiences) supply *a* syntactic form. It seems clear that one's communal context and community of origin supply one with a way(s) of making sense of the world. Where I disagree is that this supplies *syntactic form as such*, agreeing with Husserl that originally this arises in subject-world relation. It is not necessarily with an eye towards others that subjective achievements primarily function, though they certainly can do so. This chapter dedicates itself to defending Husserlian phenomenology from the common charge that it is solipsistic in nature.[6] This relates to the overall project in that a similar charge, that one undermines the social by emphasizing the individual, can be made against the sort of view being developed in relation to collective intentionality.

Sokolowski expands his view by laying out four benefits for taking syntax to be primarily or principally intersubjective. First, "We start off with an obvious realism in the use of language. We avoid the egocentric predicament."[7] Second, "We are not obliged to add communication to the use of words. The communicative dimension is there from the beginning."[8] Third,

> This intersubjective approach to syntax leads us easily and obviously into the declarative use of the first-person singular. If syntax arises when one speaker "packages" a situation for another when he raises the situation to the level of categoriality, then the speaker also emerges as *this* speaker over against *that* one.[9]

And, finally:

> This intersubjective approach to syntax permits an enrichment of what can be included in formal logic. Traditionally, logical form is said to include only those elements that are essential for predication and implication, those elements that are a precondition for truth values.[10]

I will primarily attend to the first two points, as the latter are not substantially problematic in the present context. Sokolowski's third benefit is basically that identifying one's own expressions of meanings publicly, and marking them as one's own helps distinguish us from one another and locates us in the context of the community of human persons. And the fourth claim merely adds that we ought not see logic as a reductionist or abstract game of no real relation to the world, but to embrace our exchanges and expressions of meaning in their full complex variations.

Concerning his first benefit, the avoidance of the egocentric predicament, I agree that this is a major benefit of considering intersubjectivity. However, I am not convinced that one has to place cognition in the public space or forgo a strong sense of the personal integrity of individuated consciousness to achieve this end. Intersubjectivity can be adequately addressed even if all cognition is, strictly speaking, only taking place in individual minds–albeit at times in reference to intersubjective contexts or in the we-mode. Sokolowski counts this first benefit as including the ability to avoid talk of mental representations, and dedicates a good deal of his book to criticizing the idea of mental representations as either reified or pictorial things in their own right.[11] In brief:

> Mental representations are a deadly trap philosophically: if you start with them, you will never get beyond them. They lock us into subjective isolation. The intersubjective approach we have been taking avoids the very notion of mental representations, because in it the words are used immediately by two people to refer to things and to formulate them into their wholes and parts.[12]

He brings this point home by adding: "Since two minds originally articulated the thing together, the signification of the words being used could not be a private, mental meaning. It could only be the thing that is known."[13] The problem with Sokolowski's criticism of Husserl on this point is that Husserl recognized the public nature of the expressivity of meanings. What Husserl's not willing to eliminate, however, is the subjective constitution of that meaning, i.e. the individual and individuated nature of the act of consciousness. Sokolowski overreaches here in that meanings are not necessarily originally enacted with others, even if meanings can be enacted with and by others. If meaning is originally public, a given subject merely has to come to see that and come to see that some meanings are given shape or born in intersubjective relations, not just our objective relatedness to the world–as is evidenced by child development as well. Meanings are publicly expressible but dependent on the relatedness to the world of the individual subjectivities for whom they are meaningful and by and through whom they are constituted. That is, Wittgensteinians are correct in that there is no private language but phenomenology can withhold from committing to the idea that all cognition is inherently or primarily linguistic in nature. As such, even if meanings are *publicly* articulable, their achievement and being as meaning inherently have a subjective basis. Meaning is publicly expressible, even though meaningfulness itself is, at least in a primitive way, dependent on the subjective achievement of individual consciousness. Meaning is intentional, is about something. As intentional it is about something and meaningful to someone. This basic experiential dimension, located "in" the individual, is prior to sharing of that meaning, perhaps sometimes even prior to their express recognition or contrary their self-denial.

There is a difference between whether cognition is possible without others and whether others condition all cognitive acts. For instance, one's experiences are informed by and adopt the categories operative in one's social context. It is certainly true that the presence of others influence one's cognition in everyday life. But no matter how prevalent that influence, it is still possible for there to be an enabling role based in the individual subject. Without individual subjects there is no experience at all, nor anything social to influence individuals. Individual consciousness is an enabling condition for social phenomena. Of course, the genetic development of an individual's consciousness matters, and is clearly informed by others. But in order for it to be possible there must be a basic subjective framework in which those cultural effects and meanings can first come into being.

Sokolowski is not, as many outside phenomenology are wont to do, collapsing the act-content distinction. Rather, he recognizes that acts of consciousness are conditioned by an intersubjective context. However, it being the case that how one directs one's mind and what acts of intellection one is disposed to are conditioned by one's relations to others, does not imply that one's acts of intellect are thereby inherently intersubjective. That formal and material elements of consciousness have a dynamic interrelated nature is important to note; however, that does not efface the distinction itself, only complicates the relation between distinctive elements.

This leads to the second benefit of Sokolowski's view; communication is present from the outset in relation to words. He is absolutely correct that language is primarily and necessarily an intersubjective achievement. And he has a further point, relating to the problem of mental representations, that it's not the case that one first thinks x, then publicly expresses a representation of what one thinks in either action or language. The solipsist-Internalist view, as Sokolowski calls it, is clearly mistaken: we don't first think a salute, that being the real salute; the publicly expressed salute being only an expression of the real one. One doesn't first think the word unicorn then expression in public form a representation of that thought. Sokolowski is correct that the paradigm of a solipsistically isolated consciousness is incoherent. As Zahavi has forcefully put it: "no one truly familiar with the phenomenological tradition can endorse the claim that phenomenology should have failed to recognize the philosophical significance of intersubjectivity."[14] Zahavi later points out that a view common to phenomenologists is that "subjectivity and intersubjectivity, far from being competing alternatives, however, are, in fact, complementary and mutually interdependent notions."[15] Finally, "The subject must be seen as a worldly incarnate existence, and the world must be seen as a common field of experience, if intersubjectivity is to be at all possible."[16] The experience of intersubjectivity is not merely possible, but actual. One experiences the world as bearing objective sense and such a view would be impossible if experience were on the model of *solus ipse*.[17] Phenomenological inquiries into intersubjectivity always involve examination into the relations between self, other, and world.[18] Further, scholars like David Carr have noted that the idea that Husserl was concerned with solipsism in a traditional sense is a red herring, brought on by criticisms based in misunderstandings of the phenomenological project.[19] Indeed, Husserl's goal in *Cartesian Meditations* is more one of demonstrating that the specter of solipsism is a red herring than to offer a solution to that problem. The terms according to which the traditional problem of solipsism has been framed aren't accepted on the phenomenological view. Additionally, without defining internalism clearly, it's not obvious that internalism entails solipsism and represents something of a straw-man critique.

In more specifics, Sokolowski complains about Husserl's notion of a "sphere of ownness" [*Eigenheitssphäre*] from *Cartesian Meditations*. Husserl "proposes that we try, imaginatively, to think away any dimension of other minds."[20] And, "We are to abstract from the very dimension of other persons, and see what would be left in our experiencing, as well as in the world given to our experiencing. This residue would be the sphere of ownness."[21] Sokolowski admits that to Husserl the sphere of ownness is an abstraction–not a concrete possibility. "It is a device that he uses to clarify intersubjectivity and the experiencing associated with it, and to show that his philosophy is not solipsistic."[22] The problem Sokolowski has is that Husserl believes that categorial intentionality of some sort could function in the sphere of ownness. Husserl expressly states that there are "eidetic objectivities" (essences or ideal meanings) available in that "space." Indeed, Husserl himself suggests that there would be very little difference between the meaningful articulations in the sphere of ownness as distinct from the more intersubjectively conditioned sphere of everyday articulations of or in experience.[23] To some extent Husserl may be mistaken. For example, if his position is that socially constituted objects like money or chairs are present as social objects in the sphere of ownness. But that the physical objects that bear the socially conditioned senses would vanish *in toto* could not be the case. The natives in *The Gods Must Be Crazy* interacted with a physical thing, the glass bottle, but not *qua* Coke bottle. While the cloth paper and wooden object each remain present, their socially constituted natures and connotations associated with any particular linguistic community are abstracted away. Sokolowski responds that this "would claim, however, that categorial forms and syntactically shaped experience could not be thought to occur in the sphere of ownness, because such syntax is the deposit of conversational action, and such activities could not occur without the presence, in principle, of other speakers."[24] That is the "I" is always located amongst others and our ways of articulating the world are informed by our intersubjective context. There may be a dependence relation between the possibility of meaning and intersubjectivity, what Zahavi calls the dependence of meaning on the constituting intersubjectivity. However, it's not clear that this makes individuated articulations without the involvement of others impossible. The constitution of otherness or the constitution of intersubjectivity itself must on some level be or include a significant individual subjective achievement. If that were not the case, it would be very hard to understand some neurological disorders, such as Capgras syndrome or autism spectrum disorders.

Returning to something Sokolowski himself underscores, there is a basic experiential dimension that precedes meaningful articulations. Husserl's purpose in considering the sphere of ownness is to consider how one's world would be experienced absent an intersubjective gloss into which one has been enculturated.[25] In part this asks if it is possible to transcend one's social context. Without that possibility, philosophy would be reduced to little more than social commentary and cultural determinism would be an immutable given. The more basic subject-world relation doesn't change significantly. What changes are the conventional systems of giving expression to that relation. That is, one's individual intentionality remains intact, where the socially received meaning-constitutions one has inherited are bracketed from one's attention and description. A full analysis of Husserl's view recognizes the key insights of the *Crisis* and "Origin of Geometry." Before there is a theoretical appreciation of the world we have a practical, action-oriented interaction with the world.[26] All meaning arises in the life-world, not just to coldly detached monadic-epistemological subjects. Additionally, the sedimented categorial achievements embedded in and giving structure to our present day knowledge may be retraced to their origins in an experiential basis, or set of experiential bases. Sokolowski seems to neglect these insights when critiquing the Husserlian position as too narrow on this point. Husserl isn't defending the Cartesian epistemological subject. Husserl modified the Modern epistemic subject while avoiding the excesses of the epistemological turn in Modern philosophy. He does so by recognizing that all abstractions arise in relation to and are dependent on our epistemically finite relation with the world.[27] Our physical constitution limits and constrains the constitution of our conscious experiences and establishes the range of possibilities pertaining to our knowledge. In short, our embodied natures affect the range of possibilities available to our consciousness, but our physicality in a brute sense is not the whole of the subject–only a foundational part of that whole.

A problem that Sokolowski's approach has is, while he does maintain his emphasis on the ontological subjectivity of logic, as a *praxis* of humans acting in concert with one another, he's not always careful enough to ward off the view that logic is *not* thereby epistemologically subjective. That is, even if there is no logic or meanings without subjectivity as such, that doesn't make logical findings epistemologically subjective in nature. That something is a practice in the domain of human action does not mean it is basic. Many practices we engage in during our everyday lives are institutionally situated in complex arrays of iterated intentional achievements, specifically collective intentional achievements. Those are founded on more primitive intentional achievements. Logic, as a practice, is only possible because there is some accessible phenomena in relation to which it is grounded, in this case the general syntactic articulations of meaning in experience as such.[28]

There is an associated potential problem with collectivist approaches to social ontology and their implications regarding the nature of norms. A collectivist might argue, following a view that minds are socially embedded similar to what Sokolowski is arguing for, that we receive our norms from our social contexts and that norms are in *all* cases dependent on that context in a strong sense, thereby relative to the specific social domains out of which they arise. Recall that strong notions of collectivity, such as that emphasized in the social-embedded thesis discussed in chapter two, claim the relevant issue is how individuals are formatively influenced by the collectivities with which they participate. Such views claim further that our consciousness is dependent on said collectivities. Sokolowski's position certainly resembles such a view. However, one key difference is that Sokolowski appreciates the objective nature of our relations both with the world and with others.

A difficulty with the proper handling of social phenomena is respecting that while they are ontologically subjective, being based on the beliefs and actions of subjects, they can also be epistemologically objective at the same time. There are facts about social phenomena, e.g. Barak Obama is the President of the United States, and the cartoon character Scooby Doo is a dog. Further complicating matters is that the ontologically subjective basis for social phenomena (human subjectivity) also stands in relation with ontologically objective beings, manifesting senses predicated upon complex networks of relations. As such one must resist the temptations either to fall into constructivism and treat all objects in the world as socially dependent (ontologically subjective), or classify all beings as ontologically objective and thereby deny the reality of ontologically subjective phenomena, thereby succumbing to what phenomenological philosophers recognize to be unavoidable dimension of most forms of naturalism.[29] It is imperative that one keep clear the differences between ontological and epistemological senses of subjectivity and objectivity.[30]

Collectivist motivated philosophers may, by conflating something's being subjective in ontology with its being subjective epistemologically, compromise the nature of norms. Norms are ontologically subjective; norms are norms *for* subjects. Further, norms are dependent on the nature of the phenomena to which they relate. "Every normative science demands that we know certain nonnormative truths: these it takes from certain theoretical sciences, or gets by applying propositions so taken to the constellation of cases determined by its normative interest."[31] Ontologically subjective beings like norms, where not emptily intended, are grounded in relations to objects, and given their intersubjective senses through how a community of persons stands in relation to those beings. Elaborating on this Aristotelian notion, Husserl states:

> Every normative proposition of, e.g., the form 'An *A* should be *B*' implies the theoretical proposition 'Only an *A* which is *B* has the properties *C*,' in which '*C*,' serves to indicate the constitutive content of the standard-setting predicate 'good' (e.g. pleasure, knowledge, whatever, in short, is marked down as good by the valuation fundamental to our given sphere).[32]

Any norms arising out of collective intentionality or intersubjective contexts are dependent on and imply some theoretical proposition. One should also note that, for Husserl, propositions are complex wholes, their parts include individuated meanings syntactically ordered, and, like their parts, propositions are species of mental contents. Too strong a theory of collectivity, by prescribing a status to the collective as a pre-individual locus for all normativity suggests a view that may require that one understand all norms, logical, moral, etc., as only conventions of some particular social praxis, or to be general and to only hold contingently. Such is a danger of a strong thesis of collectivity.

Following the later Husserl, one can add that the theoretical propositions on which normative propositions are dependent upon are themselves dependent on a more basic interactive experiential relation between subject and world. That subjective ground is necessary for the intersubjective agreements the collective activities are based in. We must have a shared experiential basis to engage in actions together. The experience of togetherness can be based on a wide range of subject matter; this can be anything from something very formal in nature (e.g. the shared basis of human subjectivity as such) to specific material experiences (e.g. being in a café in Buffalo, NY on a certain day and at a certain time) dependent on the nature of one's intentional formations.

Not all forms of collectivism necessarily have these problems. Hans Bernhard Schmid's collectivism avoids the necessity of such a conclusion through his relational account. Though, the denial of a constructivist approach to norms is also not necessarily entailed by his view. None of this rules out that some of the world as we experience it, and phenomena constituted in it, be intersubjectively constituted, e.g. the notion of race. Rather, it is to argue that not all norms pertaining to the world are grounded in intersubjective agreement even if their specific connotations are manifestations of collective intentional achievements, e.g. norms governing the nature of intersubjective agreement itself that arise from the objective nature of consciousness as such. There must be some basis prior to intersubjectively constituted contexts–some condition for their possibility in references to which a norm may be generated. As has been argued, the very notion of a social or collective context or broader domain of human activity is predicated on that assumption. Too often ignored in Husserl is that higher order intersubjective phenomena, those more complex than the basic intersubjective experience of an other, are dependently founded on the prior foundation of that basic experiential structure.[33] Even if subjectivity is, in some sense, intersubjective, intersubjective achievements depend also on subjectivity.

Stressing the intersubjective nature of a human activity is fine. However, Sokolowski pursues a position wherein all consciousness is primarily intersubjective. Such a view swings too far to the opposing extreme from the Modern solipsistic subject. Further, parking all cognition in the intersubjective camp seems to undermine the possibility of intersubjectivity without collective consciousness. That is, *inter*subjectivity itself is constituted by individual subjects who must be *individuals*. Consciousness is inherently individuated in each individual subject, the embodied zero-point of all experience. And it's in and through an embodied subjectivity, in a dynamic correlation with others, through our individual capabilities expanded by those relations, that there is a meaningful inter-subjective "space" whatsoever. As such, Husserl's view marks a middle ground between the extremes of solipsism and collectivism: individual subjects in dynamic intersubjective exchange with one another, liable to and responsible to one another in a common world that is accessible to us whether we accept that or not. In Sokolowski's own terminology, while intersubjectivity is an essential property of human subjectivity, intersubjectivity is dependent on subjectivity's sense-constitutional part-whole structure. Inter-subjectivity without subjectivity is incoherent.

Phenomenology is a break from the problematic framework of Modern philosophical thought. In the case of intersubjective experiences this specifically involves a break from the traditionally considered problem of other minds, and the dualist framework on which it is predicated. Two individualist-minded philosophers who have spoken to this point are Gurwitsch and Searle.

Gurwitsch begins his *Habiltationschrift* by expressing a philosophical point of view that has contributed regularly to there being a problem concerning our experiences of other human beings. By contrast, he states the basic starting point of a phenomenological view:

> Everything about which we know, considered in any sense whatever, is given to us in mental processes. In order that something be there for us as an object so that we can speak of it in some way or other, even when we might argue against its existence (e.g., a winged horse), or against its possibility (e.g., a square circle), we must have mental processes that bear upon the objects in question–no matter how the bearing might be conceived, no matter how the givenness of the object might be interpreted.
>
> Moreover, those mental processes in which we are aware of something have a relation to the ego: they are *my* mental processes.[34]

To begin with there are two potential problematics: 1) the givenness of objects in mental processes, and 2) the ego-relatedness of mental processes. Problems arise with these phenomena, or aspects of phenomenal experience in virtue of what constitutes an adequate description of them. Gurwitsch further notes that there is a sub-class of mental processes, privileged mental processes: those in which an object is given "as it itself, 'in person', and 'originalter.'"[35] And that "any proposition, any presumption, any scientific theory must be measured and verified by what is given in and through those privileged mental processes."[36] The problem for traditional theories of our experiences of other human beings is that they begin and end with descriptions of physical qualities and their changes.[37] On such descriptions, no "inner experience" or mental life of another is ever given.

Clearly, a subject-eliminative description is not adequate to one's experiences of others. Subject-eliminative descriptions are not adequate to any experience. Gurwitsch continues:

> The result of this phenomenology of consciousness stands in contrast to what is customary in our everyday lives. When in daily life someone with a radiant face tells us about something, we do not live a piece of knowledge about things intelligible to us which are accompanied, in addition, by movements of the mouth along with characteristic distortion of the facial muscles. From the other's words, instead, we *immediately* and openly witness his joy, see it *directly* in his face. In daily life the idea never arises that we do not have in perception what itself occurs in our fellow human being.

Always and everywhere our daily comportment is guided by our belief that we *directly* know what mentally occurs in the other person with whom we deal in various ways.[38]

It is a by-product of the philosophical bias that one only experiences what is immediately available to the five senses or what is physical (in a narrow sense) that leads to the counter-intuitive conclusion that we don't experience others as more than an animated piece of meat. We encumber ourselves with skeptical problems of other minds and as to the legitimacy of our knowledge in virtue of the conviction, one underlying most of contemporary philosophy, "that only something corporeal is immediately perceived and experienced."[39]

The problem is not privileged mental processes *per se*. Rather, the problem is in the idea that only corporeal objects are objects of immediate experience. That is only physical entities are real; and they are real in the manner they are given by the senses in veridical experience. This is exacerbated by an implicit acceptance of dualism, thereby assuming mentality and consciousness are non-physical and therefore not real. Where privileged mental processes are experienced in our everyday lives, so too are numbers, other people and generalities. The very structure of the problem in this traditional form makes impossible any meaningful expression of 'we' where human beings with mental lives of our own are involved.

Gurwitsch elaborates on and modifies Husserl's view of consciousness by arguing that others are always co-present at the margins of our experience.[40] One can affirm the presence of an intersubjective horizon to our experience of the world, in which the possibility of others is always live, or, as Gurwitsch puts it: others are co-present to our intentional lives. This intersubjective horizon need not be the innermost horizon of consciousness, as a more restricted range of possibilities could include one's "private" conscious life. The possibilities and actualities in our everyday lives of there being others are present as a range of possibilities built upon or "exterior" to the "subjective core." That there are experiences which are *mine* does not exclude the possibly of experiences being *ours*. But for experiences to be *ours* (yours and mine together) we must each be capable of experiences that are our own.

The bias that the only immediately or veridically sound objects of experience would be physical in a narrow sense is a by-product of substance dualism. Searle adeptly demonstrates how this developed, with specific emphasis on its reiteration and mutations in twentieth century philosophy of mind.[41] Searle identifies four factors at work in the background of philosophical traditions leading into the present:

i) "We have a terror of falling into Cartesian dualism."[42]
ii) "Along with the Cartesian tradition we have inherited a vocabulary, and with the vocabulary a certain set of categories, within which we are historically conditioned to think about these problems."[43]

iii) "There is a persistent objectifying tendency in contemporary philosophy, science, and intellectual life generally. We have the conviction that if something is real, it must be equally accessible to all competent observers."[44]

iv) "Because of our conception of the history of the growth of knowledge we have come to suffer from what Austin called the '*ivresse des grands profondeurs.*' It does not seem enough somehow to state humble and obvious truths about the mind–we want something deeper. We want a theoretical discovery. And of course our model of a great theoretical discovery comes from the history of physical science."[45]

We have inherited and continue to unreflectively operate with a conceptual framework of dualism, a categorial framework that pits two competing sets of categories against one another on roughly Cartesian terms. As such, if one favors one set of terms over another, one is often tempted to denigrate the use of the other conceptual categories as inadequate, mythical, or delusional. Like Gurwitsch, Searle believes that "The Cartesian conception of the physical, the conception of physical reality as *res extensa*, is simply not adequate to describe the facts that correspond to statements about physical reality."[46] What has been established is a false dichotomy between minds and bodies. What's more, the very terms of the division are not clear. The distinction is traditionally made on shaky grounds. Searle concludes, "once you see the incoherence of dualism, you can see that monism and materialism are just as mistaken."[47] In other words, the very categorical framework itself, in this case premised on a false dichotomy, is the problem and anything developed on that ground suffers from its incoherence. Rejecting Cartesian dualism while retaining the basic distinctions of Cartesian dualism is an inadequate response. Rather, one needs to reorder their categories and reject the basic ontological framework of Cartesian dualism itself. Husserl glosses the problems latent in Descartes, and forcefully separates his thinking from that of Descartes in just such a fashion, the results coming to a head in *Cartesian Meditations.*[48]

It is in virtue of a false dichotomy embodied in dualism as traditionally conceived, not individualism or a thesis in favor of privileged mental processes, that one comes to believe others are opaque to one. Denial of the falsely predicated dichotomy is part and parcel to Husserl's phenomenological philosophy. Critics of Husserl often fail to appreciate that even if Husserl sometimes spoke in the language familiar to the faulty Cartesian framework, Husserl's categories are not themselves subject to or predicated on that framework. Thus, most criticisms attacking Husserl from those grounds assume that Husserl did not develop phenomenology and suffer from the same incoherence. However, where Husserl's views are consistent he's not operating on Cartesian terms. It is open for dispute whether Husserl failed to remain consistent, I am not here interested in the textual question as much as the positive phenomenological insights.

Perhaps Sokolowski is operating with some remnant of the traditional Modern framework in the background of his critique. While that certainly seems plausible in the case of any number of attempts to criticize Husserl, it is more charitable to say that Sokolowski and those who are similarly schooled in phenomenological philosophy and can demonstrate comprehensive understandings of the phenomenological turn in Husserl are not directing their critiques from some vestige of Modern philosophical prejudice. Sokolowski seems, instead, to have two underlying factors that complicate his view. First, he pushes for a very strong relation between language and cognition. As such, he radically limits the domain of pre-linguistic or non-linguistic phenomena. Language is an essentially intersubjective phenomenon. If cognition is linguistic in nature or predominantly linguistic in nature, then cognition too becomes essentially intersubjective in nature. I see no reason to opt for such a strong overlap between language and cognition, preferring to maintain a more substantive pre- and non-linguistic domain of human experience. The view that there is a substantial pre- or non-linguistic base to cognition is bolstered by recent research conducted by Michael Tomasello, particularly by his work on the cooperative behaviors of preverbal children.[49] Take for instance shared musical experiences, they are not linguistically ordered, even if one can talk about them with one another. Free jazz is not a linguistic experience for either listeners or participants, yet it involves spontaneous exchanges of meaningful expressions in intersubjective "space"–directed and established through a dynamic of individuals acting in concert with one another, as it is individuals who improvise and play their respective musical instruments. Further, young preverbal children and some other species of higher-order mammals clearly have intersubjective experiences both in terms of recognizing other subjects and acting with others; yet neither group has language. As such, language must be a more complex, founded form of intersubjective experience, not its primitive basis.

Finally, Sokolowski's criticisms involve a mistake in pressing a separate epistemological point against the ontology. Husserl endorsed the claim that epistemological objectivity requires intersubjectivity.[50] Husserl identifies the set of problems concerning intersubjectivity as "concerning the constitution of the categorial form, 'Objectivity,' belonging to the world (which, after all, is our world)."[51] Objectivity, as something transcendent of the limited individual subject's capacity, and something real, is wont for some explanation. It is worth reminding ourselves that Husserl is here referring to objectivity in the sense of *Objekt* (something available to all), not *Gegenstand* (an object of experience, which may be idiosyncratic to a given subject). Husserl puts the matter in more detail:

> For me *qua* ego [*Ich*]–the world is constituted as "Objective" (in the above-stated sense: therefore for everyone), showing itself to be the way it is, in an intersubjective cognitive community. It follows that the sense of "everyone" must already be constituted, relative to which an Objective world can be Objective. This implies that the *first* and fundamental *sense of "everyone"* (and therefore of *"others"*) cannot be the usual, the higher-level, sense: namely the sense "every human being," which refers to something real in the Objective world and therefore already presupposes the constitution of that world.[52]

We experience the world as a world that has meaning available to everyone. A college campus is not something that is experienced as being what it is for me alone, but as something available to be experienced by any who wish and who have the means. The more basic sense of otherness Husserl refers to is that of an embodied subject, or as Husserl also puts it, psychophysical ego [*Ich*]. In other words, "objectivity" has the meaning of something accessible to everyone in a very basic sense, not necessarily the more specific notion of accessibility to a specific type of subjectivity.

The specifically human world, as a culturally enriched world, may have meanings that are available in a more restricted sense.

> Its Objectivity is restricted, though concretely the world is given to me and to everyone only as a cultural world and as having the sense: accessible to everyone. But, as soon becomes apparent when its sense is explicated precisely, there are essential constitutional reasons why this accessibility is not unconditional.[53]

The specifically human world, the world enriched with cultural meanings, is premised on or founded in relation to the more primitive shared natural world, as achieved through intersubjective intentional achievements or collective intentionality:

> Everyone, as a matter of a priori necessity, lives in the same Nature, a Nature moreover that, with the necessary communalization of his life and the lives of others, he has fashioned into a *cultural world* in his individual and communalized living and doing–a world having human significances, even if it belongs to an extremely low cultural level.[54]

The cultural world is given "...on the underlying basis of the Nature common to all and on the basis of the spatiotemporal form that gives access to Nature and must function also in making the multiplicity of cultural formations and cultures accessible."[55] Nature does not restrict us to one possible cultural array of meanings, but is consistent with a multiplicity of possible cultural forms. However, all cultural achievements are dependent on there being a natural world. In more general terms:

> Constitution of "worlds" of any kind whatever, beginning with one's own stream of subjective processes, with its openly ended multiplicities, and continuing up through the Objective world with its various levels of Objectivation, is subject to the law of *"oriented" constitution,* a constitution that presupposes at various levels, but within the extension of a sense conceived with maximal breadth, something "primordially" and something "secondarily" constituted. At each of the levels in question, the primordial enters, with a new stratum of sense into the secondarily constituted world; and this occurs in such a fashion that the primordial becomes the central member, in accordance with orientational modes of givenness. The secondarily constituted, as a "world," is necessarily given as a horizon of being that is accessible from the primordial and is discoverable in a particular order.[56]

When speaking of an orientational mode of givenness Husserl is referencing the intentional achievements involved in and through consciousness' relation with the world.

Husserl is also operating in terms of part-whole analyses, wherein a given whole may have several levels of constitutional achievements. That is, his analyses speak to various orders of meaning in relation to the world of experience. Consider for example how Buffalo, NY, Albany, NY, Washington, D.C., and the United States each share some meaningful correlation of kind with Vatican City. However, each correlation functions at a different level: city, capital of a state, capital of a nation, a nation-state. Those variant kinds of community bear different significances which are not equivalent to one another and the more complex of which may have dependency relations on the more basic. A similar form of analysis functions in Husserl's writings on intersubjectivity. There are many complex objects or objects with complex constitutions that we interact with everyday. Husserl's analyses excavate the parthood relations those constitutional achievements have in relation to more basic semantic-forms and achievements.

The mistake of Husserl's critics is to draw the conclusion that the ontology of consciousness must be changed in order to accept the epistemological claims that objectivity, having the sense of an open intersubjective domain, is dependent on intersubjectivity. Husserl himself saw no such modification as necessary, even calling it a mistake:

> ...it was wrong, methodically, to jump immediately into transcendental intersubjectivity and to leap over the primal "I," the ego of my epoché, which can never lose its uniqueness and personal indeclinability. It is only an apparent contradiction to this that the ego–through a particular constitutive accomplishment of its own–makes itself declinable, for itself, transcendentally; that, starting from itself and in itself, it constitutes transcendental intersubjectivity, to which it then adds itself as a merely privileged member, namely, as "I" among the transcendental others.[57]

And,

> Only by starting from the ego and the system of its transcendental functions and accomplishments can we methodically exhibit transcendental intersubjectivity and its transcendental communalization, through which, in the functioning system of ego-poles, the "world for all," and for each subject *as* world for all, is constituted. Only in this way, in an essential system of forward steps, can we gain an ultimate comprehension of the fact that each transcendental "I" within intersubjectivity (as coconstituting the world in the way indicated) must necessarily be constituted in the world as a human being; in other words, that each human being "bears within himself a transcendental 'I'"–not as a real part or a stratum of his soul (which would be absurd) but rather insofar as he is the self-objectification, as exhibited through phenomenological self-reflection, of the corresponding transcendental "I."[58]

The experiencing "I" is the starting point of rigorous analysis, and accepting this is not to endorse any old naïve folk-theory as explanation. In response to his critics, Husserl asserts, "The *illusion* of a solipsism is dissolved, *even though* the proposition that everything existing for me must derive its existential sense exclusively from me myself, from my sphere of consciousness retains its validity and fundamental importance."[59] Even in Husserl's preface to the Boyce-Gibson translation of *Ideas I*, which is the basis for a great many confusions about Husserl's analyses of intersubjectivity, Husserl claims that "the solipsistic objection [to phenomenology] collapses."[60] Referring to the embodied whole of one's subjectivity–one's finite epistemological zero-point, Husserl argues:

> Before everything else conceivable, *I* am. This "I am" is for me, the subject who says it, and says it in the right sense, the *primitive intentional basis for my world*; and, at the same time, it must not be overlooked that likewise the "Objective" world, the "world for all of us" as accepted with this sense by me, is also "my" world. But "I am" is the primitive intentional basis not only for "the" world, the one I consider real, but also for any "ideal world" that I accept; and this holds, without exception, for anything and everything of which I am conscious as something existent in any sense whatever that I understand or accept– for everything that I show, sometimes legitimately, sometimes illegitimately, to be existent–including me myself, my life, my believing, and all this consciousness-of.[61]

Searle puts the same basic point plainly: "Every conscious state is always *someone's* conscious state."[62] Consciousness always has its peculiar orientation relative to the given subject in relation to the world: "Subjectivity has the further consequence that all of my conscious forms of intentionality that give me information about the world independent of myself are always from a special point of view."[63] My history, my background, my bodily constitution, etc., all affect how I experience the world and how I structured my projections.[64] It is surprising that other self-avowed phenomenologists in particular don't recognize the basic nature of Husserl analysis and his rigorous concerns for consistency with the basic phenomenology and ontology of consciousness that substantiate and constrain his position. Add also Husserl's remarkable ability–one matched only by Kant– to maintain consistent distinction between formal and material analyses. Husserl's discussions of intersubjectivity in places like *Cartesian Meditations* and *Formal and Transcendental Logic* are formal analyses.[65] The material analyses, which only have authority on the basis of the formal analyses, are initiated only in the latter works or in the *Nachlass*.[66] As such, to levy a complaint that Husserl has not explained the material phenomena adequately, where his analysis is formal in nature and his view is that the formal analysis must precede the material in order that the material analysis may be given proper characterization, is to put the cart before the horse.

Searle, on a related point, references everyday experience in his writings: "In short, though I don't have direct access to the dog's consciousness, nonetheless it seems to me a well-attested empirical fact that dogs are conscious, and it is attested by evidence that is quite compelling."[67] In a statement Husserl would surely endorse, Searle puts the matter of the experiences of one's consciousness as individuated in conjunction with one's experience of others together: "in real life there is no 'problem of other minds.'"[68] Elsewhere, Husserl argues for the necessity of starting from one's own subjectivity. Husserl recognizes two basic components of our everyday experiences of the world: 1) consciousness is individuated and immediately or directly accessible only to the individual consciousness itself, 2) we experience others as conscious beings and live our lives in a world of socially constituted meanings. Husserlian phenomenology accepts as its starting point a world in which others are always already present. It is an achievement in the analysis of phenomena that one removes the contributions of or presence of others in order to isolate and study the nature and limits of those contributions. Instead of shying away from these, or seeking an elegant theoretical fix by denying one or the other, Husserl aims to squarely face the challenge of dealing with the complex nature of everyday life. Husserl roundly criticizes his critics for not facing the complex state of affairs as it is: "For children in philosophy, this may be the dark corner haunted by the specters of solipsism and, perhaps, of psychologism, of relativism. The true philosopher, instead of running away, will prefer to fill the dark corner with light."[69] Gurwitsch, not afraid of the dark himself, developed further a phenomenology with an individualist ontology of consciousness while accepting the epistemological dependency on intersubjectivity, thereby denying an atomistic conception of the individual.

Again, to claim Husserl's view of consciousness leads to the traditional solipsistic conclusions would seem to assume Husserl operated on Cartesian categories, which in effect denies that phenomenology is a break from prior philosophy. Husserl is clear: "Phenomenological explication is nothing like 'metaphysical construction'; and it is neither overtly nor covertly a theorizing with adopted presuppositions or helpful thoughts drawn from the historical metaphysical tradition."[70] And,

> ...phenomenological explication does nothing but *explicate the sense this world has for us all, prior to any philosophizing*, and obviously get solely from our experience—*a sense which philosophy can uncover but never alter*, and which, because of an essential necessity, not because of our weakness, entails (in the case of any actual experience) horizons that need fundamental clarification.[71]

Our basic view of consciousness doesn't have to deny that all consciousness is *my* consciousness in order to accommodate others into our experiences of the world. To do so would be to put theoretical interests ahead of one's descriptions, to engage in the metaphysical construction that phenomenology avoids. The world's complexities don't vanish in virtue of simpler theory; clearly, however, our theories are inadequate when they shy from the complex state of affairs they claim to address. As Husserl puts it "...our world in its being and being-such, takes its ontic *meaning* entirely from our intentional life through a priori types of accomplishments that *can be exhibited* rather than argumentatively constructed or conceived through mythical thinking."[72] He adds that one can make "no headway with this, and with the profound difficulties contained in it, if one hastily overlooks it and spares oneself the trouble of making consistent regressive inquiries and investigations or if one adduces arguments from the workshops of past philosophers...and carries on a game of logical argumentations and refutations."[73] The aim of philosophical investigation is not to shuffle about moves in an argumentative game, but to offer critical analysis and insight into what is otherwise taken to be obvious: to give intelligibility to the otherwise obvious as Husserl puts it, "i.e. of transforming this *Selbstverständlichkeit* into a *Verständlichkeit.*"[74]

The temptation to collectivize consciousness itself seems to stem from trying to describe how to understand our purposive activities in concert with others. That our intentions can range over, or indict, a plural subject (we) doesn't necessitate that consciousness itself is spread over an intersubjective space, even if it is "submerged" in an intersubjectively populated world. It only shows that our consciousness is capable of thinking of others and including others in our plans and goals. One's consciousness is conditioned by the presence of others–both formally and materially. Others affect how our experiences take shape and the meanings we attach to them, and in virtue of that also direct the form of our thinking either indirectly or directly when one considers the syntax passed to one through their communities.

Indeed, the effect of one's social context or milieu on one is a serious issue, one not to be looked over lightly. The existentialist analyses of oppression in de Beauvoir and Fanon, and Arendt's descriptions of the mode of totalitarianism's operations clearly ground the weightiness of this concern. It is the impact on individuals, by means of manipulating our collective states of affairs, that is the source of what is so pernicious about oppression and totalitarianism. In the case of oppression, one's choices are hidden or constrained as part of one's situation. In the case of totalitarianism, one's relation to others is undermined in an effort to atomize the individual against others. It is because these work against the individual that they are problems and it is because they work through the complicity and choices of individuals that it is so pervasive and pernicious.

One might object, finally, that something is not in being unless it is spoken through language. What those who advocate for such a position confuse are the being of the phenomena and its social recognition. Those are not to be collapsed or assumed to be equivocal. Having a name for something makes it part of socially recognized phenomena. To get the name or word to take, however, requires the assent of individuals in a collective capacity. Simply naming something by fiat, coining a term, is insufficient; a negotiation across subjects is necessary. Still, it is not a detached collective that decides, but individuals coming to collective acceptance or recognition to the legitimacy of the term and thereby a public recognition of the phenomena named. Again, however, the phenomenon named exists prior to its being named. Suffering and oppression exist, often long before they enter the awareness of many individuals. To deny this is to claim that there is no problem requiring recognition and to deny of those suffering that they suffer.

It is individual consciousness that makes collective recognition, collective action, linguistic communities, etc., possible and individual consciousness' priority over the collective is a reason why others are never wholly transparent to us, even if others are also not opaque to us. One might say that our experience of others is translucent in nature. In the language of the later Husserl, the innermost horizon of our intentional life is not intersubjective, but subjective.[75] However, intersubjective horizons are themselves essential parts, if founded parts, of our conscious lives and are deeply constitutive in relation to our experiences of the world.

"We" does not precede "I." Rather, "we" is a modification of one's intentionality expressly including others in one's relation toward the world. It also makes one liable for their relationships with others and to the world in a new way. To form a "we" however, there must first be an "I" that recognizes otherness, or at least has some level of appreciation in respect to the additive component evoked by the gesture of a "we," that it is not merely "I" and the world, but that one's intentional accomplishments can meet, at least potentially, verification in and through others. The intersubjective horizon to one's experience is ever-present in our day-to-day experience, but on analysis is found to be dependent on the individuated horizon structure of consciousness. "We" doesn't necessitate essential overhaul of our ontology of mind, nor does it demand we postulate some new entity in the world. "We" is a mode of our intentional life that calls us to greater responsibility for our relation to the world.

Conclusion

Does phenomenology itself, as critics of Husserl suggest, need to find a new starting point to being able to address the intersubjective domain of experience? I think not. Doing so effaces the proper role of the individual and thereby eliminates the essentially subjective component of intentionality: the act. This is not to assert that the Cartesian paradigm of the epistemic subject as traditionally understood is the correct starting point. It isn't that we begin as *solus ipse* and then work our way into a world with others through a series of judgments.[76] Rather, it's that one is from the outset an individual immersed in a socially enriched and conditioned world of meanings. One always already finds oneself in a world with others, that is not something Husserl denies or is unable to accommodate, it is the point of departure he consistently argued for. If one accepts the insights of the *Crisis,* the sedimented meanings permeating one's social world can in principle always be traced back to some practical relation(s) with the world. That is, meaning originates through the interactions individual conscious beings have with their world and become modified, enriched, integrated and iterated in and through our social interchanges. To assert on this basis that the social is prior to the individual is mistaken. The reactive posture of prioritizing the social over the individual fails in that it already assumes the correctness of the dichotomy, it accepts the terms of the *solus ipse* or Cartesian *cogito* as subject in opposition to the world, as something "outside" the world. The insight of Husserl and what his focus on intersubjectivity aimed to clarify and elucidate, was how to describe experience by reinvigorating the dynamic interplay between individual and social, not by trading one mummified concept for another.

Crucially, one must remain clear about the distinction between what is experienced in life and what one's analysis should look like. Husserl's critics complain, in essence, that he is not starting from experience proper, instead creating an abstraction and analyzing experience through the lens of that abstraction. This is inaccurate in regard to Husserl, and fails to appreciate the nuance of his philosophy, as well as that his writings build over the course of his career and that they more often than not report the results of the analyses, not the initial expositions.[77] Husserl is not supplanting the importance of the social on experience, he's respecting that the social world involves complex arrays of intentional constitutional achievements, while preserving the factical nature of the fundamental asymmetry of conscious experiences involving others. That's not to remove the other from experience, nor to assert that one is transparent to oneself. Rather, it is to capture the other's presence in its complexity. As such, it is more likely that Husserl's critics are the ones who oversimplify.

The preservation of the inherent complexity of the social world and its relation to the lived experiences of individuals is precisely what the addition of theories of collective intentionality can offer in expanding on Husserl's sense of higher-order pluralities. Conversely, the classical theory of intentionality operating in phenomenological philosophy can further expand and develop the collective intentionality literature, correcting for a bias towards collective action that is resultant of the English-language sense of intentionality.

To restate the overarching goal of this work, I remind the reader that one of this work's aim has been to show how some discussions of collective intentionality might be thought of as being confused in ways that could be corrected by, or at least illuminated by, engagement with Husserlian phenomenology. This has been shown in large part by applying the broader, classical theory of intentionality that is operative in phenomenology in contrast to narrower or ambiguous usages of intentionality. At the very least, an overarching agreement on the meaning of intentionality would provide some order to discussions. Some uses of intentionality in the collective intentionality literature are informed by contemporary analytic philosophy of mind and its functionalist or representationalist applications of intentionality. Others, more problematically, use the term ambiguously, running together the notions of *intent* [*Absicht*] and intentionality [*Intentionalität*].

In chapters one and two, the idea of collective consciousness was roundly criticized. Some authors might not mean by the phrase 'collective consciousness' a literal sense of a collective's having consciousness. Instead, they might mean to refer only to modifications of the consciousnesses of individual subjects, i.e.

adopting the abstraction that is a group perspective. However failure to clarify or to disambiguate motivates critiques like those offered in those chapters. Where chapter one critiqued collective consciousness from a specifically phenomenological orientation, chapter two criticized the idea with regard to metaphysical concerns consistent with contemporary philosophy of mind. In doing this, I have effectively shown two things. First, that the presence of intentionality does not imply the presence of consciousness. One only operates on this view where one fails to distinguish between intrinsic and derived intentionality. Stop signs and the words of a novel each have intentionality, but neither stops signs nor the words of a novel are conscious beings in their own right. Second, that one can speak of plural subjects without committing oneself to the existence of additional entities endowed with consciousness in their own right. This has the added virtue of not having to postulate the existence of an indefinite amount of strange entities.

In chapter three, I expanded on David Carr's initial sketch of a phenomenological account of plural subjects. Carr stresses that plural subjects are based on a shared experiential foundation, thus strongly implicating the classical sense of intentionality. After critiquing Carr's understanding of phenomenology's metaphysical neutralism as being overreaching, I supplemented the phenomenological view of plural subjects by drawing from its closest analytical cousin, John Searle's theory of collective intentionality. This served to clarify the sort of criticisms the phenomenological account is liable to in relation to the contemporary literature on collective intentionality. It also helped situate phenomenology in relation to the alternative theses at play in that literature. The chapter ended with an account of how evidence functions in relation to plural subject experiences, filling in an unfortunate lacuna in Carr's account.

Chapter four supported the view developed in chapter three and defended it from criticism. I supported a denial of formal individualism, the claim that all intentionality is in a singular, and never a plural, mode. Like Searle, I accept that intentionality can take on a plural form and is not always or ultimately reducible to conjoined sets of intentions in singular form. The bulk of the chapter, however, focused on Hans Bernhard Schmid's criticisms of subjective individualism. I argue that subjective individualism is able to offer an account of normativity and rationality, contrary to Schmid's claims otherwise, as well as offer criticisms of his collectivist approach to collective intentionality. Much as with the response to Sokolowski in chapter seven, Schmid's attack on individualism appears to express more a worry about atomism than individualism. This shows itself in that he presses for a more relational view, one that, I argue, a subjective individualist can also offer.

The fifth chapter contrasted the phenomenological account of plural subjects with that of Margaret Gilbert. The differences and comparative merits of both were shown. Criticisms of Gilbert's theory were offered. I argued that if her account is intended to be complete or basic, then her account is too narrow and needs to be revised in order to be consistent with the broader account of intentionality. Again, I want to stress that her specifically moral analyses are not necessarily problematic, only that the specifically moral emphasis of her approach may not be sufficiently consistent with a more basic analysis of social ontology. Gilbert, it was argued, appears to conflate *Intentionalität* (intentionality of consciousness) with *Absicht* (intent or volition to act). At times she appears to construe the former in terms of the latter, what I believe is inverting the proper order of this pairing. This underscores her focus on moral considerations, a criticism Amie Thomasson similarly registers against Searle. While the social world is predicated upon conscious intentional achievements of human subjects, those are not solely done from a moral standpoint or with moral concerns. The social is not necessarily coextensive with the moral, even if saturated by the moral. If one prefers, the social is not identical with the moral. Engagement with Gilbert can be instructive to forming a broader account of the social world. The chapter included discussion of Aron Gurwitsch's social phenomenology. This helps illustrate the mutually illuminative benefits possible by conjoining phenomenology and the collective intentionality literature more thoroughly. I would also add that such an exchange might serve to afford phenomenology a way to rectify its traditional difficulties in offering axiological analyses.

The sixth chapter responded to two lines of criticism brought against Husserlian phenomenology's specific treatments of social phenomena. Both are motivated by realist concerns and both worry about a potential for relativism. The first addressed was Barry Smith's critique, which hinges on how one understands the sense of "world" in phenomenology. The second was Hans Georg Gadamer's critique, which revolves around the sense of horizon intentionality, specifically concerned with social horizons manifest in one's experience. Both represent criticisms of some measure of sophistication. Yet both are given responses that take too narrow a reading of Husserl's phenomenology.

The final chapter responded to a concern about the methodology of Husserlian phenomenology. Robert Sokolowski had sharpened a perennial criticism of Husserl. Sokolowski's concern is that the methodology of phenomenology contains a solipsistic bias that needs to be rectified. I responded to Sokolowski in two ways. First, I argued that phenomenology does not assume the "Cartesian subject," the *solus ipse*. Phenomenology does not endorse an atomistic conception of the subject or subjectivity. In fact, phenomenology quite clearly rejects atomism, all while maintaining individualism regarding the nature of consciousness. Second, it was argued that Sokolowski's alternative has a problematic understanding of the nature of norms.

In the end, plural subject experiences are taken to be based on shared experiential foundations that give rise to a sense of non-arbitrary togetherness. Meanwhile, the phenomenological account preserves the importance of the individual. Preservation of the individual and accepting collective intentionality on a subjective individualist model are seen as essential to being able to account for error, to maintaining a coherent ontology of consciousness, and to reflect the complex nature of social phenomena adequately. The role of individuals and their phenomenology must be preserved in order for the possibility of change to institutional structures to be more readily recognized as real and to better empower individuals to resist and reassess social structures. To place the structure ahead of the phenomenology is like accounting for the motion of a horse in virtue of that of the cart it pulls. Emphasizing institutions or groups as prior to or wholly independent of the individuals whose complicity is essential to their very being and for their having any powers whatsoever, must be resisted in order to both maximize the efficiencies of collective endeavors and preserve the autonomy of individual persons. This appears all the more urgent in a world privileging institutions over individuals more frequently and more totally, a world also in which polarizing, pack-natured social identities are uncritically allowed to wholly define many individuals and their interactions.

As Nietzsche reminds us, if values are dependent on us then we must not be slaves to them, but revalue our values, to reassess our world anew with each successive generation.[78] His worry, one might say, was that collective intentional inheritances can be dangerous where they are accepted as facts uncritically, and given that collective intentional achievements are ultimately dependent on the achievements of individuals, collectively we are never truly impotent in relation to social institutions. A theory of collective intentionality helps inform how the development of meanings and institutions function over time. It helps disclose the underlying skeleton of our social practices. A theory of collective intentionality might serve to empower individuals, but only if the individual is given their proper place in social ontology. Phenomenology is perfectly suited to this end, serving as a counter-balance to the recent biases in analytical thought towards externalisms and subject-effacing forms of objectivism. In turn, phenomenologists and their continental brethren can find in the collective intentionality discussions that it is not necessary, where one emphasizes the place and importance of the individual, that one do violence to the importance of context and community.

The exchange I hope to provoke should be mutually beneficial. Phenomenologists benefit further by turning to collective intentionality discussions in finding a way to think about the higher-order pluralities Husserl references and to find a framework in which to speak of the role of the individual and their experience within a social or communal context. Husserlian phenomenology in particular finds a discussion that encourages one to tease out how methodological individualism does not commit one to an atomistic sense of subjectivity. Those involved in the collective intentionality discussions can benefit from the introduction of the more robust classical theory of intentionality and a systematic methodology for handling first-person experience. This will allow collective intentionality discussions to better respect consistency concerns with the ontology of consciousness. The introduction of phenomenology and its history also affords a way to expand the collective intentionality discussions beyond the narrower confines of moral kinds (rights and obligations), opening avenues for a broader and more inclusive social ontology.

Notes

1. Sokolowski 2009: 58
2. ibid: 58-59
3. ibid: 60
4. ibid: 62
5. ibid: 62-63
6. This issue represents the primary issue one finds in the mountainous literature surrounding Husserl's discussions of intersubjectivity. Allen 1978a & 1978b; Haney 1994; Hutcheson 1980, 1981, 1982a & 1982b; Lee 2006; Marsh 1979; Mensch 1988; and Tripathy 1992 are a small cast of representative examples.
7. Sokolowski 2009: 68
8. ibid: 69
9. ibid: 70
10. ibid: 71
11. See discussions in Sokolowski 2009 Chapters 10, 11, 14, 17, 18
12. Sokolowski 2009: 68-69
13. ibid: 69
14. Zahavi 2005: 148
15. ibid: 176
16. ibid: 177
17. In the terminology of Philip Pettit, phenomenology is committed to holism as opposed to atomism with regard to the horizontal relations between subjects in society with one another (Pettit 1993: 111ff.). Particularly of note is where Pettit, in summarizing how an argument from Part I of his book relates to one of the arguments of Part II, states: "...I argued that the ability to think presupposes a subject who enjoys a certain sort of interaction either with herself across time or with other subjects. I argue now that if the ability to think is required to meet a further condition, a condition that is certainly characteristic of the human situation, then it presupposes a subject who enjoys a certain sort of interaction with other people. In other words, it requires community, as the holist maintains. There is no prospect of the solitary thinker, no prospect of the sort of possibility that the atomist has to countenance" (ibid: 114).
18. Zahavi 2005: 176-177. One might add, for emphasis, that experience is always situated in a context and that context always has bodily and social horizons. The challenge, for Husserl, was to preserve the asymmetry latent in the experience of the other while allowing the contextual horizons to remain intact. What's more, there must be intentional achievements that are unique to one's self and one's own consciousness, and those achievements are independent of social horizons if consciousness is to bear the sense of mineness that it does. For example, the feeling of one's body or one's experience of hyletic contents independent of the intersubjective categorial labels and additive connotations.

19. Carr 1974: 84; see also Hutcheson 1980 & 1982a. "Phenomenologists never conceive of intersubjectivity as an objectively existing structure in the world that can be described and analyzed from a third-person perspective. On the contrary, intersubjectivity is a relation between subjects and must be analyzed, as such, from a first-person and a second-person perspective" (Zahavi 2005: 176).

20. Sokolowski 2009: 126

21. ibid.

22. ibid.

23. Husserl 1999: §46

24. Sokolowski 2009: 126

25. See also Steeves 1996

26. Searle's most recent book (Searle 2010) appears to have a claim similar to this, but distorts this relation.

27. Sokolowski himself reviews the arguments of *Crisis* (Sokolowski 2009: 112-116), emphasizing how the modern turn has led to the abstraction away from lived-experience to an extreme: where we've effectively abstracted ourselves away.

28. For more on logic's relation to the world of experience see B. Smith 1989: §5

29. This would include, then, the denial of consciousness or intentional phenomena on particularly brute forms of naturalism. Phenomenological philosophers reject the reductivism and eliminativism present in most views identifying themselves as naturalism. It is this that draws pragmatism and phenomenology close–though pragmatists are prone to still embrace some form of naturalism through their tendency to follow the empiricism of the natural science as adequate methodology for philosophy. See, for example the approach of Rockweel 2005. For a statement of phenomenology in contrast, see Husserl's "Philosophy as a Rigorous Science" in McCormick & Elliston 1981.

30. These distinctions are found in Searle 1992:19

31. Husserl 2001a: "Prolegomena" §16, 39

32. ibid: 38

33. Husserl 1999: §§55-58, though there are actually at least two prior constitutive achievements: the basic encounter of an other as other, and the constitution of an other's monadic individuality which is founded upon the former achievement.

34. Gurwitsch 1979: 1

35. ibid: 2

36. ibid.

37. ibid: 2-3

38. ibid: 3

39. ibid: 5

40. ibid: Part III

41. Searle 1992: Chapters 1 & 2; see especially Table 21 on page 53

42. ibid: 13
43. ibid: 14
44. ibid: 16
45. ibid: 17
46. ibid: 25
47. ibid: 26
48. Husserl 1999: §10
49. Tomasello 2008 and Tomasello 2009.
50. See Husserl 1978, Husserl 1999, Husserl 1973, Husserl 1970, not to mention the three volumes of *Husserliana* dedicated to notes on intersubjectivity.
51. Husserl 1978: 238
52. ibid: 240
53. Husserl 1999: 132/160
54. ibid: 133/160
55. ibid: 134/162
56. ibid: 133-134/161
57. Husserl 1970: 185
58. ibid: 185-186
59. Husserl 1999: 150/176l; also Husserl 1978: §96 b.
60. Husserl 1969: 22
61. Husserl 1978: 237/209
62. Searle 1992: 94-95
63. ibid: 95
64. This point is worked out in more detail in Husserl 1978: §8, where Husserl develops the horizon-structure of intentionality.
65. Husserl 1999 & Husserl 1978 respectively
66. Husserl 1970 & Husserl 1973 in particular, leaving aside the approximately 2,000 pages of notes in the *Nachlass* and other unpublished manuscripts.
67. Searle 1992: 74
68. ibid: 75
69. Husserl 1978: 237/210
70. Husserl 1999: 150/177
71. ibid: 151/177
72. Husserl 1970: 181, emphases mine
73. ibid.
74. Carr in Husserl 1970: 180 n.2
75. For discussion of the basic horizon structures to experience see Husserl 1973: §8
76. It is fascinating to observe infantile development. The processes of genetic transformation of their conscious states is fascinating. They are acquiring typifications in respect to objects in experience in a pure sense, and one that operates in a pre- or non-linguistic capacity.

77. This is arguably one of the chief values of Husserl's *Nachlass*, as there one finds examples of phenomenology at work, not just the ordered reporting of what has been discovered.

78. Nietzsche 1998

Bibliography

Allen, Jeffner. (1978a) "Husserl's Communal Spirit: A Phenomenological Study of the Fundamental Structure of Society." *Philosophy and Social Criticism.* 5.1: 67-82

———. (1978b) "Husserl's Overcoming of the Problem of Intersubjectivity." In discussion. *Modern Schoolman.* 55: 261-271

———. (1979) "Teleology and Intersubjectivity." *Analecta Husserliana*, vol. IX. Anna-Teresa Tymieniecka, ed. D. Reidel, 1979: 203-212

Arendt, Hannah. (1998) *The Human Condition*, second edition. University of Chicago Press.

Armstrong, David. (2004) *Truth and Truthmakers.* Cambridge University Press

Armstrong, Edward G. (1977) "Intersubjective Intentionality." *Midwestern Journal of Philosophy.* 5: 1-11

Avramides, Anita. (2001) *Other Minds.* Routledge.

Beakley, Brien & Peter Ludlow, eds. (2006) *The Philosophy of Mind: Classical Problems/ Contemporary Issues*, second edition. The MIT Press.

Block, Ned. (2006) "Troubles with Functionalism" (revised). In Beakley and Ludlow 2006: 107-131

Boghossian, Paul. (2006) *Fear of Knowledge: Against Relativism and Constructivism.* Oxford University Press.

Bozga, Adina. (2002) Review of *Husserl and Transcendental Intersubjectivity*, by Dan Zahavi. Ohio University Press, 2001. *Studia Phaenomenologica: Romanian Journal for Phenomenology.* 2.3-4:191-196

Bratman, Michael E. (1999) *Faces of Intention: Selected Essays on Intention and Agency.* Cambridge University Press.

Brentano, Franz. (1995) *Psychology from an Empirical Standpoint.* Antos C. Rancurello, D.B. Terrell and Linda L. McAlister, trans. Routledge.

Brown, Curtis. (2007) "Narrow Mental Content." *The Stanford Encyclopedia of Philosophy* (Spring 2007 edition). Edward N. Zalta, ed. URL = http://plato.stanford.edu/archives/spr2007/entries/content-narrow/

Burge, Tyler. (1979) "Individualism and the Mental." *Midwest Studies in Philosophy.* 4: 73-121

Burns, Tom R. & Erik Engdahl. (1998) "The Social Construction of Consciousness: Part 1: Collective Consciousness and Its Socio-Cultural Foundations." *Journal of Consciousness Studies*. 5.1: 67-85

Carr, David. (1973) "The 'Fifth Meditation' and Husserl's Cartesianism." *Philosophy and Phenomenological Research*. 34.1: 14-35

———. (1974) *Phenomenology and the Problem of History*. Northwestern.

———. (1977) "Kant, Husserl, and the Nonempirical Ego." *Journal of Philosophy*. 74:682-690

———. (1986) "Cogitamus Ergo Sumus: The Intentionality of the First-Person
Plural." *Monist*. 69.4: 521-533

———. (1987) "Husserl's World and Ours." *Journal of the History of Philosophy*. 25.1: 151-167

———. (1989) "The Life-World Revisted." In *Husserl's Phenomenology: A
Textbook*. J.N. Mohanty and William McKenna, eds. Center for Advanced Research in Phenomenology and United Press of America.

———. (1998) "Phenomenology and Fiction in Dennett." *International Journal
of Philosophical Studies*. 6.3: 331-344

———. (1999) *The Paradox of Subjectivity: The Self in the Transcendental
Tradition*. Oxford University Press.

———. (2003) "Transcendental and Empirical Subjectivity: The Self in the
Transcendental Tradition." In Welton 2003

———. (2004) "Rereading the History of Subjectivity." *Symposium*. 8.2:363-
377

Chalmers, David. (1996) *The Conscious Mind*. Oxford University Press

———. (2002) "The Components of Content." In *Philosophy of Mind: Classical and Conetmporary Readings*. David Chalmers, ed. Oxford University Press: 608-633

———. (2003) "The Nature of Narrow Content." *Philosophical Issues*. 13.1:
46-66

Chalmers, David & David Bourget, eds. (2007) *MindPapers*.
http://consc.net/mindpapers/

Churchland, Paul M. (2001) *Matter and Consciousness*, revised edition. The
MIT Press.

Combs, Allan & Stanley Krippner. (2008) "Collective Consciousness and the
Social Brain." *Journal of Consciousness Studies*. 15.10-11: 264-276

Davidson, Donald. (2002) *Subjective, Intersubjective, Objective*. Oxford University Press.

Davis, Michael. (1996) "Some Paradoxes of Whistleblowing." *Business and
Professional Ethics Journal*. 15.1: 3-19

De Preester, Helena. (2008) "From *ego* to *alter ego*: Husserl, Merleau-Ponty and
a layered approach to intersubjectivity." *Phenomenology and the Cognitive Sciences*. 7: 133-42

De Waal, Frans. (1997) *Good Natured: The Origins of Right and Wrong in Humans and Other Animals.* Harvard University Press.

———. (2009) *Primates and Philosophers: How Morality Evolved.* Stephen Macedo & Josiah Ober, eds. Princeton University Press.

———. (2010) *The Age of Empathy: Nature's Lessons for a Kinder Society.* Three Rivers Press.

Dennett, Daniel. (1987) *The Intentional Stance.* The MIT Press.

Depraz, Natalie. (2001) "The Husserlian Theory of Intersubjectivity as Alterology." *Journal of Consciousness Studies.* 8.5-7:169-78

Donohoe, Janet. (2004) *Husserl on Ethics and Intersubjectivity: From Static to Genetic Phenomenology.* Humanity Books.

Dreyfus, Hubert. (1993) "Heidegger's Critique of Husserl/Searle Account of Intentionality." *Social Research.* 60: 17-38

———. (2000) "A Merleau-Pontyian Critique of Husserl's and Searle's Representationalist Accounts of Action." *Proceedings of the Aristotelian Society.* 100: 287-302

Drummond, John. (2003) "The Structure of Intentionality." In *The New Husserl: A Critical Reader.* Donn Welton, ed. Indiana University Press: 65-92

Dufrenne, Mikel. (1966) *The Notion of the A Priori.* Edward S. Casey, translator. Northwestern.

Dwyer, Daniel. (2004) "Wittgenstein, Kant and Husserl on the Dialectical Temptations of Reason." *Continental Philosophy Review.* 37.3:277-307

Eilan, Naomi, Christopher Hoerl, Teresa McCormack, & Johannes Roessler, eds. (2005) *Joint Attention: Communication and Other Minds.* Oxford University Press.

Elliston, Frederick A. (1977) "Husserl's Phenomenology of Empathy." In Elliston and McCormick, 1977

Elliston, Frederick A. & McCormick, Peter, eds. (1977) *Husserl: Expositions and Appraisals.* Notre Dame.

Embree, Lester. (2009) "Phenomenology and Social Constructionsism: Constructs for Political Identity." *Journal of Phenomenological Psychology.* 40: 127-139

Fitzpatrick, Dan. (2003) "Searle and Collective Intentionality: The Self-Defeating Nature of Internalism with Respect to Social Facts." In Koepsell and Moss, 2003: 45-66

Føllesdal, Dagfinn. (2003) "The Thetic Role of Consciousness." In *Husserl's Logical Investigations Reconsidered,* D. Fisette, ed: 11-20

Gadamer, Hans-Georg. (1989) *Truth and Method,* second revised edition. Joel Weinsheimer and Donald G. Marshall, trans. Continuum.

———. (2000) "Subjectivity and Intersubjectivity, Subject and Person." *Continental Philosophy Review.* 33: 275-287

Gallagher, Shaun. (2001) "The practice of mind: theory, simulation, or interaction?" *Journal of Consciousness Studies.* 8.5-7: 83-107

————. (2005) "Phenomenological Contributions to a Theory of Social Cognition." *Husserl Studies*. 21.2: 95-110

————. (2006a) "Logical and phenomenological arguments against simulation theory." In *Minding our Practice: Folk-Psychology Re-assessed*. Daniel Hutto and Matthew Ratcliffe, eds. Springer.

————. (2006b) *How the Body Shapes the Mind*. Oxford University Press.

————. (2008) "Are Minimal Representations Still Representations?" *International Journal of Philosophical Studies*. 16.3: 351-69

Gallagher, Shaun & Dan Zahavi. (2007) "Phenomenological Approaches to Self-Consciousness." *The Stanford Encyclopedia of Philosophy (Summer 2007edition)*. Edward N. Zalta, ed. http://plato.stanford.edu/archives/sum2007/entries/self-consciousness-phenomenological/

————. (2008) *The Phenomenological Mind*. Routledge

Gallese, Vittorio. (2001) "The 'Shared Manifold' Hypothesis: From Mirror Neurons to Empathy." *Journal of Consciousness Studies*. 8.5-7: 33-50

Gilbert, Margaret. (1992) *On Social Facts*. Princeton.

————. (1996) *Living Together*. Rowman & Littlefield.

————. (2000) *Sociality and Responsibility*. Rowman & Littlefield.

Goldman, Alvin. (2006) *Simulating Minds: The philosophy, psychology, and neuroscience of mindreading*. Oxford University Press.

Gordon, Robert M. (2008) "Folk Psychology as Mental Simulation." *The Stanford Encyclopedia of Philosophy (Fall 2008 edition)*. Edward N. Zalta, ed. URL = http://plato.stanford.edu/archives/fall2008/entries/folkpsych-simulation/

Gracia, Jorge J.E. (1999) *Metaphysics and its Task: The Search for the Categorial Foundations of Knowledge*. SUNY.

Grillo, Eric. (2003) "Communal Sharing-in-Life and Collective Intentionality: The Construction of Social Reality in a Contrastive Perspective." *Phenomenological Inquiry*. 94-127

Gurwitsch, Aron. (1941) "A Non-Egological Conception of Consciousness." *Philosophy and Phenomenological Research*. 1.3: 325-338

————. (1955) "The Phenomenological and the Psychological Approach to Consciounsness." *Philosophy and Phenomenological Research*. 15.3: 303-319

————. (1956) "The Last Work of Edmund Husserl." *Philosophy and Phenomenological Research*. 16.3: 380-399

————. (1957) "The Last Work of Edmund Husserl." *Philosophy and Phenomenological Research*. 17.3: 370-398

————. (1962) "The Common-Sense World as Social Reality: A Discourse on Alfred Schutz." *Social Research*. 29.1: 50-72

————. (1964) *The Field of Consciousness*. Duquesne University Press.

————. (1970) "Towards a Theory of Intentionality." *Philosophy and Phenomenological Research*. 30.3: 354-367

———. (1979) *Human Encounters in the Social World.* Fred Kersten, trans. Duquesne University Press.

Haney, Kathleen M. (1994) *Intersubjectivity Revisited.* Ohio University Press.

Hegel, G.W.F. (1977) *Phenomenology of Spirit.* A.V. Miller, trans. Oxford University Press.

Heidegger, Martin. (1995) *The Fundamental Concepts of Metaphysics: World, Finitude, Solitude.* William McNeill and Nicholas Walker, trans. Indiana University Press.

Heil, John. (2004) *Introduction to Philosophy of Mind,* second edition. Routledge.

Hindricks, Frank A. (2003) "The New Role of the Constitutive Rule." In Koepsell and Moss, 2003: 185-208

Hintikka, Jaakko. (1995) "The Phenomenological Dimension." *The Cambridge University Press Companion to Husserl.* David Woodruff Smith & Barry Smith, editors. Cambridge University Press: 78-105

Hobson, R. Peter. (2008) "Interpersonally Situated Cognition." *International Journal of Philosophical Studies.* 16.3: 377-397

Holder, John J, ed. (2006) *Early Buddhist Discourses.* Hackett.

Honneth, Axel. (1996) *The Struggle for Recognition: The Moral Grammar of Social Conflicts.* Joel Anderson, trans. MIT Press.

Husserl, Edmund. (1964) *The Phenomenology of Internal Time Consciousness.* Martin Heidegger, ed. James S. Churchill, trans. Martinus Nijhoff.

———. (1969) *Ideas Pertaining to a Pure Phenomenology and to a Phenomenological Philosophy,* first book. W.R. Boyce Gibson, trans. Collier.

———. (1970) *The Crisis of the European Sciences and Transcendental Phenomenology.* David Carr, trans. Northwestern.

———. (1972) *Ideas: General Introduction to Pure Phenomenology.* W.R. Boyce Gibson, trans. Collier.

———. (1973) *Experience and Judgment: Investigations in a Genealogy of Logic.* Revised and edited by Ludwig Landgrebe. James S. Churchill and Karl Ameriks, trans. Northwestern.

———. (1974) "Kant and the Idea of Transcendental Philosophy." Ted E. Klein, Jr. and William E. Pohl, trans. *Southwestern Journal of Philosophy.* 5.3: 9-56

———. (1978) *Formal and Transcendental Logic.* Dorion Cairnes, trans. Martinus Nijhoff.

———. (1980) *Ideas Pertaining to a Pure Phenomenology and to a Phenomenological Philosophy,* third book. Ted E. Klein and William E. Pohl, trans. Martinus Nijhoff (*Ideas III*).

———. (1989) *Ideas Pertaining to a Pure Phenomenology and to a Phenomenological Philosophy,* second book. R. Rojcewicz and A. Schuwer, trans. Kluwer (*Ideas II*).

———. (1998) *Ideas Pertaining to a Pure Phenomenology and to a Phenome-nological Philosophy*, first book. Fred Kersten, trans. Kluwer (*Ideas I*).

———. (1999) *Cartesian Meditations*. Dorion Cairns, trans. Kluwer.

———. (2001a) *Logical Investigations*, volume 1. J. N. Findlay, trans. Routledge.

———. (2001b) *Logical Investigations*, volume 2. J.N. Findlay, trans. Routledge.

Hutcheson, Peter. (1980) "Husserl's Problem of Intersubjectivity." *Journal of the British Society for Phenomenology*. 11.2: 144-162

———. (1981) "Solipsistic and Intersubjective Phenomenology." *Human Studies*. 4: 165-178

———. (1982a) "Husserl's Fifth Meditation." *Man and World*. 15: 265-284

———. (1982b) "The Primacy of Intersubjectivity." In discussion. *Modern Schoolman*. 59: 281-286

Hutto, Daniel D. (2006) "Turning hard problems on their heads." *Phenomenology and the Cognitive Sciences*. 5: 75-88

———. (2008) "Limited Engagements and Narrative Extensions." *International Journal of Philosophical Studies*. 16.3: 419-444

Hyslop, Alec. (1995) *Other Minds*. Kluwer.

———. (2005) "Other Minds." *The Stanford Encyclopedia of Philosophy (Winter 2005 Edition)*, Edward N. Zalta (ed.), http://plato.stanford.edu/archives/win2005/entries/other-minds/

Ingarden, Roman. (1975) *On the Motives Which Led Husserl to Transcendental Idealism*. Arnór Hannibalsson, trans. Martinus Nijhoff.

Jacob, Pierre. (2008) "Intentionality." *The Stanford Encyclopedia of Philosophy (Fall 2008 Edition)*. Edward N. Zalta (ed.). http://plato.stanford.edu/archives/fall2008/entries/ intentionality/

Johansson, Ingvar. (2003) "Searle's Monadological Construction of Social Reality." In Koepsell and Moss, 2003: 233-255

Jones, Campbell, Martin Parker & René ten Bos. (2005) *For Business Ethics*. Routledge.

Jones, Mitchell P. (2000) "Transcendental Intersubjectivity and the Objects of the Human Sciences." *Symposium*. IV.2: 209-19

Kant, Immanuel. (1983) *Perpetual Peace and Other Essays*. Ted Humphrey, trans. Hackett.

———. (1987) *Critique of Judgment*. Werner S. Pluhar, trans. Hackett.

———. (2006) *Anthropology from a Pragmatic Point of View*. Robert B. Louden, trans. Cambridge University Press.

Kern, Iso. (1964) *Husserl und Kant: eine Untersuchung über Husserls Verhältnis zu Kant und zum Neukantianismus*. Martinus Nijhoff.

———. (1977) "The Three Ways to the Transcendental Phenomenological Reduction in the Philosophy of Edmund Husserl." In Elliston and McCormick, 1977

Kern, Iso & Eduard Marbach. (2001) "Understanding the Representational Mind: A Prerequisite for Intersubjectivity Proper." *Journal of Consciousness Studies.* 8.5-7: 69-82

Kim, Jaegwon. (2006) "Multiple Realization and the Metaphysics of Reduction." In Beakley and Ludlow 2006: 179-199

Koepsell, David & Laurence S. Moss, eds. (2003) *John Searle's Ideas About Social Reality: Extensions, Criticisms and Reconstructions.* Blackwell. Originally appeared as *American Journal of Economics and Sociology.* 62.1 (January, 2003).

Kwan, Tze-Wan. (1990) "Husserl's Concept of Horizon: An Attempt at Reappraisal." In A.T. Tymieniecka, ed. *Analecta Husserlianna,* XXXI: 361-399

Langer, Susanne K. (1953) *Feeling and Form.* Charles Scribner's Sons.

——. (1996) *Philosophy in a New Key: A study in the symbolism of reason, rite, and art,* third edition. Harvard University Press.

Lee, Nam-In. (2006) "Problems of Intersubjectivity in Husserl and Buber." *Husserl Studies.* 22: 137-60

Legrand, Dorothée. (2006) "The bodily self: The sensori-motor roots of pre-reflective self-consciousness." *Phenomenology and the Cognitive Sciences.* 5: 89-118

Levinas, Emmanuel. (1969) *Totality and Infinity: An Essay on Exteriority.* Alphonso Lingis, trans. Duquesne.

Lohmar, Dieter. (2006) "Mirror neurons and the phenomenology of intersubjectivity." *Phenomenology and the Cognitive Sciences.* 5: 5-16

Lowe, E.J. (2000) *An Introduction to the Philosophy of Mind.* Cambridge University Press.

——. (2002) *A Survey of Metaphysics.* Oxford University Press.

——. (2006) *The Four Category Ontology: A Metaphysical Foundation for Natural Science.* Oxford University Press.

Löwith, Karl. (1928) *Das Individuum in der Rolle des Mitmenschen.* Drei Masken Verlag.

Luft, Sebastian. (1999) "Two Themes of Husserl's Phenomenology Revisited: Responsibility and Intersubjectivity." Reviews of *Wege der Verantwortung* by Friederike Kunster. Kluwer, 1996 and *Husserl und die transzendentale Intersubjektivität* by Dan Zahavi. Kluwer, 1996. *Continental Philosophy Review.* 32: 89-99

Lycan, William. (2006) "Form, Function, and Feel." In Beakley and Ludlow 2006: 291-310

Malle, Bertram F., & Sara D. Hodges, eds. (2005) *Other Minds: How Humans Bridge the Divide Between Self and Others.* The Guilford Press.

Malle, Bertram F., Louis J. Moses, & Dare A. Baldwin, eds. (2001) *Intentions and Intentionality: Foundations of Social Cognition.* The MIT Press.

Marsh, James L. (1979) "An Inconsistency in Husserl's *Cartesian Meditations.*" *New Scholasticism.* 53.4: 460-474

Mathiesen, Kay. (2005) "Collective Consciousness." In Smith and Thomasson, 2005: 235-250

———. (2006a) "We're All in This Together: Responsibility of Collective Agents and Their Members." *Midwest Studies in Philosophy,* XXX: 240-255

———. (2006b) "The Epistemic Features of Group Belief." *Episteme.* 2.3: 161-175

May, Larry. (1987) *The Morality of Groups.* University of Notre Dame Press.

McCormick, Peter & Frederick A. Elliston, eds. (1981) *Husserl: Shorter Works.* Notre Dame.

McLaughlin, Brian & Jonathan Cohen, eds. (2008) *Contemporary Debates in Philosophy of Mind.* Blackwell.

Meijers, Anthonie. (1998) "Social Holism and Atomism: An Introduction." *Philosophical Explorations.* 1.3: 166-168

———. (2003) "Can Collective Intentionality Be Individualized?" In Koepsell & Moss, 2003: 167-183

Meixner, Uwe. (2006) "Classical Intentionality." *Erkenntnis.* 65: 25-45

Mensch, James Richard. (1988) *Intersubjectivity and Transcendental Idealism.* SUNY Press.

Merleau-Ponty, Maurice. (1958) *Phenomenology of Perception.* Colin Smith, trans. Routledge.

———. (1964) *Sense and Non-Sense.* Hubert L. Dreyfus & Patricia Allen Dreyfus, trans. Northwestern University Press.

Midgley, David. (2006) "Intersubjectivity and Collective Consciousness." *Journal of Consciousness Studies.* 13.5: 99-109

Miscevic, Nenad. (2003) "Explaining Collective Intentionality." In Koepsell and Moss, 2003: 25-267

Mohanty, J.N. (1984) "Intentionality, Causality and Holism." *Synthese.* 61.1: 17-33

———. (1996) "Kant and Husserl." *Husserl Studies.* 13.1:19-30

———. (2003) "The Unity of Husserl's Philosophy." *Revue Internationale de Philosophie.* 224.2: 115-132

Mohanty, J.N., & William R. McKenna. (1989) *Husserl's Phenomenology: A Textbook.* Center for Advanced Research in Phenomenology.

Moran, Dermot. (2000) *Introduction to Phenomenology.* Routledge.

———. (2005) *Edmund Husserl: Founder of Phenomenology.* Polity.

Moran, Dermot, & Timothy Mooney, eds. (2002) *The Phenomenology Reader.* Routledge.

Nagel, Thomas. (1974) "What Is It Like to Be a Bat?" *The Philosophical Review,* LXXXIII.4: 435-50

———. (1986) *The View from Nowhere.* Oxford University Press.

Natanson, Maurice, ed. (1970) *Phenomenology and Social Reality: Essays in Memory of Alfred Schutz.* Martinus Nijhoff.
———. (1973) *Edmund Husserl: Philosopher of Infinite Tasks.* Northwestern.
Nichols, Shaun & Stephen Stich. (2003) *Mindreading: An integrated account of pretence, self-awareness, and understanding other minds.* Oxford University Press.
Nietzsche, Friedrich. (1997) *Twilight of the Idols.* Richard Polt, trans. Hackett.
———. (1998) *On the Genealogy of Morality.* Maudemarie Clark and Alan J. Swensen, trans. Hackett.
Null, Gilbert. (2007a) "The ontology of intentionality I: the dependence ontological account of order: mediate and immediate moments and pieces of dependent and independent objects." *Husserl Studies.* 23: 33-69
———. (2007b) "The ontology of intentionality II: dependence ontology as prolegomenon to noetic and modal semantics." *Husserl Studies.* 23: 119-159
———. (2007c) "Two-Valued Logics of Intentionality: Temporality, Truth, Modality, and Identity." *Husserl Studies.* 23: 187-228
Nussbaum, Martha. (1993) "Non-Relative Virtues: An Aristotelian Approach." In *The Quality of Life.* Martha Nussbaum and Amartya Sen, eds. Oxford University Press: 242-269
Overgaard, Søren. (2006) "The problem of other minds: Wittgenstein's Phenomenological perspective." *Phenomenology and the Cognitive Sciences.* 5: 53-73
Owen, Thomas J., ed. (1970) *Phenomenology and Intersubjectivity: Contemporary Interpretations of the Interpersonal Situation.* Martinus Nijhoff.
Palma, Vittorio de. (2005) "Ist Husserls Phänomenologie ein transcendentaler Idealismus?" *Husserl Studies.* 21.3: 183-206
Pandey, Ashish & Rajen K. Gupta. (2007) "A Perspective of Collective Consciousness of Business Organizations." *Journal of Business Ethics.* 80: 889-898
Petitot, Jean, Fransisco J. Varela, Bernard Pachoud, & Jean-Michel Roy, eds. (1999) *Naturalizing Phenomenology.* Stanford.
Pettit, Philip. (1993) *The Common Mind.* Oxford University Press.
———. (2007) "Responsibility Incorporated." *Ethics.* 117: 171-201
Pettit, Philip & David Schweikard. (2006) "Joint Actions and Group Agents." *Philosophy of the Social Sciences.* 36.1: 18-39
Philipse, Herman. (1995) "Transcendental Idealism." In Smith and Smith 1995: 239-322
Pietersma, Henry. (2000) *Phenomenological Epistemology.* Oxford University Press.
Putnam, Hilary. (1975) "The Meaning of Meaning." In *Language, Mind and Knowledge.* Minnesota Studies in the Philosophy of Science, VII. Keith Gunderson, ed. University of Minnesota Press.

——. (2006) "The Nature of Mental States." In Beakley & Ludlow 2006: 97-106

Ramachandran, V.S. (2012) *The Tell-Tale Brain: A Neuroscientist's Quest for What Makes Us Human.* W.W. Norton & Company.

Ratcliffe, Matthew. (2006) " 'Folk Psychology' is not folk psychology." *Phenomenology and the Cognitive Sciences.* 5: 31-52

——. (2008a) "Touch and Situatedness." *International Journal of Philosophical Studies.* 16.3: 299-322

——. (2008b) "Farewell to Folk Psychology: A Response to Hutto." *International Journal of Philosophical Studies.* 16.3: 445-451

Ravenscroft, Ian. (2008) "Folk Psychology as a Theory." *The Stanford Encyclopedia of Philosophy (Fall 2008 edition).* Edward N. Zalta, ed. URL = http://plato.stanford.edu/archives/fall2008/entries/folkpsych-theory/

Rawls, John. (2005) *A Theory of Justice.* Reprint of the original edition. Belknap Press of Harvard University Press.

Reynaert, Peter. (2001) "Intersubjectivity and Naturalism–Husserl's Fifth Cartesian Meditation Revisited." *Husserl Studies.* 17: 207-216

Ricoeur, Paul. (1966) "Kant and Husserl." *Philosophy Today.* 10.3-4:147-168

——. (1967) *Husserl: An Analysis of his Phenomenology.* Northwestern.

——. (1974) "Phenomenology." Daniel J. Herman and Donald V. Morano, trans. *Southwestern Journal of Philosophy.* 5.3: 149-168

Rockweel, W. Teed. (2005) *Neither Brain nor Ghost: A Nondualist Alternative to the Mind-Brain Identity Theory.* The MIT Press.

Rowlands, Mark. (2008) "From the Inside: Consciousness and the First-Person Perspective." *International Journal of Philosophical Studies.* 16.3: 281-397

Russell, Bertrand. (2004) *The Problems of Philosophy.* Barnes and Noble.

Ryle, Gilbert. (2000) *The Concept of Mind.* University of Chicago.

Saaristo, Antti. (2006) "There is No Escape: Collective Intentionality and Empirical Social Science." *Philosophy of the Social Sciences.* 36.1: 40-66

Sartre, Jean-Paul. (1991) *The Transcendence of the Ego: An Existentialist Theory of Consciousness.* Forrest Williams and Robert Kirkpatrick, trans. Farrar, Straus and Giroux.

——. (1993) *Being and Nothingness: A Phenomenology of Ontology.* Hazel E. Barnes, trans. Simon & Schuster.

Schmid, Hans Bernhard. (2003a) "Rationality-in-Relations." In Koepsell & Moss 2003: 67-101

——. (2003b) "Can Brains in Vats Think as a Team?" *Philosophical Explorations.* VI.3: 201-218

——. (2006) "Rationalizing Coordination: Towards a Stronger Conception of Collective Intentionality." Published in Mark D. White and Barbara Montero, eds. *Economics and the Mind.* Routledge. URL:

http://cipp.unibas.ch/index.php?id=5416&no_cache=1&file=636&uid=5128

Schuhmann, Karl & Barry Smith. (1985) "Against Idealism: Johannes Daubert vs. Husserl's *Ideas I.*" *Review of Metaphysics*. 39: 763-793

———. (1991) "Neo-Kantianism and Phenomenology: The Case of Emil Lask and Johannes Daubert." *Kant-Studien*. 82.3: 303-318

———. (1993) "Two Idealisms: Lask and Husserl." *Kant-Studien*. 83: 448–466

Schutz, Alfred. (1953) "Edmund Husserl's *Ideas*, Volume II." *Philosophy and Phenomenological Research*. 13.3: 394-413

———. (1962) *Collected Papers I: The Problem of Social Reality*. Maurice Natanson, ed. Martinus Nijhoff.

———. (1964) *Collected Papers II: Studies in Social Theory*. Arvid Brodersen, ed. Martinus Nijhoff.

———. (1966) *Collected Papers III: Studies in Phenomenological Philosophy*. I. Schutz, ed. Martinus Nijhoff.

———. (1967) *The Phenomenology of the Social World*. George Walsh and Frederick Lehnert, trans. Northwestern.

———. (1970) *On Phenomenology and Social Relations*. University of Chicago.

———. (1996) *Collected Papers IV*. Helmut Wagner and George Psathas, eds in collaboration with Fred Kersten. Kluwer.

Schutz, Alfred & Thomas Luckmann. (1973) *The Structures of the Life World*. Richard M. Zaner and H. Tristram Engelhardt Jr., trans. Heinemann.

Searle, John R. (1964) "How to Derive 'Ought' From 'Is.'" *The Philosophical Review*. 73.1: 43-58

———. (1970) *Speech Acts: An essay in the philosophy of language*. Cambridge University Press.

———. (1983) *Intentionality: An essay in the philosophy of mind*. Cambridge University Press.

———. (1992) *The Rediscovery of the Mind*. The MIT Press.

———. (1997) "Responses to Critics of *The Construction of Social Reality*." *Philosophy and Phenomenological Research*. 57.2: 449-458

———. (1998) *Mind, Language, and Society: Philosophy in the Real World*. Basic Books

———. (1999) "Limits of Phenomenology." Review of *Being-in-the-World: A Comenntary on Heidegger's Being and Time Division I*, by Hubert L. Dreyfus. The MIT Press, 1991. Published also in *Heidegger, Coping and Cognitive Science: Essays in Honor of Hubert L. Dreyfus*, Volume Two. The MIT Press, 2000 http://socrates.berkeley.edu/~js-earle/limits_phenomenology.rtf

———. (2002) *Consciousness and Language*. Cambridge University Press.

———. (2005) "The Phenomenological Illusion." In M.E. Reicher and J.C. Marek, eds. *Experience and Analysis. Erfahrung und Analyse*. Proceed-

ings of the 27th International Wittgenstein Symposium, 2005 http://socrates.berkeley.edu/~jsearle/ PhenomenologicalIllusion.pdf

———. (2008) *Philosophy in a New Century: Selected Essays.* Cambridge University Press.

———. (2010) *Making the Social World: The Structure of Human Civilization.* Oxford University Press.

Shockley, Kenneth. (2004a) "Thinking Through Collectives: Graham and McMahon on the Influence of Membership on Practical Reason." *Social Theory and Practice.* 30.1: 127-149

———. (2004b) "The Conundrum of Collective Commitment." *Social Theory and Practice.* 30.4: 535-557

———. (2007) "Programming Collective Control." *Journal of Social Philosophy.* 38.3: 442-455

Shoemaker, Sydney. (1996) *The First-Person Perspective and Other Essays.* Cambridge University Press

Smiley, Marion. (2008) "Collective Responsibilty" *The Stanford Encyclopedia of Philosophy* (Fall 2008 Edition), Edward N. Zalta, ed. http://plato.stanford.edu/archives/fall2008/entries/collective-responsibility/

Smith, A.D. (2003) *Husserl and the* Cartesian Meditations. Routledge.

Smith, Barry. (1989) "Logic and Formal Ontology." In Mohanty and McKenna 1989: 29-67

———. (1994) *Austrian Philosophy: The Legacy of Franz Brentano.* Open Court.

———. (1995) "Common Sense." In Smith & Smith 1995: 394-437

———. (1999a) "Truthmaker Realism." *Australasian Journal of Philosophy.* 77.3: 274-291

———. (1999b) "Social Objects." http://ontology.buffalo.edu/socobj.htm Originally published as "Les objets sociaux." *Philosophiques.* 26.2: 315–347

———. (2001) "The Chinese Room Argument." Preprint version which appeared (with Searle's response) in *Philosophical Explorations.* 4.2: 70–75 (with response by John Searle, 75–77)

Smith, Barry & John Searle R. (2003) "The Construction of Social Reality: An Exchange." In Koepsell & Moss 2003: 285-309

Smith, Barry & David Woodruff Smith, eds. (1995) *The Cambridge University Press Companion to Husserl.* Cambridge University Press.

Smith, David Woodruff. (1989) *The Circle of Acquaintance.* Kluwer.

———. (1992) "The Realism in Perception." *Nous.* A.P.A. Western Division Meetings, 16.1: 42-55

———. (2005a) "Phenomenology." *The Stanford Encyclopedia of Philosophy (Winter 2005 edition).* Edward N. Zalta, ed. http://plato.stanford.edu/archives/win2005/entries/phenomenology/

———. (2005b) "Consciousness with Reflexive Content." In Smith & Thomasson 2005

———. (2007) *Husserl*. Routledge.

Smith, David Woodruff & Amie L. Thomasson, eds. (2005) *Phenomenology and Philosophy of Mind*. Oxford University Press.

Sokolowski, Robert. (1964) *The Formation of Husserl's Concept of Constitution*. Martinus Nijhoff.

———. (1968) "The Logic of Parts and Wholes in Husserl's Investigations." *Philosophy and Phenomenological Research*. 28.4: 537-553

———. (1974) *Husserlian Meditations: How Words Present Things*. Northwestern.

———. (2000) *Introduction to Phenomenology*. Cambridge University Press.

———. (2009) *Phenomenology of the Human Person*. Cambridge University Press.

Spinoza, Baruch. (1992) *Ethics*. Samuel Shirley, trans. Hackett.

Staehler, Tanja. (2008) "What is the Question to Which Husserl's *Fifth Cartesian Meditation* is the Answer?" *Husserl Studies*. 24: 99-117

Stawarska, Beata. (2006a) "Introduction: Intersubjectivity and embodiment." *Phenomenology and the Cognitive Sciences*. 5: 1-3

———. (2006b) "Mutual gaze and cognition." *Phenomenology and the Cognitive Sciences*. 5: 17-30

———. (2008) " 'You' and 'I,' 'Here' and 'Now': Spatial and Social Situatedness in Deixis." *International Journal of Philosophical Studies*. 16.3: 399-418

Steeves, H. Peter. (1996) "Husserl, Aristotle, and the Sphere of Ownness." *Southwest Philosophy Review*. 12.1: 41-150

Strawson, Galen. (2005) "Intentionality and Experience: Terminological Preliminaries." In Smith & Thomasson, 2005: 41-66

Talero, Maria L. (2008) "The Experiential Workspace and the Limits of Empirical Investigation." *International Journal of Philosophical Studies*. 16.3: 453-472

Taylor, Charles. (1979) "Atomism." In *Powers, Possessions, and Freedom*. Alkis Kontos, ed. Toronto: University of Toronto Press.

Thomasson, Amie L. (1997) "The Ontology of the Social World in Searle, Husserl and Beyond." *Phenomenological Inquiry*. 21: 109-136

———. (2003) "Introspection and Phenomenological Method." *Phenomenology and the Cognitive Sciences*. 2: 239-254

———. (2005) "First-Person Knowledge in Phenomenology." In Smith & Thomasson 2005.

———. (2007a) *Ordinary Objects*. Oxford University Press.

———. (2007b) "In What Sense Is Phenomenology Transcendental?" *The Southern Journal of Philosophy*,.XLV: 85-92

Thompson, Evan. (2001) "Empathy and Consciousness." *Journal of Consciousness Studies.* 8.5-7: 1-32
———. (2007) *Mind in Life: Biology, Phenomenology, and the Sciences of the Mind.* Belknap Press.
Thornton, Stephen P. (2006) "Solipsism and the Problem of Other Minds" *The Internet Encyclopedia of Philosophy*, http://www.iep.utm.edu/s/solipsis.htm. Spring, 2006 edition.
Tollefson, Deborah. (2004) "Collective Intentionality." *The Internet Encyclopedia of Philosophy.* http://www.iep.utm.edu/c/coll-int.htm
———. (2006) "The Rationality of Collective Guilt." *Midwest Studies in Philosophy*, XXX: 222-239
Tomasello, Michael. (2008) *Origins of Human Communication.* The MIT Press.
———. (2009) *Why We Cooperate.* The MIT Press.
Tomasello, Michael & Hannes Rakoczy. (2003) "What Makes Human Cognition Unique? From Individual to Collective Intentionality." *Mind & Language.* 18.2: 121-147
Tripathy, L.K. (1992) "Intersubjectivity in Phenomenology." *Indian Philosophical Quarterly.* 19.Supplement: 1-8
Tuomela, Raimo. (1997) "Searle on Social Institutions." *Philosophy and Phenomenological Research.* 57.2: 435-441
———. (2000) "Collective and Joint Intentions." *Mind & Society.* 2.1: 39-69
———. (2003) "Collective Acceptance, Social Institutions, and Social Reality." In Koepsell & Moss 2003: 123-165
Tye, Michael. (2008a) "Qualia" *The Stanford Encyclopedia of Philosophy (Fall 2008 edition).* Edward N. Zalta, ed. http://plato.stanford.edu/archives/fall2008/entries/qualia/
———. (2008b) "New Troubles for the Qualia Freak." In McLaughlin and Cohen (2008): 303-318
van Breda, H.L. (1977) "A Note on Reduction and Authenticity According to Husserl." In Elliston & McCormick, 1977
Varela, Francisco J., Evan Thompson & Eleanor Rosch. (1992) *The Embodied Mind: Cognitive Science and Human Experience.* The MIT Press.
Velasquez, Manuel. (2003) "Debunking Corporate Moral Responsibility." *Business Ethics Quarterly.* 13.4: 531-562
Velleman, J. David. (1997) "How to Share an Intention." *Philosophy and Phenomenological Research.* LVII.1: 29-50
Vessey, David. (2005) "Gadamer's Account of Friendship as an Alternative to an Account of Intersubjectivity." *Philosophy Today.* 49.5: 61-67
———. (2007) "Who Was Gadamer's Husserl?" *The New York Yearbook for Phenomenology and Phenomenological Philosophy.* VII: 1-23
———. (2009) "Gadamer and the Fusion of Horizons." *International Journal of Philosophical Studies.* 17.4: 531-542

Vromen, Jack. (2003) "Collective Intentionality, Evolutionary Biology and Social Reality." *Philosophical Explorations.* VI.3: 251-265

Walton, Roberto J. (2003) "On the Manifold Senses of Horizonedness. The Theories of E. Husserl and A. Gurwitsch." *Husserl Studies.* 19: 1-24

Welton, Donn, ed. (2003) *The New Husserl: A Critical Reader.* Indiana University Press.

Wheeler, Michael. (2008a) "Cognition in Context: Phenomenology, Situated Robotics and the Frame Problem." *International Journal of Philosophical Studies.* 16.3: 323-349

———. (2008b) "Minimal Representing: A Response to Gallagher." *International Journal of Philosophical Studies.* 16.3: 371-376

Wilson, E.O. (2012) *The Social Conquest of Earth.* Liveright.

Wilson, George. (2008) "Action." *The Stanford Encyclopedia of Philosophy (Fall 2008 Edition).* Edward N. Zalta ed. http://plato.stanford.edu/archives/fall2008/entries/action/

Wittgenstein, Ludwig. (1958) *The Blue and Brown Books: Preliminary Studies for the "Philosophical Investigations."* Basil Blackwell.

———. (1980) *Culture and Value.* Trans. Peter Winch. University of Chicago.

———. (2001) *Philosophical Investigations.* G.E.M. Anscombe, trans. Blackwell.

Yu, Jiyuan. (2007) *The Ethics of Confucius and Aristotle: Mirrors of Virtue.* Routledge.

Zahavi, Dan. (1999) *Self-Awareness and Alterity.* Northwestern University Press.

———. (2001a) *Husserl and Transcendental Intersubjectivity: A Response to the Linguistic-Pragmatic Critique.* Ohio University Press.

———. (2001b) "Beyond Empathy: Phenomenological Approaches to Intersubjectivity." *Journal of Consciousness Studies.* 8.5-7: 151-167

———. (2002) "Merleau-Ponty on Husserl: A Reappraisal." In *Merleau-Ponty's Reading of Husserl*; Ted Toadvine, ed. Kluwer: 3-29

———. (2003a) *Husserl's Phenomenology.* Stanford.

———. (2003b) "Phenomenology and Metaphysics." In *Metaphysics, Facticity and Interpretation: Phenomenology in the Nordic Countries.* Dan Zahavi, Sara Heinämaa, and Hans Ruin, eds. Springer: 3-22

———. (2005) *Subjectivity and Selfhood.* The MIT Press.

Zahavi, Dan & Frederick Stjernfelt, eds. (2002) *One Hundred Years of Phenomenology: Husserl's Logical Investigations Revisited.* Kluwer.

Zaibert, L.A. (2003) "Collective Intentions and Collective Intentionality." In Koepsell & Moss, 2003: 209-232

Zaibert, Leo & Barry Smith. (in manuscript) "The Varieties of Normativity: An Essay on Social Ontology." URL=http://homepages.uwp.edu/zaibert/inprogress/Social%20Ontology%20and%20the%20Manifoldness%20of%20Normativity2.doc

Bibliography

Ziman, John. (2006) "No Man Is An Island." *Journal of Consciousness Studies.*
    13.5: 17-42

Index

agency, 14-15, 18 14; derived, 39,
72n55; group, 2; intrinsic, 39
alterity, 5, 11, 31, 72n54, 108n108
analogy or analogical reasoning, 174
Arendt, Hannah, 160n18
Aristotle, Aristotelian, 15, 19n49, 23,
45n33, 91, 137, 160n1, 161n25,
181-182, 187n55, 187n58, 195
asymmetry of experience of the other,
5-6, 11
atomism, 2-4, 16n8, 65, 118, 120, 125-
127, 166n95, 211n17

beetle box argument, 72n61
Block, Ned, 55
Bratman, Michael, 13, 45n39, 110-111,
127n11
Brentano, Franz, 6

Carr, David, 14, 23-24, 31, 34-35, 77-
91, 96, 98-101, 112, 170, 192
Cartesian view, 64-65, 74n87, 105n68,
118, 157, 194, 198-199, 204, 206
Chalmers, David, 17n32
Chinese room argument, 73n61
Churchland, Paul and Patricia, 18n32
collectivism, 2, 15, 125, 161n37,
166n95, 196
collectivity, 13, 21-22, 28, 36, 139,
194-195; condition of, 34; criterion, 28-29
collective consciousness, 10, 12-14, 21-
22, 24-25, 29, 62, 66; ambiguity,
29, 53; argument from intentional-

ity, 23-24; argument from subject-
status, 22-24
consciousness; definition, 55; embodied, 45n32, 55, 83, 85-86, 203;
group, 30, 55; individual, 8, 12, 35,
19; stream of, 54, 57
culture, 63-64, 107n96, 176-177, 182,
193-194, 201

Dennett, Daniel, 18n32, 47n59
deontic power, 156-157, 159
Descartes, René, 110, 119, 158, 199
Dreyfus, Hubert, 105n68, 165n82
Drummond, John, 6, 10, 117
dualism, 198-199

embodiment , 85-88
emergence, 54-55, 74n86
emergent mind thesis, 58-60
empathy, 5, 25, 64, 181
epoché, 173, 202
evidence; apodictic, 100, 108n105,
108n109, 129n50; adequate, 100,
108n105, 108n109, 129n50; intentional fulfillment, 81, 99,180;
conditions for satisfaction, 81, 115,
162n50, 165n88; direction of fit,
83

facticity, 183-184, 207
functionalism, 55
fusion, 15-16, 137-140, 161n39,
166n89, 180

About the Author

Eric Chelstrom served as Visiting Assistant Professor in philosophy at Grand Valley State University from 2009-2012, and currently continues to teach there and in the Grand Rapids area. He completed his doctoral studies in philosophy at the University at Buffalo, State University of New York under the direction of Kah Kyung Cho. He has presented at a number of international conferences on issues ranging from the ontology of music to social ontology.

Dr. Chelstrom's current research includes work on the role of horizon intentionality in Aristotelian friendships, to be published in a forthcoming volume titled *Phenomenology and Virtue Ethics*; research in the history of phenomenology, including work on the analyses of evil in phenomenology prior to Paul Ricoeur's *Symbolism of Evil* and on the influence of Adolf Reinach's social ontology on Edith Stein's philosophy; finally, his research is beginning to turn to the implications of a theory of collective intentionality for our understanding of the nature of art, paying specific attention to arguments from Arthur Danto's essay, "The Artworld."

In addition to scholarly work, he enjoys time with his wife and children.